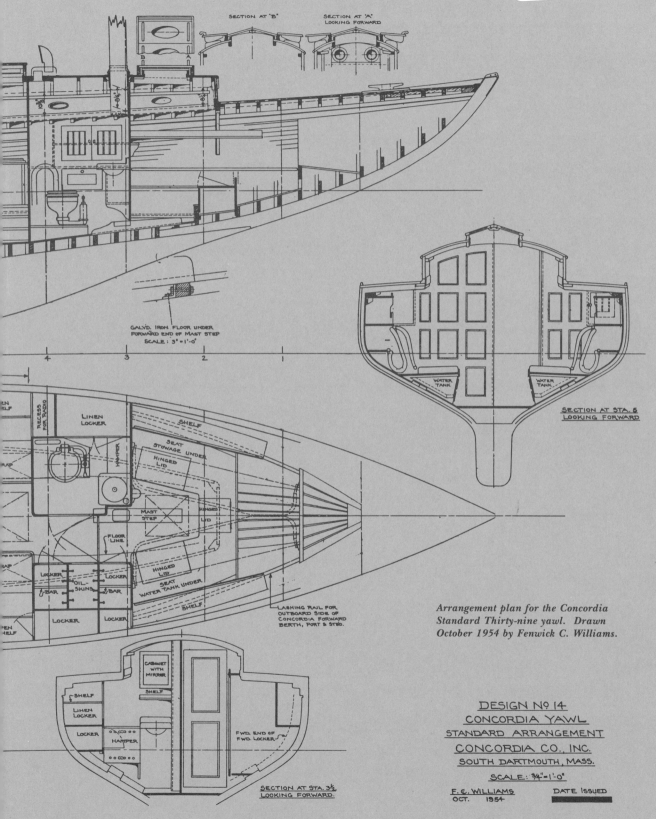

SECTION AT "B"

SECTION AT "A"
LOOKING FORWARD

GALV'D. IRON FLOOR UNDER
FORWARD END OF MAST STEP
SCALE: 3" = 1'-0"

4   3   2   1

SECTION AT STA. 6
LOOKING FORWARD

WATER TANK   WATER TANK

RECESS FOR RADIO

LINEN LOCKER

SHELF

SEAT STOWAGE UNDER

HINGED LID

HINGED LID

MAST STEP

HINGED LID

FLOOR LINE

HAMPER

LOCKER   LOCKER

OIL SKINS

BAR   BAR

LOCKER   LOCKER

HINGED LID

SEAT
WATER TANK UNDER

SHELF

LASHING RAIL FOR
OUTBOARD SIDE OF
CONCORDIA FORWARD
BERTH, PORT & STB'D.

OPEN SHELF

*Arrangement plan for the Concordia
Standard Thirty-nine yawl. Drawn
October 1954 by Fenwick C. Williams.*

CABINET
WITH
MIRROR

SHELF

SHELF

LINEN LOCKER

LOCKER

HAMPER

FWD. END OF
FWD. LOCKER

SECTION AT STA. 3½
LOOKING FORWARD.

DESIGN Nº 14
CONCORDIA YAWL
STANDARD ARRANGEMENT
CONCORDIA CO., INC.
SOUTH DARTMOUTH, MASS.
SCALE: ¾" = 1'-0"

F. C. WILLIAMS
OCT.   1954

DATE ISSUED

A LIFE IN BOATS

The Concordia Years

A LIFE

The

IN BOATS

Concordia Years

Waldo Howland

Mystic Seaport Museum
Mystic, Connecticut   1988

Published by Mystic Seaport Museum, Inc.
Mystic, Connecticut
Copyright 1988 by Mystic Seaport Museum, Inc.

Designed by Sherry Streeter
Typeset by WoodenBoat Publications
Printed by Nimrod Press

Howland, Waldo
A Life in Boats: The Concordia Years–[1st ed.]
Mystic, Connecticut: Mystic Seaport Museum, 1988
312 pp., illus. 26 cm.
Sequel to: A Life in Boats: The Years Before the War.
1. Concordia Company. 2. Yacht-building. 3. Yacht racing.
4. Yachts and yachting. I. Title.
GV 812.5.H6
ISBN 0-913372-45-5

Dedication

*To Katy (Katherine Sue Kinnaird) Howland,
my wonderful wife, who has made all things
cherished so rewarding and possible.*

*And to Martin Jackson, my valued friend and
indispensable boatyard partner for over fifty years.*

Acknowledgments

The same wonderful crew that brought forth *A Life in Boats: The Years Before the War*, which is the first volume of my sailing memoirs, has done it again for this second volume, *The Concordia Years*.

Margaret Gamble, with longstanding Concordia Company connections, has, God bless her, once more patiently and expertly transformed my handwritten pages into clear-typed manuscript.

J. Revell Carr, director of Mystic Seaport Museum, admirer of Concordia yawls, and my friend for nearly twenty years, encouraged the writing of *A Life in Boats* from the very start, and he, Gerry Morris, and the Seaport's Publications Committee have again enlisted my nephew and literary advisor, Llewellyn Howland III, as project editor, with Anne Preuss as copy editor.

That *WoodenBoat* should again be our book designer is another piece of great good fortune. Jon Wilson, creator, editor, and publisher of *WoodenBoat* magazine, understands and approves of the views I express in *A Life in Boats*. So do Sherry Streeter, Jane Crosen, Judy Robbins, Jennifer Elliott, and Maynard Bray, who have worked so hard on the typesetting, layout, editing, and design of my books at *WoodenBoat*. Maynard, one-time manager of Mystic Seaport's shipyard, has through first-hand experience and thoughtful study acquired wide knowledge of boating matters. He has assisted and guided my efforts at every turn.

I am again greatly indebted to the same photographers and organizations that furnished illustrations for my first book. For *The Concordia Years* Old Dartmouth Historical Society has supplied additional rare views of old Padanaram. Nick Whitman, a Beetle Cat owner himself, has produced outstanding photographs of Beetle Cat Boats under construction and in use. Nick has also used his exceptional expertise in producing prints from my own amateur negatives. Norman Fortier, who became a tenant of Concordia Company at about the same time the Concordia yawls made their first post-World War II appearance, has taken splendid photographs of each of them. These photographs, taken over a period of more than forty years, form in themselves a vital history of the class.

The Rosenfeld Collection of Mystic Seaport Museum has provided unique historic photographs for both volumes of *A Life in Boats*. Under the able management of Elizabeth Parker Rafferty, the Collection is being computerized in a most wondrous way, making Rosenfeld images conveniently accessible to all students of American yachting and boating.

Several sources of illustrations that I did not use in *The Years Before the War* have been of critical importance this time around. Early in our association, Abeking and Rasmussen sent me detailed photographs of their lumber supplies. Subsequently, as new Concordia yawls came into being, Abeking and Rasmussen followed up with construction photographs of each boat. These photographs provide unique documentation of Concordia yawl building procedures.

Many years ago my friend Lois Darling, a great sailor and artist, drew for me a number of sketches of various Concordia craft. Several are reproduced in *The Concordia Years*. More recently, Maynard Bray and his daughter, Kathy, have made drawings for me that illustrate certain details and features in a more telling way than the camera could ever do.

Although reference books as such have not played a large part in the writing of this book, I wish to acknowledge the use I have made of the collection of yachting periodicals at the G.W. Blunt White Library at Mystic Seaport Museum, the annual reports of the Race Committee of the New York Yacht Club, the yearbooks of the Cruising Club of America, and Lloyd's Register of American Yachts. They have all furnished information that I have relied on.

I wish I could credit here everyone else who has generously furnished information and illustrations for this book, but space is just not available. Many of them appear in the text or are noted in the list of Concordia yawl owners. One person, however, I must mention by name: Horst Lehnert, who for many years was manager of the Abeking and Rasmussen Shipyard. Were it not for his patience and kindness in sharing his knowledge with us, a whole vital part of the Concordia story would be sadly incomplete.

In short, I have had assistance of the finest kind in writing this book and preparing it for publication, and I thank my wife Katy and everyone involved, named or unnamed. Truly, *The Concordia Years* has been a very special collaboration of all members of the Concordia family.

Waldo Howland
Padanaram, November 1987

Preface

This is the second volume of Waldo Howland's sailing autobiography, *A Life in Boats*. It is also the most detailed, comprehensive, and authoritative account ever written of two of America's most popular and durable classes of one-design wooden sailboats: the Beetle Cat and the Concordia yawl.

The Concordia Years begins, as the first volume ended, in the anxious lull between the hurricane that devastated New England in 1938 and the infinitely more devastating storm that was World War II. It was in 1939 that *Escape* (later renamed *Java*), the original Concordia yawl, first went into commission and won her first race. It was in 1941 that Waldo Howland acquired historic South Wharf, a marine railway, and a homely brick storage shed in the coastal village of Padanaram, in Dartmouth, Massachusetts, and began the slow transformation of Concordia Company from a small Boston-based yacht-design and brokerage office into the world-famous yacht builder, importer, and full-service boatyard it has since become.

But it was not until Howland returned from naval service in England in 1946 that Concordia Company acquired from the Beetle family of New Bedford all rights to build and distribute the original Beetle Cat Boat. It was not until 1950 that a German-built sistership to *Java* first took shape at Abeking and Rasmussen in Lemwerder, Germany. More than 2,500 of the 12-foot Beetle Cat Boats have been built and sold by Concordia Company since 1946, making this one of the largest classes of one-design wooden sailboats still being produced and probably the oldest class in continuous production. Of the Concordia yawl class, a total of 103 boats were built, making this the largest class of large one-design wooden sailboats in the history of the sport. Although it has been some 23 years since the last Concordia yawl was built, all 103 survive today.

Waldo Howland is quick to acknowledge the role Dame Fortune played in the long-term success of Concordia Company, but, even so, the early years at South Wharf were not easy ones—and even in later years, the company faced near ruin on more than one occasion. Through it all, however, Howland held doggedly to the notion that there *is*, in fact, such a thing as a good boat—and that the creation of good boats, by hand and out of wood, is both a viable business proposition and a uniquely fulfilling professional calling.

The Concordia Years is thus fully as much the story of the men and women who helped design, build, repair, and maintain these outstanding wooden boats as it is the story of the boats themselves: their owners and crews, their races, their cruises and adventures in home and foreign waters. Howland's carefully reasoned narrative reminds us that we cannot fully understand "the way of a yacht" without knowing something, first, about the values and backgrounds of those who built her or about the conditions and uses for which she was originally intended. He helps us to understand that every element in the design and construction of a wooden boat, from keel to truck, from toerail to limber hole, has its essential function and appropriate form; and that, while simplicity is almost always a virtue on a boat, shortcuts never are.

Some of the events Howland recounts in *The Concordia Years* are already the stuff of sailing legend: the victory of Dan Strohmeier's Concordia yawl *Malay* in the 1954 Bermuda Race; the sweep by Ray Hunt's Concordia sloop *Harrier* in Cowes Week, 1955; the remarkable reign of Leo Telesmanick, master builder of Beetle Cats; and the astonishing triumph of Arnie Gay's Concordia yawl *Babe* in the 1978 Bermuda Race. But even those who have sailed in Buzzards Bay waters or stored their boats at Concordia Company for decades will find much in these pages that is new or unfamiliar. And Howland offers perspectives on the evolution of modern measurement rules and cruising boat design that are more timely and important today than they have ever been.

Part formal history, part memoir and affectionate group portrait, part meditation on the joys of sailing, T*he Concordia Years* is the story of an eventful thirty-year period in American yachting and small-boat activity. It will instruct and delight any reader who has ever aspired to a life in boats.

Contents

South Wharf and
basin at Concordia
Company about
1952. Aerial view
from the east.

Part I

BUILDING A BOATYARD

1
The Navy

i

With the dreaded arrival of a second world war, all normal yachting activity ceased. The great *Aloha*s and *Corsair*s were broken up for scrap or taken over for special Navy or Coast Guard duty. Established yacht yards and boat businesses simultaneously suffered and prospered under hastily formulated government building programs. Small-boat owners were obliged to lay up their boats wherever space was available, or limp along within strange new local restrictions.

By the fall of 1942 many of my college boating contemporaries had been swallowed up by the Navy, and, at Miami schools and elsewhere, were in short-term training for deck officer positions aboard Patrol Craft (PC's) or Destroyer Escorts (DE's). My father followed the pattern of older yachtsmen and painted large identifying numbers on the bow of his newly built *Escape*, the first Concordia yawl. With his boatman Martin Jackson as crew and his retired Marine Corps friend General Louis Little as gunnery officer, he ran a scheduled nighttime patrol of Buzzards Bay, looking for possible enemy activity. The General had as armament a venerable revolver last used in the Crimean War.

After becoming adjusted to a 1940 summer turndown by the U.S. Navy, I was in 1941 blessed with good fortune beyond all expectation. In the early winter I became married to a wonderful woman, Katy Kinnaird, and that same fall became owner of the local commercial wharf of my long-standing dreams. The future had never seemed brighter. Then came the Japanese sneak attack at Pearl Harbor. Instantly I was converted into prime material for the draft. My only hope of remaining at home with my wife and new

British practice exercises for 1944 D day landings at Normandy, being held at Slapton Sands, Devon, England, 1943. Similar exercises were carried out by U. S. forces.

son (Charles Child Howland, born in September, 1942) was a deferment job.

My first stop was Washington, D.C., where, still a civilian, I joined the staff of an organization purportedly having something to do with inter-American affairs. I understood that the project was, in fact, to build cargo ships of wood, in order to save critical metals for more urgent battle craft. It all sounded logical, and I took the assignment seriously. One of the first co-workers I came in contact with was Captain Charles Mayo, a Province-town charter-yacht owner whom I had met recently on a trip to Fort Lauderdale on boat business. Charlie was not only a complete seaman, he was a knowledgeable boatbuilder as well. Between us we devised, and laid before our new boss, a scheme aimed at setting up an operation in the Caribbean boatbuilding island of Cayman. To make the undertaking more practical and efficient, we successfully urged the additional employment of my longtime boat adviser and friend Major William Smyth.

So far, so good. But then nothing happened. Our pay kept coming, but with it one obstacle after another. Our best constructive ideas came to naught. In the end I decided to make a second attempt to gain acceptance as a reserve officer in the Navy.

Within a few weeks I found myself standing in my shorts before a Navy doctor, explaining that his findings of my advanced age, under-height, malocclusion of the teeth, flat feet, and other deficiencies, must be in error and that in fact, I was just the lieutenant junior grade that the Navy most needed. A Buzzards Bay sailing friend, John West, now a Washington-based Navy officer, had certainly done his promotional job well. The good doctor smiled and forthwith granted me the necessary waivers. Bars had definitely been lowered.

A freezing-cold four months' indoctrination at Cornell University apparently proved that I had been sufficiently subjected to information given to four-year Annapolis graduates. My navigation grade of 1.2 out of a possible 4.0 proved either that my intelligence was gravely lacking, or that I had a form of table-reading dyslexia. My seamanship mark of 3.98 suggested that the Navy course covered nearly the same material I had learned from actual boating.

Through a Boston grapevine my father learned that I was scheduled to be assigned to a converted yacht for inshore patrol duty. This would keep me close to home but would be a rough assignment in winter weather. As luck would have it, sudden new losses overseas indicated that too many of our planes and ships were being fired upon by our own guns, and that recognition training was urgently needed. A group of overaged and under-qualified deck officers like me was hastily sent off to recognition-teaching school at Ohio State University. Here, in one summer month, I discovered that the new flash system could miraculously and rapidly teach one to recognize various air and surface craft, both Allied and enemy. And here Katy and I came close to roasting to death, attempting to survive in an uninsulated attic apartment.

My next assignment came in June, 1943, and was to teach my newly learned recognition at the Great Lakes Naval Training Station. Being senior member of a small unit, I was in a position to direct each of my companions to a job, simultaneously holding myself free to accept "such other duties as may be assigned." This ploy just happened to involve me as a second-in-command at the base boathouse. Here, along with other responsibilities, I was tendered complete administrative control over a small fleet of recreational sailboats, ranging in size from 15-footers to 40-foot R boats.

In this specialized field, one of my tasks was the testing for sailing ability of each and every officer who aspired to sailing privileges. A simple routine suggested itself, whereby the one to be tested would launch a rowboat from the float, row to the chosen craft at her mooring, climb aboard, set sail, follow a designated triangular course, then pick up the mooring, secure gear, and return to shore. Most applicants easily passed the simple test; others found sailing more complicated than they realized. All had an interested and vocal audience to cheer them on.

One memorable day an imposing Commander arrived on the scene, obviously but not impolitely ill-disposed to suffer through a test given by a lowly new j.g. Naval Reserve officer. However, in the Navy, orders are orders, and I solemnly issued my instructions, while the gallery awaited results. Down the ramp went the Commander. Working the dinghy alongside with hand and foot, he stepped lightly amidships, seated himself agilely, and picked up an oar in preparation for shoving off. At this point, I sang out from my high perch on the dock that no further test was required. The Commander, a really nice fellow, was surprised but gratified, and I was relieved to realize that competent seamanship can often reveal itself in the simplest of maneuvers. My newfound friend spent that afternoon yarning with me about the many boats he had owned and the various Bermuda and other races he had taken part in. There is no doubt about it, boats have a canny way of creating their own genuine fraternities, long-term or short.

Life at Great Lakes seemed to be proceeding smoothly enough. Katy and our son Charlie, now almost a year old, arrived and in so doing transformed a small apartment into a happy home. The boathouse mechanic improved our transportation conditions by creating a fine operating auto out of a recently acquired jalopy. My immediate senior officer, Lieutenant

Don Cutler from Boston, proceeded in attitude from friendly to most cordial. He devised a scheme whereby he would acquire a long-sought-for transfer, and I would take over his Great Lakes job. Sure enough, orders did arrive, and promptly—but they were orders for me, not him. This was in the fall of 1943, and overnight big changes commenced to take place. Katy and Charlie returned home to Padanaram for the duration. I soon found myself, along with seventeen thousand others, aboard *Queen Mary*, which had been converted to the Allies' number-one troopship.

ii

Defying advice from experienced hang-back advocates and offering my services at the first call of volunteers, I was rewarded with a bridge lookout assignment, four hours on, eight off. Below decks, in our converted stateroom equipped with four triple-tier cots and in our crowded mess hall, wild rumors circulated as to where we were headed. The most persistent theory advocated a land where palm trees grow.

High on the bridge there was a complete lack of scuttlebutt on the subject, but the compasses suggested a great-circle course to the east. My watch-time sensations, beyond excitement and apprehension, were ones of chill, great height, and aloofness from reality. In the eerie nighttime darkness of our "gray ghost" ship, nothing was to be seen save the dim instrument lights, and the stream of phosphorescent waves that flashed by so very far below. During daylight hours only somber gray emptiness met the anxiously searching eye.

On the fourth day out, in the early dawn hours, *Queen Mary* majestically glided into Scotland's incomparable Clyde estuary and gave her subdued passengers a brief glimpse of breathtaking grandeur. By midday our own little Navy unit, designated as A-2 of NARU 29, had disembarked over the stark great stone docks of Gourock and was aboard a special troop train speeding south. Our final stop was at the Kingswear depot in Devonshire, where, in spite of its latitude, palm trees do definitely grow.

From previous visits I readily recognized our surroundings. Although now weirdly overhung with swaying barrage balloons and crowded not with sparkling yachts but with sullen gray naval craft, Dartmouth harbor still retained its placid waters and green-hilled beauty.

As revealed bit by bit, our unit was becoming an important link in a U.S. Navy chain of amphibious bases set up in harbors along the entire Channel coast from Portsmouth to Plymouth. With certain exceptions the local inhabitants had been evacuated, and their rolling countryside was rapidly being turned over to elements of the hastily arriving U. S. forces. Our landing-craft units were scheduled to cooperate with the army in train-

THE ROYAL NAVAL COLLEGE
DARTMOUTH, ENGLAND

This was my home from the fall of 1943 until the spring of 1945. In peacetime, English naval cadets begin their training in their early teens. Before 1905 they were quartered in the old training ship *Britannia*, which was then moored in the lower harbor just off an area known as Sandquay. After 1905 they lived and studied in the newly built Naval College set high on the hill overlooking the town of Dartmouth, Start Point, and the English Channel beyond. The great hall of the College (which had been badly damaged by bombs before we moved in) is located in its central structure. The administrative offices are toward the front; dormitory wings are attached on the two sides and in the rear. This imposing facility was designed to accommodate some three hundred cadets, plus the staff. Our operation was soon trying to cope with ten times that number, variously made up of landing craft units, construction workers, and temporary visitors of one sort and another.

Our engineering force was quickly built up to handle a large ship maintenance and repair operation. The communications and operations department, overseen by our skipper and executive officer, kept in contact with central command, and base supply officers were responsible for feeding and clothing all hands.

ing exercises organized for an eventual Allied invasion of the Continent.

Our Dartmouth group was as yet merely an advance organizational unit. It numbered some fifteen reserve officers, with a somewhat larger contingent of enlisted personnel. It was headed by an overaged maverick—up-through-the-ranks—Navy Commander.

For several weeks a few of us enjoyed the unbelievable privilege of living in the very houses that were once inhabited by some of the most famous Elizabethan voyagers, discoverers, and navigators. Sandridge, where I first quartered, was nestled in a rolling country of chestnut woods and sheep-covered meadows some five miles up on the east bank of the Dart. It had belonged to the Davis family, one member of which was John the Navigator, who for years methodically searched for a northwest passage to the riches of the East Indies. It was he who in the 1580s discovered what became named the Davis Strait, the stretch of water that runs between Greenland and Baffin Island. Somewhat later I shifted a short stretch downstream to Greenway Court, later the home of Agatha Christie, where for decades had lived the family of Sir Humphrey Gilbert, the far-sighted voyager who colonized Newfoundland and then initiated a lucrative fish trade with Dartmouth. Queen Elizabeth's great favorite Sir Walter Raleigh was a younger stepbrother of Sir Humphrey and spent many a month at Greenway Court.

I couldn't help being stirred into visualizing these famous former neighbors as youthful adventurers, sailing and rowing their little, full-bowed craft up and down the ten miles of the Dart's deep and varied waters, meeting with one another, watching ships a-building at yards in the upper river reaches, or, farther downstream, studying those differing vessels from far-off places that, for trade or shelter, had entered this safest of southern England's deep-water harbors. No finer schoolgrounds could possibly be found for the training of exceptional seamen.

In fact, our "Hooligan Navy" life had quite a few parallels with the school days of the Elizabethan period. We were on our own, and lived by instinct or upbringing rather than by major skills or possession of worldly goods. Situations shook themselves down, and invasion plans somehow proceeded. When at the end of a few weeks our entire unit was moved to—and took over—the Royal Naval College, a sort of pattern took shape that remained in force until the European war came to an end.

Rather than being worked into the recognition-teaching job I expected, I was given the assignment of First Lieutenant, which, under the circumstances, meant chief hotelkeeper: in charge of space arrangement, garbage disposal, plumbing facilities, and the like. All were fraught with storybook complications created by English customs, Navy regulations, and amateur abilities.

U. S. invasion exercises were the main reason for our existence. At frequent intervals, landing craft would be assembled on river moorings. In the darkness of night they would, on a prearranged schedule, proceed in to the cement landing hards (ramps), be loaded with the correctly synchronized Army personnel and equipment, then back off and return to station.

At the given signal, usually early next morning, they would slip their moorings and proceed in file downriver and out into the English Channel for a circuitous assault on the Slapton Sands, an area made famous by the old King Arthur sagas of the Lady of the Lake. As to be expected, all manner of snafus took place, some trivial and comical, some serious, as when German torpedo boats sneaked by the Allied patrol and inflicted losses comparable with those of the worst Allied invasion disasters.

With the passing of several months, I was shifted to an Operations assignment, the workings of which were all new to me. Again, small-boat experience came to the rescue. A major problem of the exercises was that, in the dark of night, the young landing-craft skippers, through no fault of their own, found it very difficult to locate their designated landing hard and, once there, to avoid stranding on a falling tide or getting lost on the return trip to mooring. The problem was similar, in a way, to the one that we experienced at Concordia Company in boat-moving operations. Many boat owners and yard personnel lacked the experience for safe maneuvering in cramped or unfamiliar slips. My partner, Martin Jackson, solved the yard problem by handling the whole moving process himself, doing so with his small towboat skiff. Following this technique, it simplified matters completely to train several Martins, and modify several small landing craft known as LCVP's into towboats. This way, ninety-five percent of the loading complications were simply eliminated.

In the spring of 1944 the successful Normandy landings took place. Spared all of their hardships and horrors, I had only to supervise the loading of a fair number of LCT's (landing craft tanks). The actual Navy crews and Army forces, facing a terrifying experience with unknown outcome, rose magnificently above themselves and accomplished the impossible. Several hundred LCT's filed out to sea at short intervals, all in correct order, and all on time, carrying their allotted cargo of men and materials. It was an unbelievable show of coordination. No one had been told that this particular exercise was more than another practice session, but all hands surely must have sensed that it was the Big One.

Amphibious bases were gradually closed down after D day. Being a keeper of the keys, so to speak, I was among the last of our unit to leave Dartmouth but finally after V. E. Day did return to the United States in May, 1945. Following a tedious waiting inactivity at Fort Schuyler, New York, and then in Gulfport, Mississippi, I was in November released from active duty.

2
South Wharf,
Past and Present

i

Concordia Company, as a boatyard operation, began just before the war with my most fortuitous purchase of South Wharf in 1941. As the name suggests, the property jutted out into Padanaram Harbor as a very substantial granite dock. At its inshore end were an abandoned railway and shop; the rest was in reasonably tidy, but bare, condition. Before getting into how the boatyard grew out of this, however, let me tell you about its purchase and about the wealthy and eccentric Colonel E. H. R. Green—the man who had been its last owner.

My distant kinsman Edward Howland Robinson Green entered the picture in 1915 when he bought South Wharf. He was known as Colonel Green, not because of army connections, but because he was a big landowner out in the southern state of Texas. His mother, Hetty Howland Robinson Green, was famous for her many unusual attributes, including that of being the richest woman in the world—and perhaps the most parsimonious and difficult woman, as well.

As I understand it, Hetty, who inherited a substantial fortune (from her father, whaling merchant Edward Mott Robinson, and her maiden aunt Sylvia Ann Howland) never sold anything, just kept on buying—railroads, land, banks, whatever—and thus grew rich with the expanding nation. To save money she is said to have heated her morning oatmeal on a radiator

South Wharf from the north, about 1914. The pavilion is shown here at the end of the wharf, just inboard of the oyster shell chute. William Dunn's fish shed is to the left of Laban's Folly, the main building in the center.

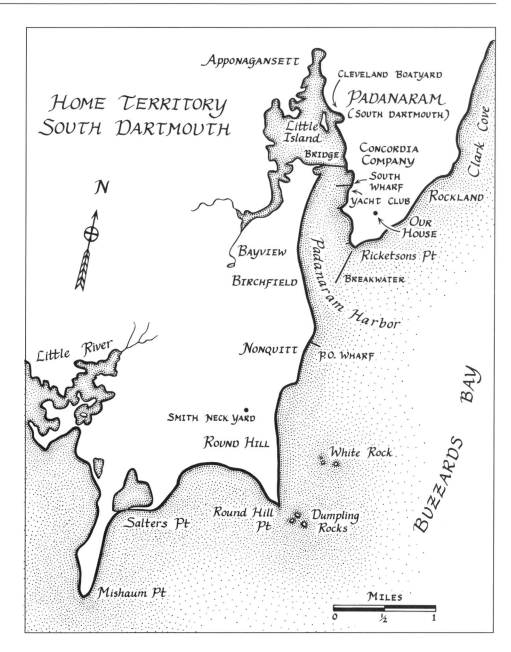

in one of her own banks. And according to my grandmother, who occasionally invited her for lunch, Hetty was pleasant enough company, but insisted on bringing her own banana and crackers for fear of being poisoned. One can say what one wants about Hetty Green, but the fact remains that she made a vast fortune, left it all to her son and daughter to do with as they pleased, and was thus, in the end, a benefactor of mine.

Edward, the Colonel, had a very different philosophy from that of his mother. He thought very little of making money, but developed a positive genius for spending it. Along with other assets, Colonel Green inherited the lovely saltwater farm known as Round Hill and located on South Dartmouth's southeastern-most point that had been settled by his and my Howland forebears in the seventeenth century. Here the Colonel built a colossal stone mansion, an airfield, a huge greenhouse complex, a radio station, and two big docks. As an adjunct to all these shore installations, he collected a fleet of boats that included countless launches, an oyster boat, a houseboat, a lake steamer, and the whaleship *Charles W. Morgan.* To support this navy, the Colonel saw the need for a private navy yard and had the good fortune to acquire South Wharf for that purpose.

Colonel Green undertook great changes there. He repaired the wharf and causeway, raising the walls and capping them with cement. Then he dredged the basin north of the wharf and installed a big marine railway. Finally, he constructed a brick-and-cement machine shop at the head of the railway. It was designed in such a way that engines could be hoisted from the beds of a hauled-out boat and slid through the big door into the shop. Although this was all taking place during World War I, the work was elaborately and expensively executed, featuring great girders and tracks overhead, a cement floor, tools and equipment of every conceivable kind, and even a big, hollow brass handrail leading down into the basement area.

This entire establishment was created largely for Colonel Green's Lakes-built steamer *United States.* Unfortunately, *United States,* with her fifteen feet of draft and forty-eight staterooms, was not a handy vessel for cruising in Buzzards Bay waters. Soon after she came to Padanaram, she sought shelter in the inner harbor as a result of war activity rumors, became stranded on a rock, and was damaged so badly that she had to be towed away. Colonel Green thereupon sold her back into commercial service.

In 1936 Colonel Green died and his major holdings, including South Wharf, were inherited by his sister, Hetty Sylvia Ann Howland Green Wilkes. For a short time thereafter, spaces at the end of the dock were rented out to local yachtsmen. Then came the 1938 hurricane, and whole sections of South Wharf and its buildings were smashed into shambles. The high chain-link fence surrounding the property was bent flat, and the machine shop was flooded. The old building on the outer end of the wharf known as Laban's Folly stood its ground, but was so badly battered that it was later taken down. Its noble white-pine timbers found their way into several new buildings in the neighborhood, including my own house.

My purchase of South Wharf from Colonel Green's estate evidently raised nagging questions to others, because some years later a small group

Colonel Green's houseboat *United States*, tied up at South Wharf in 1919. Built as a passenger steamer at Manitowoc, Wisconsin, in 1909, *United States* was lengthened from 202' to 243' by the Colonel in 1917 in order to accommodate forty-eight staterooms. She drew an unhandy 15', which compelled the dredging work depicted in this photograph.

of law partners on a yachting vacation sailed into Padanaram and called on me. Their firm had represented the Green estate in many areas, and had observed that Green assets were often retained, sometimes given away, but seldom sold. How was it, they inquired, that I was able to buy South Wharf from the estate, when others before me had tried and failed? I was willing enough to be helpful, but had to tell them I didn't know the answer myself.

With the help of my brother Louie (Llewellyn, Jr.) I had approached the Round Hill manager, Bert Hill. Hill had referred me directly to Mr. W. K. Potter, the long-time custodian of the Green empire. By appointment, Louie and I went to New York, expecting to hold our meeting in a large office complex. Not at all. Mr. Potter, with one or two assistants in evidence, held forth in a small wood-paneled room on the ground floor of a downtown Broadway building. He listened without expression to my story; who I was, why I wanted the wharf, and how much money I had to pay for it.

"That's not enough," he said when I had finished my speech. When I asked how much would be enough, he mentioned a figure just ten percent higher than mine. I could almost see Hetty Green looking over his shoulder.

And so, much to my surprise, a purchase was consummated. Thinking

14

back, I am convinced that the direct approach had been the right approach once again. But I also think that even a tight-fisted business executive has, in all probability, a soft spot in his heart and a personal slant on matters of destiny.

ii

When World War II began, the established New Bedford and Fairhaven boatyards had been compelled to sidetrack much of their regular yacht business. The efforts of Peirce and Kilburn and of Kelley's became focused on keeping New Bedford's high-priority fishing fleet in operation. Palmer Scott and Casey, for their part, took on ever-increasing boatbuilding contracts for the U. S. government. Suddenly yacht owners, instead of having a choice of yards in which to lay up, found themselves in a bind to find any storage or service facilities whatsoever. This was one of several developments in 1941 that bore directly and providentially on the postwar fortunes of Concordia Company.

In the spring of 1941 my brother Louie and his family moved to Padanaram from Marblehead and by midsummer, with the help of our builder friends Elmer Pierce and Ben Tripp, had begun their new house on family property just south of Mother and Father's house. Although still the professional on Father's Concordia yawl *Escape* for summer sailing, Martin Jackson had by now made the decision to work full-time for Concordia during the winter months. Recently married, Martin also became the owner, that summer, of a small farmhouse located on beautiful high land just north of Round Hill—a site that would subsequently be very important to Concordia Company.

Meanwhile, my own pressing goal was to raise the wherewithal to complete the purchase of South Wharf, which figured so prominently in the plans of Louie, Martin, and myself. First, I approached the New Bedford Institution for Savings, which wanted no part of any youthful boatyard dreams. The attitude of the Fairhaven Institution for Savings was of a different kind. Its six-member mortgage committee took positive action at their very next meeting. Impressively ensconced in an ancient and stylish twelve-cylinder Packard touring car, they arrived en masse at South Wharf and concluded their deliberations right on the spot. This was a wonderful boost to my self-confidence at a time when I sorely needed it. I will always be grateful for their faith in me.

With financial backing now assured, my next move was to make a final arrangement with Padanaram's only operational boatyard at that time, the Cleveland yard on Shipyard Lane. The yard's founder, Captain Al Cleveland, had by then joined his ancestors, but his son Harold and his grandson Alfred were still in business. Because Harold was under doctor's orders to slow his pace, it worked out to the benefit of all concerned for Concordia to take over the whole Cleveland plant—hauling gear, cradles, workboat, moorings, supplies, and all—and also to sign on Harold himself and his crew, youthful Al and old-timer Tony Anderson. (Cleveland's Shipyard Lane real estate was soon sold to a local resident. Some years later it was bought by Breckinridge Marshall, the originator of the now famous fiberglass Marshall Catboats. Breck became associated with Concordia Company at the time it was acquired by William Pinney in 1969.)

By the summer of 1942, Louie and Martin were essentially carrying the whole burden of all the boatyard operations. I was in the Navy, and my free time for South Wharf was limited; but I was granted temporary leaves in which to engineer a few classic mistakes and enjoy a certain amount of yard planning. In the course of cleaning up the big brick building, I displayed notable brilliance by towing Colonel Green's 1908 Benz limousine off to the dump. With its gold brocade interior, silver-plated wheel covers, custom engine #6124, and special high body, it was already, had I only realized it, a priceless collector's item. Fortunately, Katy had the foresight to remove the circular amber window strap-handles for the teething of our children to come. And Martin salvaged the two front wheels and parts of the front axle, from which he fabricated a marvelous dolly for moving masts and spars. Throughout the following thirty years Concordia made daily use of this unique rickshaw. Then there was the graceful lapstrake pulling boat

South Wharf as it appeared just after I acquired it in 1941. The New Bedford Yacht Club dock is at far left. Only the foundation of Laban's Folly remained after South Wharf was cleaned up following the 1938 hurricane.

Harold Cleveland and his son Alfred, about 1942. Harold's father, Al, had been a yacht captain, and his grandfather a ship captain. The Cleveland family played an important part in the maritime history of Padanaram for more than a century.

Looking toward shore from the end of South Wharf in 1941. This photograph shows Colonel Green's machine shop and the converted oyster boat *Lydia*, hauled on the railway beneath the steel gantry crane. The New Bedford Yacht Club clubhouse had recently been repaired and its porches enclosed after sustaining heavy damage in the 1938 hurricane.

that Colonel Green reportedly had used on the Adirondack lakes. This museum piece I gave to a friend, who, sadly, never had time to repair or use it. Although its memory lingers on, it, too, was lost to posterity. As a final folly, I drew up plans for a long, high storage shed to be built on the all-too-narrow strip of land that ran parallel with, and to the north of, the railway. Fortunately, we lacked the money to build this error. It would never have been practical.

During that first wartime fall at South Wharf, Martin and Louie had no choice but to concentrate on essentials. For manual help, Ben Tripp and Uncle John Waldo, now freed from house-building projects, came down to the yard to augment the Cleveland crew.

The first priority was to create facilities for tying up boats for storage in a basin that was of good length but of limited deep-water width. Having been around boats since childhood on a working, practical basis, Martin knew well how to "make do."

After assembling several available pieces of big ship's chain into one long length, he anchored its outer end around the northerly hook of the dock, led it to shore in a line parallel with and to the north of the dock, and then secured its inner end to an existing crane footing ashore. From this main creation, lighter and shorter pick-up units were attached at about 30-foot intervals. Thus, eight to ten or more 40-foot boats could be moored stern-to between dock and pick-up line.

This initial basic system and, for that matter, most of the old chain itself, remains in constant use to this day. The general design worked better for our conditions than any expensive arrangement of pilings could possibly have done. The chain automatically compensated for the rise and fall of tide, its very weight acted as a shock absorber, it made maneuvering in close quarters very flexible and damage-proof, and it also permitted considerable option as to the number of boats accommodated. From the start, stern lines were securely shackled to the dock, and bow lines likewise to their pick-up floats. Thus the yard had no occasion to use or damage a customer's dockline, and owners in turn had no easy way to mistakenly run off with one of ours. For pick-up floats, Martin made up inflated tires mounted on special plate wheels, in the hub of which was a through-bolt, with one eye for chain below and another for dockline above.

The next need was for gear to unstep masts and haul small boats. For this Uncle John raided his barn of treasures, and came up with the rugged iron fittings for a big three-legged boom derrick, which we assembled on the protected inside corner of the outer wharf. Hand-operated, this old-time former quarry gear served Concordia well for some thirty years. There were, to be sure, those who had to turn the windlass crank and who understandably cussed the tedious labor, and there were other engineering types who shook their heads at our lack of progressive thinking, but our own eyes saw only that the investment was small, and that a careful working of the windlass handles resulted in a very fine and gentle up-and-down adjustment of precious loads. To the best of my knowledge, the old derrick never damaged a mast or dropped a boat (except for a little one of my own). A modern mobile crane can doubtless perform lifting jobs with greater ease and speed, but it requires skill and training to operate and maintain, and its initial cost may well be out of reach. At least in the 1940s it appeared to us that a few extra willing hands were more versatile and practical for our overall yard picture than any expensive specialized equipment.

For hauling the larger boats we had a ready-made head start, in that

New derrick for spars and small craft at the outer end of South Wharf, 1942. A shed for spars and small craft is going up just behind the four Herreshoff Twelves.

19

Colonel Green's railway, its big steel cradle with sprocket-and-chain drive, and the splendid hauling winch were all in working order. The preliminaries needed to make use of this gear did involve a lot of bull work and several "good-enough-for-the-time-being" methods, as Martin would say. First the silted mud had to be cleared off the little-used track. Then, the old oyster boat *Lydia*, which sat half-dismantled on the cradle, had to be demolished. Finally, someone had to learn how to coax the ancient cherry-red hauling diesel into action. As usual, Martin and Louie had the energy and imagination to get on with it. Atop the cross-members of the big freed cradle, they directed the building of a turning platform approached by a

LLEWELLYN HOWLAND, JR.

Llewellyn Howland, Jr., a director of Concordia Company and my business partner after the war. This photo shows him sitting on the front doorstep of his newly built home in Padanaram, 1942.

My brother Louie is only four years younger than I, and as boys growing up in the Boston area and attending day school and Milton Academy, we lived very similar lives. During those early years, Louie enjoyed his share and more of good boating. Initially it was daysailing and racing in his Herreshoff Twelve, *Cutty Sark*, off Padanaram. Then in the late 1920s he did a great deal of cruising, especially aboard Ralph Williams's 52-foot Alden schooner, *Fearless*. Racing, formal and informal, was all part of it as well, and Ralph's younger brother, Tom, who had the 34-foot Crocker-designed ketch *Pole Star*, and our friends Bill, John, and Roger Hallowell, with their 52-foot Crowninshield schooner *Winnebago*, were ever-ready rivals. In 1930 Louie took in the Bermuda Race aboard *Shimmo*, an old Crowninshield schooner that belonged to his classmate John A. White's father.

As I think back on it now, Milton Academy certainly had its share of boys from boating families. Another of Louie's classmates was Nathaniel Goodhue, whose family summered in Marblehead and owned a 34-foot Alden yawl, *Cadenza*. Louie and Natty spent much of their vacation time aboard *Cadenza*, cruising to Maine or sailing closer to home. It was through Natty that Louie met his wife, Sally Ives. Sally was Natty's cousin, and her family also had a summer place in Marblehead.

In the summer of 1933, at the end of his sopho-

temporary wooden ramp. By using a heavy manila line on the winch drum, a boat, once floated into its own cradle, could be hauled up the main railway tracks, then moved on wooden rollers up the ramp to the platform, then turned ninety degrees, and, finally, with the help of Cleveland's old hand windlass, be persuaded into the brick building, the Colonel's onetime machine shop.

The first new structure on South Wharf was a simple, pitched-roof shed in which to garage our pickup truck and to store various equipment. Located just to the west of the brick building, it remains in place today, although disguised and partly hidden by locker shed additions. Out

more year, Louie left Harvard and went to work for the Merchants Bank in Boston. In 1934 he and Sally were married and settled into a small, but charming, old house on Lee Street in Marblehead. Right across the way was Oxner's Boatyard, and a few houses down the line lived L. Francis Herreshoff. At this time Louie owned one of those greatest of daysailers, a Herreshoff Fish-class sloop that he named *Harbinger*.

After three years with the Merchants Bank, Louie grew disenchanted with commuting. In 1936 he became the North Shore agent for Benjamin C. Tower, a well-known Boston real estate broker — and, I might add, a great sailor-man. This new undertaking automatically involved Louie in the insurance business.

In 1941, Louie and Sally decided to move to Padanaram. Our mother's passing and an inheritance of family property made the move practical for Louie. It was a godsend for Father and me. In Padanaram Louie continued his real estate and insurance business under his own name.

It was obvious during these prewar months that my own immediate future was in for a big change. And when I joined the Navy in the fall of 1942, all my boatyard plans would have come to a screeching halt if Louie and Martin Jackson had not come to the rescue and taken over the day-to-day management of Concordia for the duration.

It was only the year after I returned to private life in 1946 that Louie and I worked out a formal partnership arrangement. In general the idea was that we would divide the responsibilities and share the profits; Louie was to concentrate on real estate and insurance, and I on the boat business. To accomplish these tasks in an orderly fashion, we set up two additional partnerships: W. & L. Howland, to handle the insurance business; Howland & Howland, to handle real estate. Louie was to manage both of these entities. Concordia Company, Inc., was to handle the boat business, and I, with Martin's participation, was to manage this end of things. It was a good arrangement, and we had little trouble communicating, because we were all in a small office area and could keep track of what was going on merely by keeping our ears open. If I sold a boat, Louie was soon discussing marine insurance with the new owner. If Louie sold or rented a house to a new arrival in town, I was soon trying to sell that person a boat.

To cement further our joint involvements, the Waldo Howlands received rent from their original South Wharf property, the Louie Howlands received rent from their newly bought sail loft property, and Martin also received rent from his Smith Neck property, when Concordia expanded part of its operation to that location. The whole setup was unusual in many ways. But it worked.

21

on the end of the dock we built three low, connected spar and storage sheds in the area where the building known as Laban's Folly had once stood. With these few preliminary moves Concordia was immediately in business and took on its first storage customers.

From early on we sensed that owners who enjoyed traditional small daysailers and sound family cruising boats would be our best and most compatible customers, that enlarging our facilities to handle bigger boats would create an impractical mixture. Our only compromise was our decision to maintain Colonel Green's big cradle for the temporary haul-out of some special bigger boat, if circumstances ever warranted.

iii

Having seen the first storage boats safely under cover, I had to leave the scene completely for a three-year Navy tour. Louie remained as business manager, Martin as foreman. Both took on additional civic duties. And Martin, in addition to his yard responsibilities, joined the Coast Guard Reserve for a four-year, part-time stint of coastal patrol, ship inspection, and airplane-spotting duties. Indeed, Father's *Escape* was legally transferred to Martin for the duration of his patrols.

During the yard's second summer, in 1943, Louie and Martin made two permanent facility improvements, as well as going into a brief venture that had wartime priority potential. As a result of expensive basin dredging done for Colonel Green's yacht *United States*, the center of our wharf's north wall had collapsed into the deepened water. Father came to the rescue and had the Fairhaven marine contractor Frank Taylor repair the damage and then add a series of closely spaced reinforcing pilings. Good granite wharves have always been monuments to durability and strength, but for this very reason are all too often taken for granted. Be well advised that there are do's and don't's that every stone-dock owner should learn and keep in mind. We were fortunate to receive an early warning.

The second capital improvement was the replacing of the makeshift wooden hauling ramp with the first stages of an excellent turntable-and-track system that Martin and Louie worked out after a visit to the Peirce and Kilburn yard in Fairhaven. Tracks of the right weight were readily available from the recently dismantled New Bedford trolley lines; for a pivot mechanism the stern bearing and propeller shaft of the old *Lydia* served to perfection. The toughest part of the job fell to Mr. McGowan, the New Bedford blacksmith. He had the task of bending the supporting track into a complete circle. The success of this track arrangement encouraged my dream of eventually attaining a yard surfaced with mowed grass, one such as I had admired at Dooley's yard in Fort Lauderdale. Most conventional

South Wharf from the second-floor verandah of the New Bedford Yacht Club, late fall, 1942. Father's Concordia yawl *Escape* (later named *Java*) lies in the basin, third from right, alongside the Crocker-designed sloop *Amantha*, a Concordia 25' sloop, and an S boat. My own Hunt-designed fin-keeler, *Koala*, sits in a cradle underneath the derrick.

boat-moving methods result in a ground base of dusty gravel or greasy planks; neither of these please the conscientious painter or the aesthetic owner.

To conserve space between tracks, and inside sheds, final storage moves were accomplished with wooden rollers and big automobile-type roller jacks. The wooden rollers that Uncle John turned out for us were of tupelo (or snag oak, as we called it), a locally grown tree with a beautiful shape and, in the fall, lovely red leaves. More important, for us, tupelo has a very gnarly grain, doesn't split, and seems impervious to the crushing weight of a boat or to directional blows from a sledgehammer.

Before being made ready for winter, each boat was always leveled up both fore-and-aft and athwartships, to prevent water from pocketing. A boat stored outside had its own fitted canvas cover, securely fastened over a wooden frame that formed a pitched roof to shed snow and rain and to allow for accessible crawl space on deck. The covers were of untreated

Concordia's railway and track setup, about 1960. The turntable is in the right foreground.

HAULING, MOVING, AND LAUNCHING

Although the grass-surfaced boatyard I envisioned never materialized, we held throughout the years to this original track layout. Each boat had its own wooden cradle (the white yawl in the foreground is hauled out on the original Colonel Green steel cradle) and was floated into same with the help of removable and adjustable supporting arms. Once the boat was up on dry land, short, fitted shores took the place of the arms. Ballast-iron weights were removed from the cradle, and the boat, securely in place, was hauled up to the turntable and shunted off on radiating tracks to its general storage location.

Every cradle had slots in each of its two runners to accept two removable steel axles. This simple four-wheel design made it possible to haul boats around modest curves or over shallow hollows or bumps without binding of wheels or undue stress on the cradle. The old second-hand, hard pine mill timbers that we first used for cradles lasted indefinitely, while new hard pine bought later from the lumberyard rotted out quickly. Old growth just has a quality that second-growth trees seldom seem to have.

white cotton canvas to reflect sunlight, avoid daytime heat, and permit breathing. They extended down below the waterline to protect the boat's topsides. Even when synthetic materials were developed in later years, we never used them because they did not breathe and therefore tended to cause an undesirable buildup of condensation on the boat's surfaces.

The major 1943 yard project that turned out to be temporary was a commercial fish business. Louie worked out a practical agreement with our neighbor Bob Sylvia of the Apponagansett Fish Company, whereby Concordia built and leased to them a small, raised, fish off-loading and packing shed, with concrete floor, drains, water, electricity, etc. This enterprise on the north end of the dock served its purpose and was quite successful for a time. As many as forty thousand pounds of fish were landed during a single September day. But by July of the following year, the Apponagansett Company had changed hands and moved to New Bedford. That boom was over.

The fall of 1943 saw an appreciably larger and more organized boat storage business at South Wharf, but finding labor to handle it all was challenging, to say the least. Even our few regular yard workers were often called away for one civic or military duty or another. After a single wail of the local volunteer fire department siren, half the men in the yard dropped everything to race across the street and board the fire engines, Louie and Martin in the lead.

Miss Shine, our faithful secretarial manager of all departments, had by this time moved down from Boston to work each day in a makeshift stockroom-office tucked away on a balcony in the brick building. She boarded at our house to keep Katy company and catch up with the boatyard bookkeeping. The mechanic work was handled on a part-time basis by Len Tripp, whose regular job was at the Grove Street garage in New Bedford. Johnny Carr accomplished an endless succession of essential blacksmith jobs for us. And as a final addition to our regular crew, Mike Hanson came over from Hadley Harbor to be our head rigger.

iv

In times of war or general stress, people pull together, necessary work somehow gets done, and lasting loyalties develop. On what was at best a frail shoestring, Louie and Martin were making noble progress. Then, out of the blue, came the terrible 1944 hurricane, which swept up and across the southern New England coast on the evening of 14 September—only six years after the hurricane of 1938.

What the damage would have been in peacetime beggars the imagination. As described by Louie, Concordia Company was a strange and shock-

25

ing picture of devastation. South Wharf had been swept clear. The three new storage sheds and all the small boats and gear within them had vanished. Only the fish shed remained, battered but intact on its raised footings. Surprisingly, the boats tied in the basin were still there and not badly damaged. But inshore the new garage shed and the small, metal, paint and mooring shacks had been twisted off their foundations; the brick building had been flooded. With no insurance for this type of flood damage, the question confronting Martin and Louie was, where and how to begin again.

A search of the waterfront revealed some of the lighter small craft, thrown high and dry ashore. Others, such as the keel Herreshoff Twelves, apparently had sunk and then been washed away or covered by sand and mud. Few of these were ever found. Boats that could be salvaged were brought back to the yard for rebuilding. Although such work had its depressing side, it nonetheless made a busy winter for the yard crew.

Of the larger boats, Father's Concordia yawl *Escape* was among the most seriously damaged. She, like several others, had been washed from her mooring and dashed against the riprap of the bridge causeway. Her entire starboard side was gone. Fortunately for Father, Captain Harold Hardy had, at my brother's urging, come to work full-time on *Escape* that summer as the replacement for Martin. Captain Hardy undertook the salvage of her hull, rig, and gear, and then made arrangements to trailer the wreck over to Casey's boatyard in New Bedford. Here he and the grand old shipwright Bert Briggs did a superb rebuilding job. Even before the boat was launched the following spring, Father, having lost a boat named *Escape* in each of the two hurricanes, renamed this boat *Java*. *Escape* had proven an unlucky name for him.

v

Slowly things again began to look up for Concordia. Just as the onset of war had sent us good customers, so its termination now sent us a number of peerless craftsmen. For while other yards were shifting downward from priority and labor-intensive government work back to the slower and different pace of peacetime activity, Concordia's own demands for skilled workers increased. In the personnel shuffle, we were the clear gainers.

Proper boatyard folks as I have known them are a rare breed. For better or worse, no real money is ever in their future, just a continuing desire to work with boats and a lifetime satisfaction in doing so. Their addiction is sometimes obviously inherited from fathers and grandfathers, but in other cases must have developed all but spontaneously. Many lucky people realize that working with one's hands can be a source of very real satisfaction. And I find that, for a fortunate few, working specifically on or with boats has a doubling urgent and binding appeal. It seems that the more genuine and perfect the boat, the more lasting is the gratification brought by owning her. Consciously or unconsciously, fine craftsmen seek boats of their liking and then take pride and responsibility in working on them. To preserve a masterpiece is more inspiring than ordinary work. It's hard to explain this phenomenon. But believe me, it's worth pondering.

On Saturday morning right after the 1944 hurricane, Leslie Randall, a top boat carpenter at Peirce and Kilburn's and later at Palmer Scott's, wandered down to the Padanaram bridge to survey the damage. There he ran into Martin. Shortly thereafter Randy came to work for Concordia and, with but one short interruption, remained with us until his retirement in 1968. His great knowledge of yacht construction, sparmaking, and joiner-work became one of Concordia's greatest assets. At about the same time Randy's friend and one-time schoolmate Wilton Butts joined us. He was a young South Dartmouth fellow of many skills who had been working on boats owned by Dr. Demarest Lloyd, a notable yachtsman and summer resident of nearby Potomska. Butsy's superlative carpentry work, his ingenuity, and his boat-handling ability were a boon to Concordia and all its customers from the day he came until his sickness and death in 1963.

When the Casey boatyard changed hands in 1946, their patternmaker and carpenter Byron Briggs moved down to Concordia to help with the special fittings and equipment we were trying to develop. Also in 1946, Nick Demers, a former Scott worker, came to head up our expanding paint department. George Montigny, formerly a rigger at both Peirce and Kilburn's and Casey's, became available, and Martin put him in charge of our rigging department. Byron and George stayed on with us until retirement, and Nick was with us until his death many years later.

I could continue about Concordia's remarkable crew, but will add here only the important fact that in these early years Martin also gave what were their first jobs to two young friends of his, Arthur Correia and Louis Verissimo. After forty years and more, both men are still at Concordia Company. Yacht owners and sailors may or may not realize it, but their pleasure on the water and sometimes their very lives depend on the skill and integrity of such men as Concordia has been privileged to employ over so many years.

South Wharf, about 1890. Laban's Folly is the large building in the center of the picture. To the right is the coal pocket, with a coal schooner and two fishing sloops tied up alongside. The fish shed in the lower left was taken down during the building of the New Bedford Yacht Club's Padanaram Station in 1901.

EARLY TIMES AT SOUTH WHARF

It couldn't have been chance alone that led Concordia Company to establish its final boat business at South Wharf in South Dartmouth. Happenings of long ago and Howlands of earlier generations had played their part in the arrangements, I'm convinced.

Dartmouth, Massachusetts, is one of the oldest New England towns, and has a long tradition of the sea and ships. Purchased in 1652 from the Indians by Governor Bradford and a score of his friends, it was named for the English Dartmouth, whence the Pilgrims took their 1620 departure for the New World. Originally, new Dartmouth covered a large area. It was subsequently divided into several townships, including New Bedford, Fairhaven, Acushnet, and the current Town of Dartmouth, which, itself,

consists of several different villages, including South Dartmouth.

The original Dartmouth settlers must have been rugged individuals indeed to venture their lives and fortunes in this remote country. One of their number, Henry Howland, brother of John Howland of *Mayflower* fame, became the principal progenitor of the Dartmouth and New Bedford Howlands, from whom my family is descended.

Accounts of early Dartmouth boatbuilding are all too sketchy, but at least six shipyards are known to have operated on the Apponagansett River shores at one time or another. And in his *History of the American Whale Fishery*, Alexander Starbuck notes that in 1807 the successful and long-lived whaleship *George and Susan* was built at the head of the river (on what

Saltworks at Ricketsons Point. Windmill pumps have suction pipes leading below the low-water mark. The evaporation trays shown have movable "covers," or roofs. Sections of the Ricketson farm at the outer easterly side of Padanaram Harbor were leased in 1810 for 99 years to individual salt makers.

The Howland brush-type saltworks on the west shore of Padanaram Harbor, about 1900. The seawater evaporated very rapidly as it dripped through the brush and was thus very salty by the time it reached the shallow evaporation tanks below. The last Padanaram saltworks to continue in operation, this Howland saltworks finally shut down in 1907.

was then the Wing farm) for my great-great-grandfather George Howland.

A second industry of local importance was the retrieving and processing of various salts from seawater. From early days shallow-tank evaporation saltworks were set up in neighboring settlements such as Mishaum Point, Salters Point, and Nonquitt. The War of 1812 and new taxes on imported salt added impetus to local salt production, which flourished right through the nineteenth century.

In 1805 a Harwich boatbuilder named Laban Thatcher moved from Cape Cod to the little Dartmouth village later to be known as Padanaram that was taking shape along the east bank of the Apponagansett River. Some fifteen years later Thatcher, seeking to supplement his shipbuilding business, attempted a new wrinkle in salt processing. In hopes of creating a special all-weather salt-grinding mill, he built a massive granite pier well out in the river, the outboard end paralleling the east side of the channel and positioned about halfway up the harbor. On this unique, rectangular manmade island of rough-dressed stone, Laban constructed, as only a boatbuilder could, a very strongly framed, two-and-a-half-story pitched-roof mill building. With its classic proportions and weathered shingled exterior it remained for over a century a distinctive harbor landmark and a durable and handsome example of New England craftsmanship.

The main power for his operation was supplied by windmills, but to supplement these Laban added a huge wooden tank to the second floor of his mill. The plan was that, when the winds blew fresh, he could grind his coarse salt crystals and at the same time pump water into his tank. In periods of calm he would then have reserve water power with which to continue the grinding. Unfortunately for the scheme, hours were required to fill the tank, whereas minutes alone would empty it. The mill was soon memorialized forever as Laban's Folly. The island itself gradually became a wharf by the addition of a pile-and-plank runway from the shore. By my day this wooden structure had been replaced by a stone-walled causeway with gravel fill.

In spite of his mill miscalculations, Laban must have been quite a fellow. Not only was he involved in all manner of local businesses and land ownings, he is credited with being the inspiration for the surviving name of the Apponagansett settlement and its harbor. The name Padanaram first appears in the town records on an 1828 deed given by Laban. It is a biblical reference that can be found in Genesis 28:2. For, like Jacob of old, young Laban Thatcher had left the home of his father to make a new start in a far country.

After the completion of a wooden bridge, which in 1834 replaced the ferry service across the Apponagansett River, several shipbuilders found it advisable to move their operations farther southward to land at the foot of Laban's Folly. This building site logically came to be known as South Wharf. Here, in the years between 1845 and 1858, the firm of Mathews, Mashow and Company built a veritable fleet of schooners, barks, and other craft, including the schooner *Bouquet* (1855), the firm's first and only yacht. These forty or more vessels were not small boats by any means; many were whaleships and merchantmen that made fame for themselves and fortunes for their owners. Alonzo Mathews was a member of an already prominent shipbuilding family. His major partner, John Mashow, was a Negro who as a boy came from Georgetown, South Carolina, to Dartmouth. Mashow learned his trade from Laban Thatcher. He was soon recognized as one of the finest builders in the country, and a Mashow-built ship was one to be proud of.

The Civil War and other exigencies brought an end to shipbuilding in Padanaram. Thereafter South Wharf was utilized for many diverse enterprises. In 1870 a South Wharf Company was organized, and some ten years later Laban's Folly was joined by other buildings, including a great coal pocket which occupied the whole northwest corner of the wharf. By the 1890s, one Charlie Howland— clearly a relative of mine, but at some remove— held a major interest in South Wharf. As bakemaster supreme he produced top-notch clambakes which attracted patrons from far and near. Depending on the weather, he served his feasts either in, or on the west side of Laban's Folly. He himself lived upstairs where the tank had been. Outside, to the east, he had a small building in which to store his clambake gear. Farther in on the dock, my friend Leon Dunn's father, William, owned a fish house. Local boats brought in fresh fish and landed them at his door on the south side of the dock causeway. They were then packed in boxes and shipped by trolley car to New Bedford. The newly completed electric car line ended on the east side of Elm Street, conveniently right at the foot of South Wharf.

At about this time, 1901 to be exact, the New Bedford Yacht Club built its Padanaram station immediately south of South Wharf, and only a year after that came the completion of the new village bridge. With all this local activity, Charlie Howland put in a water system with well and windmill tower, and then built a pavilion on the west side of Elm Street. This was the same land that the Mashow shipyard had occupied. Here, for New Bedford trolley trippers and others, he furnished entertainment and sold a variety of knickknacks, food, and drinks.

Like most good waterfront locations, South Wharf was from the beginning a center of activity. About 1908 Charlie Howland's pavilion was moved out onto the wharf to replace the by-now-abandoned coal pocket. Other small businesses were set up on the wharf, including even a clothing store. Then, about 1911, Charlie Howland's interests in Laban's Folly came to an end, and, according to Leon Dunn, the wharf and shoreward land that went with it were offered to the Town of Dartmouth at a very modest price. The town fathers failed to take any action; their one chance to get a good town wharf was lost, so it seems, for good. Meanwhile, a small group of nearby landowners formed a second South Wharf trust and gradually bought out various interests, consolidating them into the single wharf unit which Colonel Green purchased in 1915.

Padanaram Station of the New Bedford Yacht Club, perhaps during its commissioning day ceremony in 1901. The pavilion at left would soon be moved out to the end of South Wharf.

3
Martin Jackson:
Harbor Master

Before World War II, Padanaram Harbor sheltered a picturesque little fleet of work and pleasure boats, with ample room for all. The small craft were uncrowded in the shoal water close in and to the south of the yacht club. The 30- and 40-footers were moored just across the channel on the west side, where there was ample depth of water. The schooners and other bigger boats, generally cared for by professional crews, lay in the outer harbor to the east, and in the lee of the breakwater.

There were only two government markers in the harbor. One was a bush buoy (a spar, to the top of which a small cedar tree had been nailed) that was later replaced with a nun; this marked a rock on the outer east side of the harbor. The other, and far more important, marker was a nun located about midway up the harbor and well over toward the west side of the natural deep-water channel. Its main purpose was to create a mooring and anchorage area in the handier and more protected east sections of the harbor.

Through long-standing riparian right, an owner with an established mooring retained his location privileges year after year, and might even hand them down in the family. An experienced harbor master not only recognized this custom, but adhered to it, and made only those changes

Martin Jackson at the tiller of the yard's workboat *Gracie II* in 1965. Our guesthouse for customers, nicknamed the Waldo Astoria, is at the water's edge at the extreme left of the picture, and stacked-up cradles show at center.

33

necessitated by special contingencies. By law the Padanaram harbor master was—and is—elected by Dartmouth voters and given very substantial control over boat traffic, moorings, and fishing regulations. As with countless other seafaring towns up and down the coast, it meant a great deal to Dartmouth to retain as harbor master an able man who habitually worked in the environs of the harbor and who had the temperament to maintain good public relations with all concerned. Such a man would know personally local boats and boatowners, depths of water, characteristics of holding ground, potential for storm damage, and much else besides.

Concordia's foreman, Martin Jackson, was first elected Padanaram harbor master in 1940. With good reason he became the town's most-elected official and was returned to office term after term until he retired from Concordia Company in 1969. Adhering to workable, established custom and playing no favorites, he held the confidence and backing of the yacht club directors and most individual boat owners. Having himself done a fair amount of quahoging, scalloping, and fishing, he readily understood the problems of the working fisherman. For his daily attendance and all his wisdom and effort, Martin received the munificent yearly salary of one hundred dollars. For the use of a yard boat and other equipment, he received nothing. His thirty-year reign was a noble record that all Padanaram sailors should remember with gratitude. Certainly it was a boon to Concordia.

ii

The 1938 hurricane dramatically highlighted some old truths about the characteristics of Padanaram Harbor: that the west side of the harbor, although exposed in an occasional southeast blow, furnished the best holding ground; that the bottom of the east side was soft, meaning that when high flood waters rushed out, they took with them mud, moorings, and all; that certain moorings, regardless of their location, were just plain inadequate and real troublemakers: dragging loose early on and causing the release or damage of well-moored boats unfortunate enough to be in their path; that most moorings had insufficient scope to withstand the extreme rise of water—ten feet or more above normal high tide—that we experienced in the 1938 hurricane; that the most damaging wind direction was south-southeast—or straight up the harbor.

Although it was a costly investment at a time when cash was scarce, we felt it would be of benefit to all concerned if Concordia owned or managed as many of the moorings as possible. This would allow us to control their design, location, and maintenance. In addition to Padanaram moorings that we inherited with the purchase of Harold Cleveland's business, we

gradually took over the ownership or management of others in the harbor, at Nonquitt and Salters Point, and at a few more distant locations. War conditions thrust additional moorings into our hands, when some owners abandoned their equipment without notice or offered their moorings to us.

Some yachtsmen believe that renting a mooring is the expensive way

Aerial view (from the south) of the east shore of Padanaram Harbor and the south shore of Ricketsons Point, about 1950. The boatyard and basin are visible just to the right of the bridge.

35

of doing things. In fact, however, this system can be the most practical arrangement of all. Certainly, it was in our case. For with Concordia owning most moorings, Martin could work consistently toward an orderly mooring system. The small daysailers would continue to be located within easy rowing distance of the yacht club and in shoal water not adequate for large boats. Powerboats, which swing differently from sailboats to wind and tide, could in general be located in an area of modest water depth. Larger vessels needing more swinging room and depth of water would naturally be best provided for in the outer harbor. Knowledgeable sailors understood this practical philosophy, even if they did not always get their first choice of mooring assignment.

Keeping track of numerous mooring locations is never easy. Using his own ranges, Martin knew instinctively where certain primary moorings lay; he listed others on paper and in his mind, according to bearing and distance from them. For most of us this system would be difficult, almost impossible, but Martin played his moorings as a pianist plays his keys. A seaman's sense, like a bird's compass, may be hard to understand, but is very real.

Management of the whole Padanaram mooring system fell primarily on Martin's shoulders, and after a period of trial and error he developed arrangements that proved substantially satisfactory not just for local boat owners, visiting yachtsmen, and yacht club directors, but for the Coast Guard and even for the town tax collector.

The handling of guest moorings was a matter of the greatest sensitivity. As I have said, Concordia owned, or was responsible for, the majority of the moorings in Padanaram, very few of which were specifically for guests to the harbor. The yacht club, on the other hand, owned few moorings, but the club's launchmen were always on duty to direct a visitor to a suitable available mooring. Concordia and the yacht club therefore agreed to split their responsibilities and share the guest fees. There were always mooring owners or renters who felt it was unfair that they didn't receive any recompense for the guest use of their moorings. However, it was definitely to their advantage to keep the mooring line out of water, and to know that moorings were not being used by oversized boats that might drag or damage them or by visitors who did not know when to leave.

The Coast Guard had occasion one year to lift and repair the outer channel marker. Their original range marker, a candy stand at the west end of the bridge, had been washed away by a hurricane, and they reset the nun well west of where it had been. Martin, who had done his share to make the government service welcome at our dock, brought this buoy misplacement to their attention. The Coast Guard most courteously cooperated by moving the nun back where it would best serve harbor interests.

The tax potential of pleasure boats has always been of great interest to waterfront towns. In Dartmouth the selectmen turned to Martin to make up a list of boats stored in the town as of each January first, and to place opposite each one a value. If the boats were assessed at full value, the tax would be excessively high and drive boat owners to more hospitable towns; whereas a reasonable percentage of value would result in good revenue for Dartmouth from the greatest possible number of boats. Martin was scrupulously fair and impartial in setting his valuations. The boat owners were happy with the results—or as happy as they could be with taxes of any nature.

But Martin was not immune to criticism. One group of disgruntled individuals insisted that they had citizens' rights to set their moorings where they pleased. Receiving no satisfaction from Martin, they organized a political campaign to replace him with a man of their own choosing. They hired a lawyer, issued stickers and buttons for their candidate, and even gave away promotional combs. (Martin was bald.) On election day the votes went to Martin. So that was that.

As head of the boatyard, I too was handed a few mooring problems. These tended to come from new owners who resented, quite understandably, being placed on the outer rim of the established mooring area. My most persuasive response was that we would have to kill off Mr. Stanton, Mr. Wing, my father, and other senior yachtsmen before we could steal their mooring locations. Even my most adamant critics realized that this would be going a bit too far. A more specialized complaint came from an owner who refused to pay a fall bill for the winter staking of his mooring. He claimed he had never ordered the work to be done, which was absolutely true. With no charges involved, we agreed to remove the stake and put back the summer pennant. The following spring the owner did give us an order: to find his sunken mooring and make up a new pennant for him.

Another owner made a habit of complaining that our mooring bills were too high. He regularly insisted that we take off ten percent. The hassle was unproductive and time-consuming; I eventually resorted to the practice of adding ten percent to the troublesome annual bill, which we gladly took off for the owner each spring. As the old-timers say, there's nothing so queer as folks.

Concordia's mooring tripod set on pontoons. The buildings in the background are just north of the Concordia property. The gull, although never on Concordia's payroll, was a frequent inspector.

MOORINGS

Moorings come in many different forms, some good, some bad. At Concordia we inherited a few old-timers, such as big, flat rocks with bolts through them. In soft bottom, these worked their way down into the mud and held just fine, but they were heavy and difficult to service, and a diver was often required to check them for us. Freightcar wheels, big blocks of cement, and even old engines did their job under the right circumstances, but again they had their fouling and servicing problems. A few interesting old ships' anchors came to light and seemed to have served well, but these generally ended up with many turns of chain around their exposed flukes, which is not a good situation.

It was soon apparent that, although expensive, adequate mushroom-type anchors were the best. These tended to work their way down in most bot-

toms. Once under the mud, they deteriorated very little—in fact, they seemed to last more or less indefinitely.

Up through the 1920s the Fairhaven Iron Foundry made a special "bulb" mushroom. Designed with a long shank, it had a heavy, oval-shaped, bulb cast to its head, just below the shackle eye. This extra weight tended to keep the anchor lying down on its side as intended. Without the bulb, conventional mushrooms sometimes stand up with their shanks in a somewhat perpendicular position, and thus lose much of their holding power.

The closing of the Fairhaven Foundry was a sad loss for boat owners, because their mushroom anchors were certainly the very best. To create a substitute, Concordia made up necessary patterns and arranged with Mr. Gardner at his iron foundry in

Easton, Massachusetts, to produce for us Fairhaven-type mushrooms in various weights ranging from seventy-five to twelve hundred pounds. (The base and bulb were cast onto a steel shaft.) Having more holding power for their weight than standard mushroom anchors, these bulb anchors were by far the easiest to handle and maintain.

In general, our preferred moorings were made up with a bulb mushroom anchor, shackled to a galvanized chain, which in turn was shackled to a custom-made nylon (originally manila) pennant. Into the lower end of the pennant was spliced a heavy galvanized thimble. The upper end of the pennant was made into an eyesplice so dimensioned that it would slip comfortably over the particular boat's mooring cleat, bitts, or windlass. The pennant was of such a length that the chain itself could never chafe on the side of its boat, even when the boat rode forward on it. There is virtue in having a pennant on the large side to allow for some chafe, but, regardless, it had to fit comfortably in the boat's bow chocks. To prevent the buildup of barnacles and other growth, the pennant, all but its upper end, was parceled with strips of canvas, seized in place, and then painted with antifouling paint. Finally, attached just below the pennant's

mooring loop, there was a light pickup line, the outer end of which was secured to a small buoy. This had the double purpose of floating the mooring line and clearly identifying it.

There is nothing unusual about this general design of mooring, and I go into a discussion of it only to emphasize the importance of correct and custom detail. As a rough guide for those who might be interested, I have, with Martin's guidance, made up the chart on the following page which suggests mooring dimensions for different-sized boats that might be moored in a harbor such as Padanaram.

There are, of course, all kinds of variations that should be considered for particular situations. For instance, moorings that we set off exposed South Nonquitt or Mishaum Point had especially heavy anchors and chains plus additional scope. In the harbor, scope is unfortunately limited by the close proximity of too many boats. In certain cases, Martin compensated for this by dividing the chain into two sections. The upper two-thirds was of standard variety; the lower third (just long enough for its shackle to reach the surface) was of really heavy old ship's chain, preferably stud link. Due to its great weight, this section normally just lay in the

The Concordia mooring shed, built on the foundation of Laban's Folly. Both standard mushrooms and bulb-type Fairhaven Foundry mushrooms are shown in weights varying from seventy-five to twelve hundred pounds. In the foreground are two winter mooring stakes. Navy surplus steel balls (at left) were used for large mooring floats. Our mooring boat of later years operated from a float on the south side of the wharf, just out of the photo to the left.

Standard Concordia Moorings

Boat length	Weight of mushroom	Galvanized chain size	Nylon pennant size	Nylon pennant length
12'–15' (Beetle Cat)	75 lbs.	$3/8''$	$5/8''$	15'
15'–20' (Herreshoff 12)	100 lbs	$3/8''$	$5/8''$	18'
20'–25' (S boat)	300 lbs.	$1/2''$	$3/4''$	25'
25'–30'	400 lbs.	$1/2''$	$7/8''$	25'
30'–40' (Concordia)	500 to 750 lbs.	$3/4''$	$1''$	30'
40'–50'	750 to 1,000 lbs.	$3/4''$	$1^1/4''$	35'

Assuming: Bulb-type mushroom anchors; harbor conditions like those at Padanaram; length of chain three times the depth of water (3:1 ratio), plus 5' for extra-high tide.

mud. Only under the stress of extreme high water or wind would it ever straighten out, and, even then, little jerk or lifting effect would be transmitted to the anchor.

For an insurance-oriented customer, Martin designed a special mooring setup that retained a reasonable swinging circle, yet achieved a long scope when needed. As shown on the hurricane mooring sketch, two widely spaced and lined-up mushrooms were connected by a chain arrangement, in the taut length of which was a heavy iron ring. To this ring was shackled a conventional mooring chain and pennant. The tremendous holding power of this arrangement more than compensated for its possible fouling of a visitor's anchor. Note on the sketch that the bigger mushroom and heaviest chain were laid to the southeast of the ring and the lighter mushroom.

Another feature of this special mooring in later years (when the materials became available) was a big, Dacron-covered nun-shaped buoy, which was shackled between chain and pennant. Under storm conditions, this acted like a shock absorber, in that to straighten out the chain-pennant unit to

the ring the buoy itself would have to be forced under water. The big-buoy theory was not new. Many moorings off exposed beaches used a heavy floating mooring log between chain and pennant. Martin merely substituted the special fendered buoy for the old log type that could often damage topsides in a tideway.

Few who have not made up and handled their own moorings for a number of years realize how much more there is to the process than first meets the eye. Even a fifty-pounder requires most of the elements of a larger unit: proper lengths and sizes of chain, shackles that will fit, nylon line of special dimensions, harbor master approval, splicing ability on the owner's part, and more.

Good mooring maintenance is an annual chore of some considerable proportions and responsibility. In the fall the pennant must be removed, brought ashore, immediately cleaned, rinsed off with fresh water, coiled, hung up to dry, and then, as time permits, repaired as necessary. To take the place of the pennant and to mark the mooring for the winter months, a wooden stake has to be prepared and painted—with antifouling paint for the underwater portion, and with white above for good visibility. It must also be identified with a suitable tag or nameplate (Martin used out-of-date dog tags). The stake, preferably round in section, must be of sufficient length and diameter to float the chain-end and keep its own head out of water. You may ask, why a stake? The answer is that this deep-floating form of buoy withstands ice and other winter ravages better than types that float mainly on the surface.

Springtime requires the reverse process. The winter stake comes off for cleaning, repair, and repainting. Simultaneously, the pennant (its lower end having been freshly dipped in an antifouling mixture of copper paint mixed with kerosene) is shackled into the chain. This changeover should

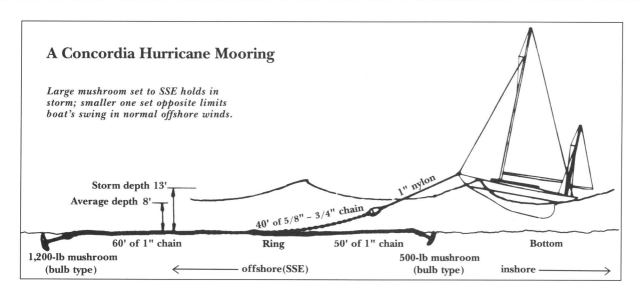

A Concordia Hurricane Mooring

Large mushroom set to SSE holds in storm; smaller one set opposite limits boat's swing in normal offshore winds.

Storm depth 13'
Average depth 8'
1" nylon
40' of 5/8" – 3/4" chain
60' of 1" chain
Ring
50' of 1" chain
Bottom
1,200-lb mushroom (bulb type)
← offshore(SSE)
500-lb mushroom (bulb type)
inshore →

not take place until a few days before the mooring is to be used, because the exposed and unpainted pennant loop and pickup line tend to become foul when in the water unattended for any length of time. Slime or barnacles on the nylon are not good for topsides, deck, or hands. All in all, taking care of a mooring is a hard and messy job and entails a number of complications learned only by thoughtful experience. I suggest that a would-be mooring tender's wife should have some extra bandaids on hand and save a day or two for extra laundry.

Equipment for handling and servicing moorings doesn't have too many components, but items needed are somewhat specialized. A good, rugged skiff, preferably oar or inboard powered, one with plenty of stability, is mighty useful. Concordia's skiff, inherited from the Clevelands, had a one-lung, make-and-break United States engine. Her big outboard rudder was fitted with a strong tiller that could be operated by hand, foot, or knee. Her equipage included a long galvanized pump, a strong boathook, a box of rusty tools including a heavy ball-peen hammer, pliers, a stilson wrench, a marlinspike, a dirty rag or two, a fish knife, and some copper wire for seizing shackle pins.* This

* Our friend Captain Swift advised using stainless-steel wire, but Martin found this rusted right out, and the copper did little damage to the iron pins.

skiff of ours came with the lovely name of *Gracie*, but she was better known as "Greasy."

From the Clevelands also, we acquired a set of pontoons, straddled by a few platform planks, and two structural beams on which was mounted a tripod derrick arrangement with rope tackle and windlass. If the latter would not release a mooring from its hold on the bottom, Martin set the gear up taut and let a rising tide cope with the situation. Mud gives up slowly, and a steady tension over a period of time will do a lot more than a quick pull of short duration. Martin endeavored to check all moorings on a rotating basis so that every few years each one could be raised and repaired as needed.

For setting a heavy mooring, our wharf derrick lowered the mooring to just below water level, where it was tied with some old line to a beam of our pontoon rig, from which suspension it could be cut loose when in position.

On shore was our mooring shed, which changed in location and grew in size as the years went by. Its major piece of equipment was a huge standing vise that at one time had graced the on-deck workbench of a whaleship. Other tools included hammers and steel marlinspikes of various sizes, and other ingenious shackle persuaders, like a blow torch. Then there were kerosene, machine oil, a heavy wirecutter, hacksaws, and ropeworking tools.

4
Beetle Cat Boats

i

When I returned to Concordia from the Navy, I found myself rather like a fifth wheel on a cart. The yard operation was running smoothly, with Martin managing outside and Louie in charge of the office. It was not the right time for intrusions. Therefore I focused my initial attention on brokerage and sales.

Realizing that boatyard springtimes are always too busy and boatyard wintertimes always too slack, it seemed to me worthwhile to explore the practicability of a small-boat building program that might ease this seasonal problem. Father mentioned the recent closing of the Herreshoff yard in Bristol and suggested the sad possibility that the deservedly popular Herreshoff Twelves might be no longer in production. With the vague thought that Concordia might build several Twelves each winter, I went to see my helpful friend Fred Barden in Marion. Before the war he and his boatyard had had a special agency arrangement for sales of the Twelves. As it turned out, Fred could only advise me that E. Leslie Goodwin at Cape Cod Shipbuilding in Wareham had finally acquired building rights to the Twelves (along with a number of other Herreshoff designs).

Les Goodwin, with whom Concordia had already had happy dealings, was most cooperative and seemed quite prepared to work with Concordia on a royalty basis. However, it finally appeared that, after paying the required royalties, our end selling price might well be too high for the market. Herreshoff Twelves, with their lead keels, special hardware, and fine workmanship, were expensive boats to build. It would be especially expensive to build new Twelves that would be acceptable for competition in the existing Herreshoff-built one-design class.

Cruising Beetle Cat (owned by Nicholas Whitman) among the marsh grass on the Westport River. The shrouds are optional equipment, called for mainly by racing enthusiasts.

43

At this time Father was enjoying frequent communication with his friend L. Francis Herreshoff (who, in fact, later dedicated his book *The Compleat Cruiser* to Father). These boat-minded authors were both writing articles for Boris Lauer-Leonardi, editor of *The Rudder*. Because of Padanaram's location partway between New York (where Boris lived) and Marblehead (where Francis lived), the three often gathered at Father's house for congenial overnight conferences. Early on, Boris had acquired one of Francis's great, Twelve-inspired H-28 ketches, and it was natural enough that Father should now commission Francis to design for him a version of the Herreshoff Twelve that Concordia could build as a new class, unhampered by restrictions.

We might well have proceeded with the newly designed Buzzards Bay Fourteen, had we not become aware of a growing demand for new Beetle Cat Boats. This unanticipated development prompted me to visit Carl Beetle of New Bedford, the current owner of building rights to these splendid little centerboard catboats.

I already knew Carl well as builder of the Crocker-designed New Bedford Thirty-five sloops that raced so competitively against Father's *Java*, and on my first business approach, Carl was very much his old determined self. No, he had no used Beetles for sale. No, he wasn't building any more new wooden Beetles. No, he wouldn't build any for us, even if we did have buyers for them.

These answers were not just for the sake of being contrary; they were the result of deep conviction. Carl was by nature a capable, inventive, forward-looking sort of boatbuilder. During and immediately following the war he had become the first to go seriously into the development and use of fiberglass for boat construction. With financial backing from a group of prominent New Bedford businessmen (among them Dick Gee, Fred Towle, Ike Dawson, Judge Crowe, Seabury and Otis Stanton, and Edmund Rigby), he had formed a new corporation expressly to build fiberglass boats. Using the trade name "B. B. Boats," Beetle Boat Corporation was already well into production. In addition to a marconi-rigged fiberglass version of the original Beetle Cat, it produced an 8-foot dhow-shaped dinghy (this before the days of the fiberglass Dyer Dhow) and several powerboats designed for bass fishing in the 20- to 24-foot range.

The fiberglass craft were revolutionary to the trade and created a big stir. They were selling well, they promised to be both long-lasting and maintenance-free, and on top of that they appeared to be relatively inexpensive to produce. Carl truly felt, and with reason enough, that wooden boats would soon become a thing of the past.

Momentarily discouraged, I withdrew from any argument, but I was back again at Carl in a couple of weeks. Still no luck! Finally, on my third visit, Carl came forth with a suggestion. "If you are so damn sure about the future of wood," he said, "why don't you just take this whole blessed wooden Beetle business out of here." Carl pointed around toward the back of his newly acquired South End shop, at a number of half-finished wooden Beetle hulls, oddments of parts, lumber, and other materials, and the all-important original Beetle Cat mold and patterns. (There never had been any formal Beetle Cat plans on paper.) I asked Carl what he wanted for it all. He grabbed a scrap of paper and quickly totaled up the lot on some basis or other, added a mysterious extra of minute proportions, and said, "There, and good luck, and don't use the name Beetle Cat. Call your boats Wooden Beetles." A handshake from him, a check from me, and that was about it. In essence Concordia acquired the original Beetle Cat Boat business for nothing, and Carl had his shop cleaned up for free.

The Rainbow Fleet rounding Brant Point at Nantucket, about 1924. One of the earliest fleets of Beetle Cats, all of these Nantucket boats had different-colored sails.

ii

Although much smaller than the working Cape Cod cats, the wooden Beetle Cat Boat had most of their basic virtues. It was shoal draft, to get over sandbars and to run up on sandy beaches. Its rudder was designed not to extend below the keel and skeg line. Its centerboard (unlike a dagger-board) automatically pivoted up on grounding. Its beam was wide, to attain good initial stability and to afford ample carrying capacity. Its forward deck was intentionally long, to deflect wave water whether the boat was underway or moored in a rough anchorage, and further to minimize the tendency of an open boat to swamp in heavy rainstorms. Its bow had a slight hollow at the waterline, but was full on deck to balance its wide stern, to support a forward position of mast, and to allow a person to get forward without fear of capsize.

Its gaff rig and sail proportions were tried, true, and basically suitable for a proper Cape Cod cat. With short mast and long boom, this type of boat tends to come head to the wind and stop as soon as the tiller is released. This virtue can become very important for general work and fishing operations and likewise for many pleasure-boating situations.

The throat and peak halyards led aft to allow the crew, without moving their weight, to adjust the shape of the sail to suit the conditions: well peaked up for going to windward, peak slacked off slightly for squaring away to leeward, peak scandalized (slacked away completely) as a most effective emergency reef.

The fact that the boat was to be built entirely of wood and to require no ballast other than human made it nonsinkable. In case of a capsize or flooding, a tow from the bow, especially with crew dragging astern, would (and does) tend to right the boat and gradually and automatically free her of overburdening water.

Complete equipment was simple enough, consisting of spars and sail, anchor and warp, bucket and pump, a paddle or oar, and whatever equipment was required by the Coast Guard.

In fact, this catboat was a complete little ship, having a shape that has been proven by generations of experienced boatmen. As early as 1880, the English yachting authority Dixon Kemp had written that "these wonderful little craft [catboats] were extremely handy and useful and would always be popular." Charlie Beetle claimed that as long as man married woman and had children, the Beetle Cat would continue to be in demand. Certainly it has been my own observation that if any boats whatever are sailing in Padanaram Harbor, one of them is almost sure to be a Beetle or at least a catboat.

Beetle Cats racing at
Padanaram, about 1952.

These and other plans, drawn up by B.T. Dobson from existing boats, became the standard to which all future Beetle Cats would be built.

iii

When Concordia fell heir to the wooden Beetle Cat business in 1946, events did not work out at all as I had anticipated. Instead of eight or ten Beetle Cat orders, we received six times that many, a volume we were totally unprepared to handle with our limited facilities at South Wharf. So, as I had done on previous occasions, I turned to the New Bedford boatbuilder Palmer Scott for help. And as always, Palmer generously gave it to me. By putting Leo Telesmanick in charge of the actual building, all Palmer had to do was line up more oak, pine, and cedar and increase his production lines to include Beetle Cats as well as the Rhodes-designed Wood Pussys he was building on contract for other interests.

For the following fifteen years the wooden Beetle Cat business went along very smoothly, with Concordia handling sales and service and Leo, as an employee of Palmer Scott's, doing the building. Volume ran about seventy boats a year, sometimes a few more, sometimes a few less. Most buyers came from the South Shore of Massachusetts Bay, Cape Cod, and Narragansett Bay. Several fleets also developed on Great South Bay, Long Island, thanks to the Richard Perkins family who summered at Mishaum Point. Prices crept up annually, but never drastically, from four hundred to six hundred dollars, in that period of low inflation.

Also during that period, and always under Leo's direction, several modifications were made in Beetle Cat construction. The major change was undertaken the better to assure the uniformity of the hulls. Slight hull variations had been possible with the traditional whaleboat plank-first, frame-afterwards system, and owners sometimes suggested that it was the boat and not their child that was out of shape for winning races. To eliminate this uncertainty, Leo built one boat with special care, checking out every measurement against a number of older boats. Then the meticulous New Bedford naval architect Ben Dobson was commissioned to take off the lines of this special hull and to draw up for Concordia a set of formal architectural plans that would thereafter be standard for all future wooden Beetle Cat Boats. In addition to lines and offsets, Dobson drew construction, sail, deck, and parts plans.

Adhering precisely to these Dobson plans, Leo made up a new and different type of mold—solid, fixed, and upside-down—on which the frames were first steamed and wrapped on, then firmly locked into position. Each pre-shaped plank was then sprung over and around the frames and fastened with screws. (Galvanized clench nails, which had been used up until then and had been most satisfactory, were no longer possible, because there was no way for a human hand to get inside the new type of mold to clench them.)

We made several other minor improvements. We also got a number of interesting suggestions from well-wishing professionals and amateurs that were pertinent enough but didn't promise improvement. One recurring suggestion was that we use plywood for the decks. Our primary response to this was that plywood could not comfortably tolerate the needed compound curves of both sheer and crown. Second, it was expensive material. Third, its exposed end-grain edges could soak up water, to its own detriment. Fourth, there were always pieces of cedar left over that made first-class material for the deck, but were too short for planking or ceiling. And fifth, I didn't—and I still don't—like plywood.

A second suggestion was that we fasten the oak guardrail (Leo called it half-round) around the sheer with screws instead of common galvanized wire nails. This, at first, might seem like an improvement, but Beetles are meant for all members of the family to use and may, through error, run into floats, pilings, sisterships, or whatever. The half-round guardrail acts like a fender and absorbs the blow, sometimes getting ripped off in the process. Such an accident rarely does damage to the sheerstrake, deck edges, or canvas, as it surely would do if the guardrail were screw-fastened. Replacement rails, all varnished and ready for use, were kept in stock. With them any carpenter could easily and efficiently make most repairs resulting from collisions.

And we were asked why we didn't use standard marine hardware, instead of going to the trouble of making up our own. Again, the answers were revealing. Stock hardware has a way, over the years, of changing in style, going out of production, or becoming unavailable when needed. Although our rough bronze castings were expensive, our labor costs for finishing them were minimal. Any time one of the crew had a few minutes, at the end of a day or during a pause between jobs, there was always a hole to drill, or a grind to do that would finish up a rough casting in fine shape.

I could go on about Beetle Cat details, because details do make up the whole. However, the real point to be made here is that Beetle construction (materials and methods included), as well as Beetle design, was thoughtfully and thoroughly worked out in the first place. It is always difficult to improve upon a good thing.

A companion factor in the longevity of Beetle Cat Boats individually and as a class is the builder's determination never to make a change in the original design or construction that might outdate an older boat. A twenty-year-old Beetle continues to retain the same chances of winning races as a new one, and its value therefore keeps pace with the gradual advance in new boat prices. Obsolescence has never been a Beetle Cat objective.

The Beetle–Scott–Concordia arrangement might well have continued indefinitely had Palmer Scott not decided to retire. In 1960 the whole Beetle Cat operation, including Leo, part of his crew, and the molds, patterns, and Palmer's blessings, was bodily shifted from the Palmer Scott yard to Concordia. To make room for it, and to add sorely needed storage space for other small boats, Concordia rented from Martin Jackson a half-acre of land behind his house on Smith Neck Road. For boat storage, lumber storage, building, and work of all sorts, the high ground of the Smith Neck yard soon proved to be a godsend.

Since the early 1960s, production of Beetle Cats has run about thirty boats a year. The media (including *The New York Times Magazine* and *The New Yorker*) has "discovered a living boatbuilding legend" in Beetle Cats that has given the boats something of an international reputation. More and more individual boats are being shipped to faraway sailing grounds—Florida, Washington State, Hawaii, and beyond. And, thanks to the influence of Mystic Seaport Museum, a strong new fleet has developed in that Connecticut area. One forward-looking grandfather went so far as to order a 1984 Beetle to be saved for a grandchild yet to be born. Although Leo Telesmanick semi-retired in 1985, he still lives just a few yards from the shop on the Smith Neck Road and still contributes help and guidance to Charlie York, who is now in charge of the program.

Throughout the years, the New England Beetle Cat Association (which was officially organized in 1937) has kept its various fleets together and their racing activity humming, growing in membership from six clubs to nearly six times that many. In 1948 the Association adopted two regulations that were of considerable importance, both to the class and to Concordia Company. First, it offered membership to any organization that schedules regular Beetle Cat races for three or more boats. Second, it stated that boats must be standard Original Beetle Cats (wooden), built by Concordia Company, Inc. or by its licensee. The main reason that the second regulation has been adhered to thus far is that no one with profits in mind has figured out how to compete with Concordia's Beetle Cat prices.

But perhaps the primary objective of the New England Beetle Cat Association is "to foster a feeling of good will and neighborliness between Beetle Cat Boat sailors." That it has succeeded so well in this effort is a wonderful testament to the vision and practical ingenuity of John and Carl Beetle, who first worked up the model for the Beetle Cat more than sixty years ago.

The old Beetle boatshop, located on the east shore of Clarks Point on the southwestern side of New Bedford Harbor, about 1914. The tall smokestack and the long row of windows of a cotton mill loom in the right background.

THE BEETLES OF NEW BEDFORD

As with our acquisition of South Wharf, I can't help feeling that the Howlands had somehow been destined to acquire the old catboat business from the Beetles. The two families had already worked together in one way or another for three generations, so why not a fourth?

At eighteen years of age, Carl's grandfather James Beetle, like many another young boat-builder, migrated from Cape Cod to New Bedford, intent on taking advantage of the growing whaling industry. This was in 1830. After an apprenticeship at Crampton's whaleboat shop, James went to work for the Hillman Brothers shipyard, which at the time was building the whaleship *Charles W. Morgan.* For his next move

James set up a whaleboat shop of his own. It was here that my great-grand-uncle George and my great-grandfather Matthew Howland, as joint owners of a fleet of whaleships, became two of his best customers.

By 1879 James Beetle had moved his shop south a mile or so, out of New Bedford's inner harbor and onto the east shore of Clarks Point. With this change he brought two of his sons into the picture. The older one, John, became lumber surveyor for the prosperous nearby Greene and Wood Lumber Company. The younger one, Charles, stayed with the family boatbuilding shop and not only took over the business in due course, but expanded its operations. (A third

Beetle's boatyard at Clarks Point, about 1900. Father's ketch *Fox* (without a winter cover) is the hull with dark topsides in the upper right-hand corner of the picture. Several Beetle-built whaleboats lie next to the boat shed.

son, or close relative, named James Beetle moved about 1890 to San Francisco to set up a successful whaleboat shop there.)

It was Charles Beetle who in 1896 built the beautiful 54-foot Will Fife-designed yawl *Flying Cloud* for my grandfather William D. Howland, and shortly thereafter the little Block Island ketch *Fox* for my father. It was also Charles Beetle who, a few years earlier, had given Father his first paying job: doing chores around the yard and putting bungs in planking at a pittance apiece. At the time, Father was a schoolboy living but a half mile away, over the hill on the west shore of Clarks Point.

Although the Beetle shop continued to build whaleboats until well after the turn of the century, these later craft were mainly special-purpose orders. In 1920, as a fill-in project for the yard, John Beetle and his son Carl modeled a 12-foot Cape Cod-type catboat that they were convinced would make a safe, useful, and pleasurable boat for young members of the Beetle family and, they hoped, for other young-

sters as well. It would be known, quite naturally, as the Beetle Cat.

Carl Beetle was scheduled to be the builder of the first production Beetle Cats and was, in fact, involved in setting up the Beetle Cat building program in 1921. This was in essence a continuation of the ingenious and efficient whaleboat production system the Beetles had devised years before. Under the system, whaleboat parts had been prefabricated and kept on well-placed wall pegs so that they would air-dry evenly and be ready for use at a moment's notice. Permanent station molds were carefully designed to fit into a form. These molds could be placed more closely together for a shorter whaleboat or slightly farther apart for a longer one. With a stem and stern-post attached to a keel of the desired length, and with the station molds placed accordingly, the right set of pattern-shaped planks could be wrapped from stem to stern around the molds. After this the steamed oak frames were bent into place, and the planks were fastened to them with clench nails. My father in his book *Sou'West and By West of Cape Cod* gives a first-hand account of helping to complete one of these Beetle whaleboats within a period of thirty-six hours, paint and delivery included. Speed was of the absolute essence, if the ordering whaleship was standing by ready to sail.*

Such haste was, of course, not essential for the building of a Beetle Cat, but, naturally, the fewer hours involved, the more economical the finished product. Certainly, a low initial sales price has historically been a strong factor in the selling of Beetle Cats, as it had once been in sales of Beetle whaleboats.

Once the word had passed around, the new catboats were in good demand as single boats and in small fleets. They became very popular both for general use and for racing, especially in shallow harbors such as Duxbury, Nantucket, Bass River, Barnstable, and other Cape Cod towns. Although Carl Beetle was both builder and salesman, he seemed to lose interest in the project early on, switching his capabilities elsewhere and toward the building of larger boats. Fortunately for the little cats, his father, John, came to their rescue and worked on them evenings, after finishing his day's work at

*For a full account of whaleboat building, see *The Whaleboat*, by Willits D. Ansel, Mystic Seaport Museum, Mystic, CT, 1978; also *To Build a Whaleboat*, by Erik A. R. Ronnberg, The Old Dartmouth Historical Society Whaling Museum, New Bedford, MA, 1985.

Greene and Wood. Production went along on this limited scale until 1928, when John Beetle himself joined his ancestors.

At this critical point John's brother Charlie Beetle took over the management of the program, set up his son-in-law, John Baumann, as master builder, and his niece, Ruth, daughter of John Beetle, as treasurer and bookkeeper. Shortly after this, in 1930, he apprenticed as helper Leo Telesmanick, a lanky fifteen-year-old who lived up the hill a short walk west of the yard.

Like many other New Bedford families of the time (including the Howlands), the Beetles had Quaker roots and believed in hard work every day, except Sunday. From Charlie Beetle, Leo learned that there was to be no smoking or drinking or going out with the gang; that hard and conscientious work would be the making of the Beetle Cat Boat operation. Never forgetting this prophetic conclusion, Leo has for some fifty-five years practiced and preached these lessons of his youth.

The year 1936 turned out to be a special milestone for Beetle Cat Boats. Both Charlie Beetle and John Baumann passed on, leaving John Beetle's two daughters as owners and managers of the business. They had the wisdom and courage to retain young Leo and put him in charge of the building end of things. Simultaneously Leo took another step up life's ladder by marrying Alma Marcioni. In later years she was to take over the very important re-

Charles D. (Charlie) Beetle at the age of ninety-one, at his boatshop on Clarks Point. Sitting in front of him are his grandsons Walter (left) and John Beetle Baumann (right).

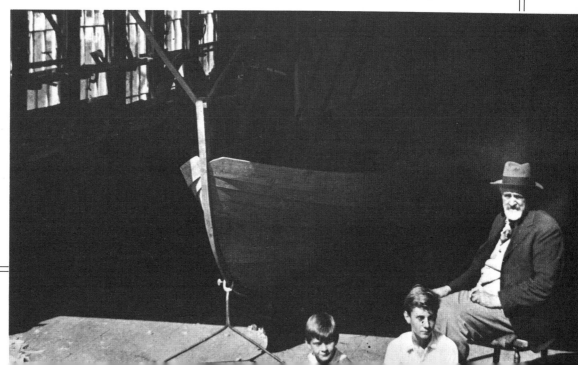

sponsibility of handling Beetle Cat correspondence.

During the years of World War II, Beetle Cat production, like other yacht work, came pretty much to a halt. Leo first worked for Carl Beetle on early government orders. When these were completed he transferred over to Palmer Scott, who still had boats to finish for the Army and the Navy.

As war operations slowed their pace, Palmer gradually reverted to general boatyard work, buying and building up the old Billy Wood boatyard that was located just north of the Beetle yard. During this period, Palmer made several attempts to buy the original Beetle Cat business from Ruth Beetle and her sister Clara, who turned down his offers because they had every intention of making Leo owner of the operation

My grandfather William Dillwyn Howland's yawl *Flying Cloud*, New Bedford Harbor, 1896. She was designed for my grandfather by William Fife, Jr., of Fairlie, Scotland, and built by Beetle in New Bedford the year this photograph was taken. The beauty of Fife-designed boats may well have inspired certain features of the Concordia yawls. *Flying Cloud*'s dimensions were 53'9" LOA; 36' LWL; 11' beam; 7'6" draft.

in due course. This thoughtful and practical solution would probably have come naturally to pass had not Beetle family finances dictated the transfer of the catboat business from the sisters to their younger brother Carl.

Here the story becomes a bit more involved. Having been disappointed in acquiring the Beetle Cat, Palmer went to the popular New York naval architect Philip Rhodes for the design of a similar catboat, one that could be built and sold in competition with the Beetles. As I learned the details from Palmer, Rhodes felt that the Beetle-type cat with full bow and gaff rig was outdated, which accounts for the fact that the new Scott cat—the Wood Pussy—came out with a fine bow and a tall marconi rig.

Although this new boat was undoubtedly a nice design, it has always been my opinion that the hull should have been rigged as a sloop and not as a cat. My Captiva Island friend Allen Weekes bought a Wood Pussy from Palmer, and during many sails I enjoyed with him on Florida's Pine Island Sound, Allen and I discussed and agreed on this point. Not only did the tall mast so far forward in the narrow bow make the boat somewhat prone to capsize when her anchorage became rough, but it made conventional reefing underway very difficult. As one lowered the sail, strong windage on the tall mast tended to blow the bow to leeward, the very consequence that one hopes to avoid when struggling to claw off a lee shore.

Also to my thinking, Palmer's agency system of selling Wood Pussys was probably a mistake, in that Palmer carried the major risks and the work load, while the agents enjoyed what little profit there was in this kind of project. Be that as it may, a goodly number of Wood Pussys did get sold (especially on Long Island Sound, where winds are light), during a period of ten years or so after the war. One of the reasons that they were so well and economically produced was that Leo was still on Palmer's payroll and was in charge of their construction. His methods quite logically followed many of the Beetle procedures.

BUILDING BEETLE CATS: INSIDE THE SHOP AT SMITH NECK

We sketched out a building (above) large enough to take care of foreseeable needs. The long, post-free center is a simple, pitched-roof affair that is narrow enough for a light, efficient roof-truss construction. The lean-to sheds on either side are equally straightforward to build—and tend to brace the main building. The fact that the lean-to roof line is below a set of high windows on the main building allows for light in all areas.

Lumber sheds at the Smith Neck yard (which show to the left of the boat shed) store the wood used in building Beetle Cats. The basic principle behind Beetle construction was and is the practical use of local woods.

Native cedar from nearby winter-frozen swamps is the lumber most constantly needed. All milled to a strong 1/2-inch thickness, the best of the stock is used for planking, less versatile boards are used for the cockpit floor and ceiling, and the odd-shaped and shorter leftovers, as we have said before, are perfect for decking. Practically speaking, all that is left is fragrant kindling to be enjoyed at home on cold winter evenings.

Forest-grown white oak (not pasture oak) is the best for keels, frames, sheer clamps, cockpit coamings, rubrails, and smaller components like maststeps, tillers, boom crotch assemblies, gaff jaws, and mast hoops. Careful sawing and milling can make very good use of selected logs.

Eastern white pine, grown near enough to the sea to have absorbed some rot-resisting salt air, is chosen for deck framing and centerboard trunks. This special pine (we call it Acushnet mahogany) is really the primary lumber product of this area, but, even so, it can be so selected, cut, milled, and stored as to be especially economical and useful for Beetle Cat boatbuilding.

Local sawmills, such as Gurney's in Freetown, Delano's in Dartmouth, Acushnet in Acushnet, and Hartley in Rochester, have for years (generations, in fact) gone out of their way to help with special needs of the Beetle Cats. But just the same, collecting boatbuilding lumber continues to be a two-way affair that requires understanding and constant cooperation.

BUILDING A BEETLE CAT

Since the 1950s, in true production-line fashion, Beetle Cat hulls have been built upside down beginning with an oak keel steamed to proper shape over a form (shown below at right). The boats move to completion through distinct stages, five at a time. A hot cedar plank, fresh from the steam box, shows here about to be hung on the next-in-line hull.

Beetle stems of oak are now built up in layers (early
ones were steam-bent), glued together and clamped
over a bending form for curing. Here, Leo Telesmanick marks three stem laminates for cutting by
means of a pattern—one of the many that help
make the shop so productive.

Although the early Beetle Cats more-or-less followed whaleboat-building practice (an upright setup using clenched boat-nail plank fastenings), the sturdy building jig or mold now in use makes these later boats more uniform in shape, and the conveniently positioned, down-hand hull-building process takes less time.

Except way forward, the frames are in one piece from sheer to sheer, and serve to stiffen the boat throughout, much as floor timbers would. Limber holes for fore-and-aft drainage of bilgewater are formed naturally below the frames on each side of the keel timber.

For stem-to-keel fastenings bolts and screws are now used, rather than nails and drifts. Centerboard trunk construction has been improved; the sides of the trunk are especially grooved and splined to ensure tightness.

The cedar planking (shown at left as pre-cut planks hanging in racks on the wall) is air-dried with just enough moisture content so that when the boat is in the water for the season, the planks won't warp. All loose knots are reamed and plugged. Before plugs are driven, they are dipped in glue to ensure that they will hold.

Leo and his key helper, Donald Moser (Moe), fasten the first broadstrake after clamping it tightly into place. During hull construction, the steam box (not shown), in which many of the cedar planks and all of the oak frames are softened for bending, is kept "at the ready," being supplied with steam from the shop's heating plant. Only the box's end-loading door is actually in the workshop; the rest of it is located out-of-doors, where the inevitable leakage of steam won't be troublesome and where the considerable space the box occupies won't be as objectionable.

Before they're turned over, Beetle Cat hulls are smoothed, caulked, puttied, primed, and have their waterlines scribed for painting—these operations being much more easily accomplished with the hull upside down. Interior painting takes place as soon as the boats are right-side up; this is followed by installation of the oak sheer clamps. The maststep is next, made of oak and bridged over stem and keel and bolted, for added support of these members. The mast partner is oak, 1 1/2 -inch in thickness, and is reinforced by a 2-inch-by-3-inch strongback that runs fore-and-aft and fastens (forward) to the extra-heavy deckbeam that helps support the mast partner, and (aft) runs along the top of the centerboard trunk. The deckbeams rest on top of the strongback and the sheer clamps and fasten to them. This construction, using the centerboard trunk for support, gives a solid deck to walk or jump on.

Cedar too short for hull planking usually finds its way into the decks of these boats. A standard 1/2-inch thickness is used for both planking and decking as well as for the ceiling and floorboards; thus, there is very little waste. After Moe finishes nailing on the deck, it will be faired and sanded, then covered with #10 canvas duck. Subsequent installation of the oak coamings and guardrails and the bronze hardware will complete the structural work on the hull. Spars are of clear, dry, straight-grained Douglas-fir. Gaff jaws are of steam-bent white oak for maximum strength; mast hoops are also steam-bent around a form.

Because pre-cut pieces are on hand and available from Concordia, worn-out boats like this can be readily rebuilt. Photographer Nick Whitman started with this derelict and, with some work, made it into the boat shown on page 42.

61

Besides racing, Beetles are
great for exploring inland
reaches, sandy shores...

...or rocky coasts. Fitted with
boom tents, they make wonderful
children's cruising boats.

5
Java, Father, and Captain Hardy

i

My father and his yawl *Java*, the first of the 103 Concordia yawls, form a central chapter in the story of the Concordia years. During the war and in the decade that followed, Father fortuitously had the opportunity and inclination to live with his boat under many and various conditions. He had, equally, a vital interest in sharing with us the details of his life with *Java*. In retirement from conventional business he was, at an important stage in the development both of Concordia Company and of the Concordia yawl class, enjoying the simple luxuries of a lovely year-round home—one that lay only a few steps from boat and boatyard, Buzzards Bay, and the Atlantic Ocean. Surrounding him was an extended family of all ages who gently broadened and tempered his thinking, all the while caring for his daily needs, worldly and spiritual.

Under these unique and almost idyllic conditions, it suited all concerned that Father should spend at least part of each day sailing, and thinking, reading, writing, and talking *boats*. What made this existence so productive (and practical) was the presence of Captain Harold E. Hardy, who during the fall of 1944 became an essential part of it all.

My brother Louie tells me how he brought about this most happy connection. When the boatyard, undermanned because of the war, became so busy that Martin could no longer be available for summer yachting and still manage the yard, Louie inherited the difficult task of finding a replacement crew for Father. During his search he learned that Captain

Java, the first Concordia yawl, about 1950. Father is at the helm, and Captain Hardy is in his usual position at the forward end of the leeward cockpit seat. This photograph, perhaps Father's favorite of *Java*, shows the loose-footed jib and *Java*'s bateka (bow just visible) towing astern. The special sail insignia was created for Father by Lois and Louis Darling.

65

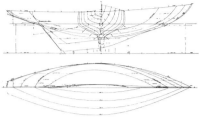

Java's working sail area—some 680 square feet—was modest, even a bit on the short side for light-weather racing, but perfect for Buzzards Bay. It was also divided just right for a small crew to handle with minimum effort. With her easily driven hull shape, *Java* really did not need light-weather sails to keep her going, and precise trimming of sail could be accomplished simply and with very little extra equipment. The mainsail could be trimmed in several ways. Being double-ended, the sheet could be released from the windward or leeward lead block and dead-ended on the base of one of the others, either to bring the boom down or inboard. (A track and slide on the bridge deck would do the same thing, but for daily use it has its disadvantages. It also can be dangerous during a jibe.) If the afternoon breeze came on strong, reef number one was just to drop the mizzen. Although small in area, its absence really reduced the pressure on boat and helm alike. If home-going squalls called for a more drastic reduction of sail, the mizzen remained set, and the complete main was lowered. Of course, if *Java*'s morning schedule called for a trip to the eastward against a strong wind, then the shortening of sail was handled quite differently. Captain Hardy would then tuck in the deep reef that brought the top of the main opposite the head of the jib. With this combination and no mizzen, *Java* really enjoyed showing what she could do.

Hardy might be available. So far, so good. However, signing up Captain Hardy was not so easy.

Born on Deer Isle, Maine, and bred aboard working schooners there, Harold Hardy fell heir quite automatically to that wonderful built-in understanding of the sea and its ships that can come only with lifelong experience. When the sailing coaster trade faded after the end of World War I, Captain Hardy gravitated to New Bedford, married, and went to work as a carpenter for a top local contractor, Zabina Davis, who at the time—1919—chanced to be building Colonel Green's machine shop at South Wharf. But Captain Hardy was a seaman at heart. He gradually drifted away from the carpenter trade and, like many another Deer Islander, found his way into the yachting fraternity, within which he soon became a professional yacht skipper of the finest quality.

At the time Louie made his approach, Captain Hardy confessed without hesitation that he did not fancy working on a small sailboat and furthermore already had received the grapevine word that Llewellyn Howland was a tough man to work for. Still, never blind to basic facts, he realized well enough that good opportunities in the yachting field were at that moment far from plentiful. In the end he agreed to sign on, but with the understanding that it would be for one year only, and that certain rules would be strictly adhered to—especially that there would be no cooking required of him under any circumstances whatsoever.

Given the right author, a delightful, instructive, and very moving novel could be written around the saga of Skipper Howland and Captain Hardy. For an enduring partnership did gradually develop between them that became a well-known Padanaram tradition, one that not only prolonged Father's life, but also served as a living inspiration for younger sailors in Buzzards Bay, among them would-be or actual owners of Concordia yawls.

Each of the men being a strong sailing personality, it did take some years of fancy sparring before either one knew exactly where he stood with the other. But as so often happens between great men, no matter how divergent their paths, a certain mutual respect existed from the start, and an understanding cooperation soon developed. Before long they had evolved a workable *Java* routine that grew more and more rewarding as one season faded into another. Local racing and Maine cruising dwindled over time. Daily sails and occasional overnight trips continued unabated.

ii

Early every summer morning, Captain Hardy, lunchbox in hand, drove down to the yacht club. He picked up the dinghy oars next door at Concordia, which gave him a chance to get the latest waterfront news. Then he proceeded to Father's yacht club float space, where he tipped rainwater, if any, out of the dinghy, dried off her thwarts, and rowed out to *Java*.

After opening up *Java*'s hatches, his first chore was to mop the decks and chamois the brightwork before the God-given dew had evaporated. (Only fresh water is suitable for washing off salt rime. But hosing down *Java* would have entailed bringing her in to the yacht club dock under power—a needless waste of time and effort, in Captain Hardy's view. For as his philosophy had it, "There is no end of trouble a lazy man will go to, to save himself work.") Captain Hardy also took advantage of the dew to wipe off *Java*'s topsides, working from the dinghy with her big padded fender.

Next he sent the working sails up on the dry deck and swept and tidied the main cabin. On likely sailing days he bent on the mainsail and gave it

Captain Harold E. Hardy rowing *Java*'s tender, a bateka with slightly more beam that Captain Hardy himself built.

Llewellyn Howland, c. 1952.

a light furl, then replaced the short harbor mainsheet with the working mainsheet. (This was in the days before synthetics, and undue exposure to the elements very rapidly aged natural-fiber running rigging.) After the mainsail, he bent on and hoisted the mizzen and sheeted it flat, then hanked on the loose-footed jib, which he lashed, loosely furled, over to port and clear of the mooring line.

Although everything aboard *Java* was shipshape and spotless, the only brass Captain Hardy ever shined were the two sheet winches in the cockpit and the two halyard winches on the mast. According to Father, there was already enough dazzle off the water to suit his old eyes. According to Captain Hardy, there were better things to do with one's time than rub brass.

By half past nine, Captain Hardy was ashore again to chair the morning gam for recognized skippers and other early-rising habituals. At the appointed time, but not a second before, Father showed up at the club dock, and Captain Hardy rowed him out to *Java*.

Once aboard, the dinghy secured astern and the weather carefully considered, the two men got *Java* underway smoothly, rapidly, and wordlessly. Captain Hardy hoisted the main and tacked it down to his satisfaction. Father cleared the mainsheet, lifted the boom from its crotch, and stood by to slack off the mizzen sheet. At Father's signal, Captain Hardy dropped the mooring clear, hoisted and momentarily backed the jib, then tacked it down and made his way aft. By the time he returned to the cockpit, Father had trimmed both jib and main to suit. *Java* was off. There exist soul-less people who fail to appreciate the quiet satisfaction of a simple maneuver well executed. Neither Father nor Captain Hardy was one of these.

Once they were fully underway, Father, wearing his favorite felt hat, collarless blue shirt, and red bandanna neckband, seated himself comfortably to windward. Captain Hardy, in his khaki uniform of cap, shirt, and trousers, and sporting his white summer mustache (to protect his lips from the sun), stationed himself on the end of the leeward cockpit seat facing forward. From this secure and comfortable vantage he could, without rising or blocking the skipper's view, easily handle the jib, main, and mizzen sheets—and also, without getting a single ash on deck, smoke his cigarette. Although a small man (he got his shoes from the boys' department), Captain Hardy could from a sitting position get a good brace with one foot against the bridge deck and exert a lusty heave on the sheet as needed. (It seldom was, however, for Father could usually give him a luff.)

The most natural sail was across Buzzards Bay and return. Sometimes *Java* anchored for lunch, but more often Father and Captain Hardy trimmed her to sail herself as they ate their sandwiches. Father was consumingly interested in how different sails and varying conditions of wind and wave affected *Java*, and he would frequently time *Java*'s progress with some precision. He found that, using working sails only, *Java*'s speed remained very constant, whether going across to the Islands close-hauled or reaching back home well off the wind. Even with the addition of a genoa jib or a spinnaker, *Java* gained surprisingly little time on crossings in an average sou'west breeze. *Java* had her own good pace and didn't demand pushing, just a little understanding. This was great for two old gentlemen who conscientiously avoided confusion but secretly enjoyed keeping up with the best of them.

Father's involvement in sailing was so deeply rewarding that invariably *Java* was late heading for home. After ten years of his tardiness, Father's cook, Mary Harkness, took little stock in his standard excuse that the wind had quite unexpectedly petered out. Even Father sensed the inadequacy of his excuse, and once within the harbor limits he and Captain Hardy became beautifully adept and expeditious in catching the mooring, stowing gear, and getting ashore.

Again, no words were necessary. After passing the breakwater, Father hauled up to the westward toward the old Clifford house, all the while flattening in the main. He then bore off sharply dead before the wind so that Captain Hardy, standing by the mast, could drop the jib on the run and completely in the lee of the main. There was no flapping of sail or grabbing overside. Within seconds the submissive jib was secured with a lashing.

By this time Father had eased off the main, and with a clear view of the channel ahead he was back on course and proceeding at a good pace up the harbor. This provided the interval that Captain Hardy needed to lower, unbend, and stow the mizzen, and square away her running rigging.

The final turn up to the tide-ridden mooring buoy was the critical one. With the tiller controlled by his body (you can't do this with a wheel) and using both hands on the main sheet (conveniently right in front of him) Father made his move, always watching wind, tide, and neighboring boats. Ninety-nine times out of a hundred, *Java*'s bow came to a gentle stop directly over the buoy. Captain Hardy hooked it up, easily set the mooring splice over the mooring cleat, and immediately reached over to cast off the main halyard, always at the exact moment when *Java* came head to wind with the main flat in. With no reel winch to slow its progress, and with well-tallowed track, the sail dropped in a flash right amidships, where it could be smothered before a beam breeze could catch it.

Still near the mast, Captain Hardy slacked the main outhaul (cleated purposely well forward on the boom) and then commenced leading the luff slides out through the mast track gate. Standing aft on the cockpit

Java's main cabin, looking forward.

BELOW DECK ABOARD JAVA

Although general conditions above deck on *Java* were, for a crew of two, pretty hard to fault, the setup below might be considered a bit too primitive by the uninitiated. Nonetheless, the essentials were all there.

The layout was ample in length, restfully proportioned, and symmetrical in design. The general motif of knotty pine bulkheads, dark painted and spattered floor, and white overhead was harmonious and pleasing in a neat, New England sort of way. The bright-finished locust table, countertops, and trim added a sunny touch.

On dark days the lack of any ports in the cabinsides made things rather dark, even with the main hatch open and with a skylight overhead. However, Father did not trust potentially leaky ports and noted that he spent most of his days in the cockpit. At suppertime the bright checkered tablecloth with its setting of two candles, well-polished silver, and blue Canton china obviated the lack of ports. The big, mirror-backed brass wall lamp amply lit the main cabin, and the cockpit port, wide companionway, and main skylight furnished God's fresh air in abundance. Why would anyone ask for more?

Over the years *Java*'s basic design, and the thinking that went into her arrangements, changed but little. Although numerous useful refinements gradually merged into what became the standard plan of later Concordia yawls, obsolescence as such never became a class problem.

seat, Father released the clew of the mainsail from its outhaul, and, while there, lashed the tiller up out of the way, to the mizzen strut stay. With only two steps forward, he could reach the boom crotch from its stowed position on the housetop and set it in its socket. To help him raise the boom into the crotch, Captain Hardy, without coming aft, could give a helping pull on the topping lift. While Father replaced the working mainsheet with the harbor sheet, Captain Hardy unhanked the jib, coiled the sheets still attached to its clew, and tossed the lot down the forehatch.

Then came a bit of joint effort amidships to ease the mainsail below, where, loosely spread out on the cabin sole, it could dry itself off or stay dry, as the case might be. Now there was little left to be done: no sail furling or bagging, no covers, no deck gear to stow; just the main hatch to be locked by Father, while Captain Hardy brought the dinghy alongside.

Watchers on the yacht club porch were divided between those timing, in admiration, the quick but apparently deliberate *Java* procedure, and those hoping to witness the rare occasion when Father failed to make a perfect mooring. It was not in the cards at all for Captain Hardy to make an awkward reach with his boathook or to struggle with a taut mooring line and flapping sail. But Father did, for whatever reason, miss a mooring once in a while. When he did, Captain Hardy would solemnly shake his head, then move smartly to raise and back the jib to help Father position *Java* for a second pass.

iii

As soon as the cold winds of November closed down summer activities for *Java*, new off-season operations commenced for her in Father's upstairs home office. Big casement windows made the room cheerful and light. Great-grandfather's flat-top desk, an impressive collection of nautical books, and a beautiful eighteenth-century Philadelphia side chair (reserved by Father for privileged guests) made it workable. It was here, at ten o'clock on prearranged off-season mornings, that Father and Captain Hardy convened to discuss the world situation in general and boat matters specifically and in particular.

For the first few years there were many details to be figured out or perfected and then added to the *Java* action list. Included were such items as anchors, their handling and stowage; reefing gear that involved boom and sail; lifelines with removable stanchions; bow pulpit with special features; engine exhaust improvements; alcohol, kerosene, and spare oil storage; painting schedules; tapered locust sail battens for special batten pockets.... On and on went the discussions, from which *Java* and her later sisterships shared the benefits.

Professional skippers can, merely by their continued presence, become a problem at a small yard. However, in Captain Hardy's case, those involved well understood the situation and developed practical guidelines that worked so smoothly that everyone gained and no one lost.

The first move was for Concordia Company to build a narrow extension to the west end of the truck shed. Ideally located for sunlight and a harbor view, the shop was designed to be long enough for working on *Java*'s spars, wide enough for the building of a dinghy. Overhead in the center was a small, peaked attic reachable only by drop ladder and trapdoor. The attic was perfect for storing sails, rigging, equipment, and whatever, and keeping it free from dust, sight, damage, or disappearance.

Java herself was stored inside the yard's main brick building at South Wharf, where, at its own schedule, Concordia could do all the necessary topsides and bottom painting, the plumbing overhaul, and the engine maintenance. By dividing the responsibilities in this way, Concordia avoided any chance of having a sanding job take place next to a varnish job, the untimely borrowing of a ladder, or the interruption of a yard worker—whose time, after all, was money.

In "Hardy's shed"—and that's what it was called—conditions could be more flexible. Its manager was free to choose his own gray days for sanding and his clear, dry, dust- (and people-) free days for varnishing. He could always call on Martin (never, however, directly on other yard workers) for needed help or materials. Guests could come or go at his discretion. Though outside pressures were never a problem for Captain Hardy, he always had some interesting and constructive operation in progress, from which a visitor could always learn, if he cared to watch and listen.

During the sacred noon hour all work ceased, and Hardy's shed became a lunch and meeting hall of some significance. Displayed on every available inch of wall were pictures from the Hardy collection: photographs of the whaleship *Charles W. Morgan* coming in from her last voyage, the schooner *Niña* at the start of the race to Spain, Grandpa Howland's Fife-designed and Beetle-built yawl *Flying Cloud, Java* as a new boat, and so on. And, true to the Maine aesthetic, there was also a section of wall devoted to such scenes as that of four strong men struggling to roll a mammoth potato up onto a railroad flat car. It mattered not whether the day was sunny and warm with doors and windows open, or whether it was a raw winter day with the coal stove lit and drawing: the general atmosphere in Hardy's shed was always ideal for enjoying one's vittles, swapping opinions, or now and then swapping an exaggerated yarn.

The years passed all too quickly. During the 1957 sailing season Captain Hardy noticed that Father tired more easily and that he had fallen into the habit of polishing whatever was at hand with his red bandanna handkerchief. Something was definitely amiss. With only a gentle plea that Father not tell Mrs. Hardy, the captain unobtrusively (and with great skill) assumed the *Java* cooking detail.

The work-list conference that fall became more of a ceremony than a business affair. It all proceeded according to custom, but the only item to appear on the action pad was a rough sketch of a shelf about three inches long to hold the kitchen matches. After twenty years, *Java* was now complete. A few weeks later, in his eightieth year, Father died of a stroke.*

---

* This was a sad change for all of us. Captain Hardy retired to build a small boat for himself. Louie and I reluctantly sold *Java*, and Hardy's shed became Concordia Company's rigging loft.

THE DEVELOPMENT

Concordia yawls #8 and #9, *Moorea* and *Whisper*, being loaded in Bremen. The temporary stub mast and heavy beams across *Whisper*'s deck forward and aft will be used to secure the boat to her cradle. *Moorea*'s rectangular portlights were called for by her owner, as was her slightly higher-than-normal deckhouse.

6
Abeking and Rasmussen and Drayton Cochran

Between 1950 and 1966, without benefit of a single contract or disagreement, the German shipyard Abeking and Rasmussen built for the account of Concordia Company some ninety-nine sisterships of *Java*, along with an equal number of 8-foot bateka-type dinghies to go with them. Drayton Cochran was the person directly responsible for launching us into business with Abeking and Rasmussen. Draytie's association with Concordia goes back to 1948—and a fortunate one it has been for all Concordia owners.

I first got to know Draytie Cochran during a cold midwinter trip to Brown's yard in Gloucester, where Phil Rhinelander's prewar Lawley-built Concordia yawl *Jobiska* was in storage and had just come on the market. Draytie looked the boat over with a professional eye, made a comprehensive list of every item of gear that went with her, bought her without further delay, changed her name to *Ina*, and early that spring of 1948 sailed her home to Southport, Connecticut. For the next few years Cochran cruised and successfully raced *Ina* along the coast from Long Island to Maine.

About the time he bought *Ina*, Cochran asked his friend Walter McInnis to design him a cruising boat along the lines of a Maine sardine carrier—long and comparatively narrow, seaworthy but easily driven—that would be shoal enough to travel the canals of Europe. Complete plans for *Little Vigilant* soon materialized.

High-quality yacht-building projects of all types were to be found in Abeking and Rasmussen's shop in the years following World War II. Abeking and Rasmussen hull #5577, whose backbone has just been set up, will become the Concordia yawl *Westray*.

For a builder Drayton first approached several Nova Scotia yards and received bids ranging from forty to fifty thousand dollars. The specifications called for commercial construction and finish, everything strong but plain in order to hold costs down. Before coming to a final decision he sent a set of his plans and specifications to Abeking and Rasmussen. Their quote was twenty-seven thousand dollars for the boat complete less engine, which was to be an American General Motors diesel. The price was more than just tempting.

Abeking and Rasmussen redrew all the plans, as was their standard practice, and then went immediately to work. At an early stage of the building Cochran made a preliminary inspection visit and found the quality of the workmanship and materials well above his expectations. In spite of this early encouragement, he was in no way prepared for the superlative excellence of the finished boat. She was not a plain, simple, commercial job at all, but a first-class yacht in every respect, with teak trim and decks, and exquisite joinerwork below. Fully found, with all sails and rigging, she was carefully equipped with all tools necessary for engineroom and bosun's locker. In fact, she was delivered absolutely complete and ready for sea. As a final touch Mr. Rasmussen himself, together with a close friend, Mrs. Velhagen, accompanied Drayton to Bremen to select the cabin upholstery covering material. They chose beautiful sturdy cotton corduroy (designated in Germany as Manchester cloth) of a soft green color. This choice was important, because future Concordia owners were to enjoy their comfort on cushions covered with this identical material.

Just to complete the *Little Vigilant* story, Draytie used her in Europe for the next thirteen years, cruising widely to Turkey, Africa, Scandinavia, and European ports and canals. If written up, these voyages would constitute a saga in themselves.

It was while he was in Germany commissioning *Little Vigilant* that Draytie, with our most hearty approval and even urging, submitted Concordia yawl plans and specifications to Abeking and Rasmussen. They thought well of the boat and gave a building quotation of seventy-five hundred dollars. This represented another opportunity much too good to let pass, and the first Abeking and Rasmussen-built Concordia yawl was delivered to Cochran in New York during the fall of 1950. As soon as she was launched off the freighter's deck in Brooklyn, Drayton took charge. His local contractor friend Tom Thorson towed her across to Fulton Fish Market, and then, with the help of his small lighter and two old sailormen from the nearby Seaman's Church Institute, the spars were stepped and rigged. Everything was there, everything fitted, and Draytie straightaway sailed his new boat home to Southport.

A steel motor ship, just completed, on the launching ways at Abeking and Rasmussen, Lemwerder, in 1952. Some four hundred of Abeking and Rasmussen's work force were building commercial vessels while only about one hundred were doing yacht work.

I was passing by Southport shortly thereafter on my way to New York and stopped to have a look at her for myself. Perfect in every respect, the new yawl was a completely faithful reproduction of Father's *Java*: lead keel, canvas decks, slatted cockpit seats, low house with one port only on each side. Only the rigging was different, the spar tangs and shrouds being of galvanized steel rather than bronze and stainless.

Unfortunately for me, the boat was locked. I crawled into the cabin through a cockpit locker door. When I tried to worm my way back out, I got stuck. Only Abeking and Rasmussen's thoroughness saved me. Under the fo'c's'le locker seat, there was a set of tools that included, among other essentials, a screwdriver. Using this, I easily removed some of the skylight fittings and made an ungraceful exit without further damage to my ribs or any at all to the boat.

Granted permission by Cochran, and at his price, we sold this first Abeking and Rasmussen Concordia yawl to Father's friend Edward Cabot of Westerly, Rhode Island. Cabot named her *Suva*. Now Draytie ordered two more sisterships from Abeking and Rasmussen. One of these he named *Sheila* and kept for himself, the other he allowed us to sell for him to Hobart Hendrick of New Haven, Connecticut. Several other similar transactions followed in the same way, with Draytie doing the financing and Concordia the selling. This was how it all began.

DRAYTON COCHRAN

Drayton Cochran was directly responsible for putting us in touch with Abeking and Rasmussen. Pictured here, at the wheel of *Little Vigilant* (shown at above right cruising France by way of the Doub River to the Mediterranean), Drayton, as usual, was his own captain, engineer, and shipkeeper, as well as navigator and cook, when necessary.

Philosophies and abilities of a boating nature came to Drayton Cochran quite naturally. His uncle Alexander was the bachelor head of the Cochran clan and a legendary figure of the Gay Nineties yachting world, who, in his short life, owned and raced many of the largest and finest yachts the sport has ever known — including the Herreshoff schooner *Westward.*

Drayton's father, Gifford, was also a prominent sportsman. But although Gifford Cochran enjoyed sailing, his particular interests centered on race-horses. Of importance to Draytie, he maintained at their summer home in Sorrento, Maine, a proper Wilbur A. Morse-designed Friendship sloop. In this little vessel, Draytie early learned the joys, arts, and responsibilities of the mariner.

At St. Paul's School in Concord, New Hampshire, Draytie displayed a somewhat greater interest and prowess in sports and outside activities than in the formal academic curriculum. Even before he graduated, he converted part of a legacy from his uncle Alexander into a contract with Shelburne Shipbuilding Company in Shelburne, Nova Scotia, for a 105-foot, fisherman-type schooner. Designed by Francis Sweisguth, she cost $16,000, completely equipped and ready for sea. At her launching in 1927, Draytie christened her *Mabel Taylor*, in honor of his mother.

During his three years at Yale, Cochran spent the summers cruising extensively aboard *Mabel Taylor*, sailing her in the third summer, 1931, across the Atlantic via the Azores and into the Mediterranean, and returning to Cuba by way of Madeira, the Canaries, and Puerto Rico. Arriving home too late for the fall semester of his senior year at New Haven, he chartered out *Mabel Taylor* with himself as captain to the Bingham Oceanographic Foundation and spent the winter of 1932 studying ocean currents and other scientific matters in the Gulf of Mexico.

Taking after his uncle Alexander, Drayton always had a deep-rooted interest in large sailing vessels, and in 1932 became greatly intrigued with plans for a 128-foot brigantine. The designer of this handsome craft was one Henry Gruber.

Right here I want to add some background information about this young German naval architect, because, in a way, he fits positively into the subject at hand. Henry came to the United States in the mid-1920s, and for six or seven years worked in New York, primarily with Starling Burgess. In addition to being an excellent designer in his own right, he possessed special expertise in the area of structural stresses and strains, and he was of great assistance to Burgess in working out construction details for Paul Hammond's *Niña* (1928) and, more important, for the Cup defenders *Enterprise* (1930) and *Rainbow* (1934). Olin Stephens tells me that in 1936, when he himself was collaborating with Burgess on the design of the J boat *Ranger*, they together solicited Gruber's help in producing certain needed plans. Unfortunately, Gruber had by this time returned to Germany and was no longer available.

Once back in his own country, Gruber came to know Hitler personally. It was not long before he was called upon to design yawls for the German navy, and, in fact, he turned out some very fine ones that bore a striking similarity to the then-current Sparkman and Stephens type of ocean racer. Two of these, *Roland von Bremen* and *Peter von Danzig*,

which were designed more to the Royal Ocean Racing Rule than to the Cruising Club of America Rule, participated in the 1936 Bermuda Race.

During World War II Henry Gruber remained in Germany, where he worked as chief designer for the big Burmeister yard on the Lesum River. Shortly thereafter, he disappeared from the active boating scene.

Gruber was understandably anxious to further Draytie's interest in the brigantine and arranged to conduct him on a survey trip to a number of likely European boatbuilders. Abeking and Rasmussen of Lemwerder was one of the yards they visited, and Draytie in this way had his first opportunity to absorb the potential of this unique organization. Henry Rasmussen quoted him the very favorable price of $126,000 to build the brigantine, but by this time Draytie had decided that the project was well beyond his scope. He continued to sail *Mabel Taylor* until 1935, when he took her to England and sold her.

Cochran worked for a short time in the highly successful family-owned Alexander Smith Carpet Company. However, his heart was never in the routine business life. By 1939 he was building a second vessel at Shelburne Shipbuilding Company — the 93-foot (waterline), Walter McInnis-designed diesel ketch *Vigilant*. In *Vigilant* he undertook a series of venturesome and interesting expeditions, including three of a scientific nature in the West Indies. Then came World War II, and five years of eventful naval service. In 1942 Cochran commanded a PC in the Aleutians. Later, he commanded a destroyer escort in the Atlantic. Finally, he was a senior officer on the escort carrier *Block Island* and saw action off the Canaries.

At war's end Cochran still owned *Vigilant*, but she had seen government service and needed a complete overhaul. Jakobsen's yard in Oyster Bay converted her back to yacht condition, and Draytie used her for a few more years. However, she was really too big for his needs at that time. It was then that our mutual friend John West told Draytie about Concordia yawls and urged him to consider buying a sistership to Father's *Java*.

HENRY RASMUSSEN

Henry Rasmussen (1877–1959) at the wheel of *Landfall*, 1932.

Fine wooden yachts, and the designing, building, and sailing of them, were throughout Henry Rasmussen's life a prime objective. The products of his yard brilliantly reflected this personal interest and understanding.

Born in 1877 in the Danish port town of Svendborg, Rasmussen came of an old and respected Danish shipbuilding family.* His boyhood home, ideally situated amid fields and woods, lay close to the sea at the southern tip of Fyn. Nearby was the modest Rasmussen shipyard, where the whole family worked and made their living. For a boy there was always plenty to be done, and one of Henry's earliest memories was of collecting wood to feed the steam box.

The Rasmussens were primarily builders of heavy trading vessels, usually ketch-rigged, but sometimes three-masted schooners. They used time-honored methods of designing by half model (taking hull shapes from carved models, rather than from lines drawn on paper) and sawn-frame

construction. The Rasmussens also built the occasional lighter and smaller boat—of lapstrake construction and with the graceful lines of most Scandinavian double-enders. These double-enders might be designed for work or pleasure, and they varied in length from 10 to 30 feet. No matter what size the boat, the Rasmussen tradition was always one of good workmanship and a careful selection of materials.

From a very early age Henry longed to become a professional boatbuilder and designer. He even thought seriously about moving across the ocean to America, the land of great opportunities. However, in the end he honored his mother's wishes that he seek his livelihood somewhat closer to home.

After a five-year apprenticeship at the yard of his maternal grandfather, Hans Poulsen, and a

* For this account of Abeking and Rasmussen's history I am greatly indebted to Mr. Horst Lehnert, for many years manager of Abeking and Rasmussen's yacht-building operations.

short stint as a shipwright at Hansen's yard in nearby Odense, he went to Copenhagen, where he studied ship engineering and construction at Burmeister and Wain, a world-famous producer of ships and engines. Although Rasmussen advanced to the position of assistant to the yard director at Burmeister and Wain, his interest remained with wooden boat construction, and he decided, after some additional study at Ships Academy, to leave Copenhagen and seek work in the trade of his choice.

When he received a job offer from Schömer and Jensen to join their yard in Tönning (north Germany), he immediately accepted. Here he became seriously involved in design work and also developed his consuming interest in sailing. Unfortunately or otherwise, Schömer and Jensen failed. Henry moved on to Vegesack, a small town on the Weser River about halfway between the North Sea port of Bremerhaven and the city of Bremen itself, where he took a job as naval architect at the Bremer Vulcan shipyard.

According to Rasmussen, the next few years were the happiest of his life. He was married, and moved from an apartment over a bakery shop into a house of his own. Besides working at a trade he enjoyed, he found time and opportunity to get in a lot of sailing with friends and to organize an active rowing club.

In 1903 the Vulcan yard sent Rasmussen to the North Sea port of Emden to help establish a new steel shipyard. This was an especially fortuitous assignment that put him in touch with many keen sailors, a number of whom gave him the chance to get into the type of design work he loved. In his off hours he drew up plans for his new friends and soon became recognized as an excellent designer of yachts and small craft.

One of his new boating acquaintances was Herr Abeking, a German businessman from Schmalkalden (inland in the Thuringer Forest area). As each had plans to go into business for himself, they decided to form a partnership, and in 1907 they established a boatyard at Lemwerder, just across the Weser River from Vegesack. The arrangement was that each would invest in the venture, that Abeking would take care of the business end of things, and that Rasmussen would handle the boat designing and building.

The new firm of Abeking and Rasmussen launched its first boat in 1908 and during the next six years built many small wooden work and pleasure boats, often designed by Rasmussen, and usually for German customers. Among the boats were some very lovely sailing yachts, including 75-square-meter boats (similar to my father's first *Java*), Six-Meters, Eight-Meters, and the like. During World War I, yacht building naturally ceased, and the yard turned to producing a hundred and fifty or more wooden utility craft of sizes varying from dinghies to 50- and 60-footers.

Starting in 1918, and for the next year or two, the firm had a very hard go of it. One of the chief problems was to procure suitable lumber, a situation Henry never forgot. Commencing in 1921 and continuing on through 1924, the relatively new yard really came into its own and each year built some two hundred and fifty boats of various types and sizes. Then, for two years, production fell off materially. Not only was inflation a serious problem, but labor union demands created a very unsettled state of affairs. Mr. Abeking withdrew from the partnership in July 1925.

The year following Abeking's departure, Rasmussen himself made a combination business and pleasure trip to New York as a guest of Starling Burgess, Linton Rigg, and Jasper Morgan. These individuals were not only prominent sailors, but were also associated together as a New York yacht design and brokerage firm. During Henry's stay, he enjoyed some great sailing and racing and thus met many substantial yachting figures, quite a few of whom were soon to become customers. In fact, the prospects for new orders appeared to be so promising that he set up an Abeking and Rasmussen sales office at 11 Broadway, which remained active for several years.

The Abeking and Rasmussen yard had already built a boat or two from Burgess plans, but from 1925 on orders for more of the same came in very rapidly. Beginning with a fleet of Bermuda one-designs, which were delivered to Bermuda in 1926, there followed some fourteen International Ten-Meters in 1927, six Twelve-Meters, and eleven Eight-Meters in 1928. These meter boats were all one-design classes, and to save importation duties many of them were delivered in Halifax and then sailed to United States ports. Names of their owners, mainly New York Yacht Club members, read like a "who's who" of yachting, and included Mallory, Maxwell, Stewart, Goodwin, Stuart, Harding, Forbes, Iselin, Roosevelt, Bedford, on and on. I remember the excitement at the time, because my father helped to sail Charles Goodwin's Twelve-Meter down from Canada. In 1928, 1929, and 1930 came some one hundred Atlantic one-design sloops, 28-footers that have been one of the most popular and long-lasting of Long Island Sound racing classes.

Burgess one-design class boats were not the only American orders that Abeking and Rasmussen received during these years, but they accounted for a large portion of the total. For the German yard not only showed that it could offer a good quality of workmanship, at prices that were highly competitive, but that it had the capacity to build a number of boats at one time.

As the year 1930 approached, Abeking and Rasmussen's production began to change. The yard continued to build modest-sized yachts for German customers, but few orders were forthcoming from America: the Depression was taking its toll. In 1931 the only American boat of consequence built by Abeking and Rasmussen was Paul Hammond's Francis Herreshoff-designed ketch *Landfall*; in 1932, the small schooner *Starling*, built for Burgess's and Hammond's close friend Elihu Root; in 1933, Vadim Makaroff's big ocean-racing ketch *Vamarie*, for which Burgess's former partner Jasper Morgan helped design the so-called wishbone rig.

By 1934 Abeking and Rasmussen were mainly engaged in producing sailboats for German navy training schools. These boats varied from dinghy types and Star Boats on up to 45-foot (waterline) ocean racers. (The German-owned yawls *Bremen* and *Hamburg*, designed and built by Abeking and Rasmussen, sailed in both the Bermuda Race and the Transatlantic Race of 1936.) By 1939 even the building of small yachts for German civilians was giving way to demands of the German navy. As events developed, Abeking and Rasmussen concentrated their efforts on the production of minesweepers. These 100-footers had to be strong, nonmagnetic, and have a speed potential of some 18 to 20 knots. Basically, their construction included framing of aluminum and laminated planking of wood, hastily assembled from European sources. Prefabrication methods were soon developed to a point where one of these craft could be launched every two weeks.

With the defeat of Hitler's forces in 1945, this military building program came to a sudden and complete halt, and Abeking and Rasmussen took what work they could find. My old schoolmate Horace Fuller tells me that when his army unit moved into the Bremen area the firm was building wheelbarrows. (Horst Lehnert confirms this, and adds to the list clothes pegs, kitchen trays, sewing boxes, and mahogany bedroom furniture. According to Draytie Cochran, the yard also did some beautiful work restoring the damaged interiors of historic buildings.) In fact, conditions were so tough at the yard that American military personnel were able to buy beautiful small wooden boats for next to nothing.

Then the Marshall Plan went into effect, and Abeking and Rasmussen began getting orders for big diesel-powered steel coasters and motor freighters of up to 400 and 500 tons and over 100 feet in length. So the yard turned to commercial work in steel and away from yacht work in wood. I am told that, as of 1952, only about one-fifth of the yard's five-hundred-man work force was involved in yacht construction.

In spite of this trend, Henry Rasmussen's personal interests remained with the creation of fine wooden yachts. To quote from a recent letter from Horst Lehnert, Rasmussen's "first knowledge of lumber was acquired from his grandfather, who took him into the woods when selecting lumber for merchant ships (beech trees for keels, oak and/or fir for frames, fir for planking). Later, as a yacht builder, his knowledge of the right kind of lumber was the basis for quality yacht building. (The varnished hulls of Six-Meters and R-class yachts and shiny cruisers had to be spotless Tabasco, Mexican, or Honduras mahogany.) When visiting the United States, American oak was a matter of special interest to him....Certainly, Henry Rasmussen always found a way of keeping on hand the variety, quality, and quantity of special lumber that was needed for the construction of strong hulls and the finish of beautiful cabin interiors."

Although we at Concordia continued to import our yawls from Abeking and Rasmussen

until 1966, serious inflation in Germany raised prices and had the effect of curtailing orders from the United States. At the same time, aluminum construction was gaining in popularity in the yachting world, and Abeking and Rasmussen were able for several years to take advantage of this by using their expertise in metal fabrication. As of this writing, however, the yard is almost entirely out of the yacht-building field and is concentrating on international naval construction.

Yacht yards tend to blossom and fade in reflection of the spirit of their founders. So it was for Abeking and Rasmussen of Lemwerder, Germany, whose founder, Henry Rasmussen, died in 1959 at the age of eighty-two.

JOHN WEST

John West was an enthusiastic benefactor of the Concordia yawl class from its very beginning. His opinions were based on years of active sailing and cruising on many a splendid 30- and 40-footer. John was still a student, summering at Quisset on Buzzards Bay, when his father gave him the New York Thirty sloop *Phantom*, together with a membership in the New York Yacht Club. Thus equipped, John cruised widely and raced often against top competition. When the Great Depression put an end to this style of yachting life, *Phantom*, which had originally cost John's father $3,000, was sold complete with a new mainsail for one-third that amount.

Among the various boats John chartered during the 1930s was a Herreshoff-designed Newport Twenty-nine, a Herreshoff-designed New York Forty, a Gardner-designed Larchmont O boat, and, most important for this story, the little *Cinderella*, designed by Concordia. It was during one of his vacation charter cruises that John West came across my father in Cuttyhunk Harbor and had the chance to inspect and sail aboard *Java*. He was convinced this was a very special boat, and in conversations with Drayton Cochran he strongly urged Draytie to consider a sistership. John subsequently owned several Concordia yawls himself and became a leading promoter of the class.

7
A Visit to Lemwerder

Following my convincing exposure to the first three German-built Concordia yawls, I felt an irresistible urge to see for myself the shipyard that was capable of such outstanding workmanship. Liberating our nine- and seven-year-old sons, Charles and Kinnaird, from five weeks of school, we set sail for Europe on 10 November 1951, aboard the *S. S. Ryndam*.

At Bremen and headed for our final destination, the boys and I climbed aboard the Lemwerder special. This was a miniature train. One of its two cars was carrying a consignment of lumber for Abeking and Rasmussen. The other, equipped with rough wooden benches, was rapidly filling up with a happy group of young schoolchildren. The fact that they all carried English primers brought them gradually but surely into communication with Charlie and Kinny, who never lacked for German playmates the rest of their stay in Germany.

Henry Rasmussen conducted me on the initial inspection tour of the yard. He made me feel at home from the start by reminiscing about his early contacts in the United States. Especially, he had been impressed by Nathanael Herreshoff, whose yard and boatbuilding program he had seen, studied, and admired. Rasmussen pointed out with justifiable pride the well-planned and precise workmanship of his own craftsmen; he stressed the important point that perfect joints and fits are in fact the very strength and life of a boat. Over a mid-morning glass of sherry he had kind words about the design of the Concordia yawl and assured me of his earnest desire to work with Concordia on a continuing building program. On that note he left me with his blessing and the understanding that Elo Poulsen would do the yard honors for the remainder of my visit. And indeed, Mr.

A building shop at Abeking and Rasmussen, in which five Concordias are in various stages of construction. The boat in the left foreground has its backbone set up and is awaiting a ballast keel. Boat #5001 is partially planked, with sheer clamp in place. Behind her are three Concordias—one fully planked, another decked, and a third boat painted and ready to move. The tracks facilitated moving the boats and their keels, and the wood sleepers embedded in the floor made possible the firm shoring of the hulls while under construction.

Elo Poulsen with my sons Charlie and Kinny in Lemwerder, 1951.

Poulsen went far beyond the call of duty to make the Howlands' stay pleasant, memorable, and worthwhile.

When our stay came to an end, Mr. Poulsen crowded us and our luggage into his Volkswagen and breezed us back to Bremen and our train, all the while singing the then popular American song, "Give Me Five Minutes More." Although we parted with fond promises of future meetings, sadly they never materialized. About four years later our friend lost his life in an automobile accident.

Leaving Germany, the boys and I made our way back to England for visits to London and Torquay. In Torquay, as expected, I received a letter from Camper & Nicholson, Ltd., of Gosport and Southampton. J. W. Nicholson suggested that I pay them a visit and discuss the possibility of their building Concordia yawls for us. It was a wonderful and hoped-for opportunity for me to see this world-renowned shipyard that had for generations designed and built England's finest yachts. I immediately made reservations to stay a few days in Southampton.

The day of my appointment was drizzly and raw, but the reception given us by Camper & Nicholson was quite the reverse. Charles Nicholson, whom I had had the privilege of meeting twenty years earlier aboard *Landfall*, was now retired, but he greeted us from the warmth of his day room, and his son John, who was currently in charge of yard affairs, gave us his undivided attention for the remainder of the morning.

During an introductory tour I sensed everywhere the specter of royal yachts, great activity, and unmatched craftsmanship, but what I actually observed was a depressing scarcity of boats, sail or power, sheds that appeared largely empty, and machinery well cared for but mostly silent. On a more positive note, Mr. Nicholson was happy to point out with understandable pride a handsome new 92-foot ketch named *Aries* which the yard had designed and had just finished building for Richard Reynolds of tobacco fame.

He also discussed with me the Camper & Nicholson-designed and built schooner *Creole* that had been at the yard recently. This great three-masted schooner-yacht had been built as *Vera* in 1926 for Drayton Cochran's uncle Alexander Cochran. During the war she had been operated by the British Navy as a degaussing ship, but recently had been acquired by the Greek shipping magnate Stavros Niarchos.

Drayton told me later that at the time of *Creole*'s building, his uncle declined any formal contract arrangements, saying that he might wish to make changes along the way, that he was well aware of the yard's good reputation, and to please just proceed with the work, and send him the bills. To some, this approach might sound casual, even dangerous, but it has been my experience that with reliable parties, a pay-as-you-go procedure can work to the best interest of all concerned.

With the coming of morning teatime we retired to John Nicholson's private office, and, in surroundings of homelike comfort, took up the main purpose of our visit. We discussed at length the practicality of having Camper & Nicholson build boats for Concordia Company. Mr. Nicholson had at hand plans of our Concordia yawls, and seemed much interested to work out arrangements to build some for us. He suggested that in spite of actual costs, his firm was prepared to meet competitive figures, for at least one boat.

I was equally keen to have a Camper and Nicholson yacht, not only for sentimental reasons, but also because I was confident that their construction would be of top quality. However, under the circumstances, the project seemed in some ways to be nonproductive. I even felt it might be unfair for me to accept a one-sided proposition that in all probability could not be repeated. Reluctantly, we agreed to postpone any action for the time being, and with feelings of some sadness on my part, we bade our farewells.

A visit with my *Landfall* shipmate Uffa Fox and a tour of the Ratsey and Lapthorn sail loft at Cowes completed our business in England. Charlie, Kinny, and I sailed for home on the *Maasdam* on 15 December.

FROM LOG TO PLANKS: THE STORING,

During my tour of Abeking and Rasmussen in 1951, the feature that impressed me most deeply was the tremendous supply and variety of good boat lumber. Equally important were the efficient methods for handling it and the well-understood routine for processing it.

Quality boatbuilding lumber—mahogany from Africa and South America, teak from India—is not acquired merely by picking up the telephone or writing a letter to the local sawmill. Even though Henry Rasmussen had, over the years, developed close and valuable connections with top international lumbermen, the time lag between an order placed and a delivery made was often a matter of several years.

Finding the right trees, felling them, and assembling them as a full shipload could take many months, and, for the yard, it meant months of planning ahead. Once the logs reached Germany, they had already been partly seasoned. At the yard the logs were carefully sorted, then placed in outside storage for later processing. (Although I didn't see any lumber in water storage, I was told that as a matter of convenience, logs were occasionally left in the brackish river water until other space was available. During World War II, Abeking and Rasmussen hid many of the big logs in nearby shallows to save them for peacetime boatbuilding. Certainly it was a miracle that these logs survived the war in excellent condition and were ready for use in postwar yacht construction.)

Logs were taken from storage as needed and brought into the mill, where, by the use of a huge, horizontal frame saw, they were accurately sawed into full-length, live-edged planks. A thickness of 3 or 4 inches was usually maintained to avoid the ever-present tendency of thinner boards to warp or check. The planks were branded on one end with their own reference numbers, then stacked outside again in the shape of the original log, with spacing sticks approximately 1 inch thick placed between the planks to permit circulation of air for seasoning.

Most of the lumber was stored outside—row upon row of huge logs and systematically stacked planks.

For moving the big logs, the yard had an elaborate system of tracks, heavy-wheeled dollies, and special gantries.

SAWING, AND SEASONING OF WOOD

Sawed logs usually remained out in the air from six to eighteen months, depending on plank thickness and wood density.

If, during sawing or handling, any rot or worm holes were discovered in the center part of the tree, the affected planks were discarded. The tree's outer layer of less durable sapwood was never used. Abeking and Rasmussen knew from experience that any disease observed at this stage had actually started while the tree was still alive or as it waited in the woods to be transported. Once the select lumber was correctly stacked at Abeking and Rasmussen, it remained in good condition indefinitely.

Although I have been talking mainly about mahogany and teak, many other species of wood were in use at Abeking and Rasmussen. Each type was seasoned and treated by the yard according to its makeup and intended use. In general, all trees regardless of species were cut into planks of predetermined thickness and stored as a unit, either inside or out.

When a boat such as a Concordia yawl was to be built, the office lumber files were consulted and the required planks from a specific log were taken from storage, resawed, and then planed to the desired thickness. Before being built into the boat, they were placed for a time in a special, air-conditioned chamber to ensure that they contained a correct percentage of moisture—twelve-and-a-half percent, to be exact. Obviously, wet lumber built into a boat will, in time, shrink and cause trouble through the opening of joints and seams. Not so obviously, the same wood will, if too dry, swell with use and become equally troublesome in its own way.

Abeking and Rasmussen engineers customarily redrew all plans received from outside architects.

The heavy planks cut from each individual log were retained as a unit; when stacked with spacing sticks, the reassembled log became egg-shaped in cross section.

If properly protected on top from rain and sun, the sawed logs could safely—and often did—wait eighteen months or more before being restacked, still as a tree, but without the sticks, in big lumber sheds.

They did this both to convert English measurements to the metric system and, where permission was granted, to adapt plans to their own construction methods. Having great faith in Abeking and Rasmussen's engineering ability, and believ-

The specific planks required for each new boat were removed from storage. Here the planks are going into an air-conditioning chamber.

ing that this approach would reduce costs and not quality, I had readily given my approval for their recommended modifications of the Concordia construction plans.

In regard to wood to be used in building the Concordia yawls, we agreed that African mahogany, being available in quality and quantity, was the logical choice for planking, and that teak would be best for cockpit floor and cabin sole. Our specifications called for locust trim both on deck and below. Abeking and Rasmussen had never before used locust in this way but said that there was no trouble in procuring it, and that it could easily be used as requested. The same situation existed in regard to knotty pine for the cabin interior. The German white pine was not exactly like our Eastern pine but appealed to me as very attractive. Abeking and Rasmussen expressed approval for using it, because it was inexpensive and available. The only comment they had about it was that it required quite a bit of time and material to match up the panels, have the right number of knots and grain in each, etc. This lovely refinement of matching panels, however, is something they insisted on and that I was delighted with.

After being sawn from logs, the planks were individually branded: 81 indicates that sawing took place in 1981. 420 is the width of the plank in millimeters. 740, 680, 850, 880 give the different lengths in centimeters. 65 is the thickness of the plank in millimeters.

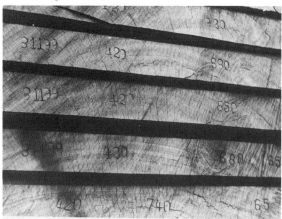

BUILDING THE YAWLS

The stem, keel, sternpost, deadwood, and horn timber of the Concordia yawl—the backbone, as this white oak assembly is often called—were sawed and shaped, fastened together, and rabbeted by Abeking and Rasmussen in a meticulous but conventional way. Patterns and templates with the necessary reference marks on them had been carefully made and were reused again and again as additional Concordia yawls were built.

The Abeking and Rasmussen full-framing method was entirely new to me, but very appropriate—that is to say, extremely efficient as well as accurate—for the prefabricated construction of identical sisterships. Each pair of frames (originally steam-bent, but in later years laminated) was bent over an individual form of the correct shape on the framing table. After beveling, these frame pairs were assembled in a finished frame unit that included an attached floor timber, shaped and pre-drilled for its bolts, and a finished deckbeam (or a pair of half-beams), likewise permanently fastened in place.

To complete the framing operation, the 'midship frame was leveled, plumbed and squared, then braced to a timber strongback overhead. Working both forward and aft from amidships, about every third frame unit was similarly leveled and braced, after which full-length marked battens were temporarily attached to these "control" frames at deck level and at the turn of the bilge.

Construction begins with the white oak backbone assembly consisting of the stem (scarfed from two pieces), keel, deadwood, sternpost, and horn timber.

The backbone is set up on its ballast keel and deadwood, with the floor-timber bolts in place, awaiting installation of the frame units. Cheek pieces fastened to the stem and horn timber provide extra strength and the necessary additional wood to receive plank fastenings.

The intermediate frame units were then brought to the marks on the battens and temporarily fastened. Thus, in a few short hours, the structure was transformed from backbone only to a completely framed, floored, and deckbeamed skeleton, ready for structural clamps, shelves, and bilge stringers.

Two hefty ribbands, one at the tuck and another at the bilge, strengthened the hull framing and held it fair for the work that followed. Inside the hull, permanent full-length bilge stringers and sheer clamps and shelves provided still further stiffening. Transom installation was delayed so these longitudinal members could be loaded aboard from aft.

Abeking and Rasmussen's planking system was also their own, and one with which I was not familiar. There was no conventional caulking seam; rather, both the top and bottom edges of each plank were given a compressed, mid-placed groove, done with a simple round-headed tool (perhaps a quarter of an inch wide) that depressed the grain of the wood to form the narrow groove, much as a dull pencil leaves a hollow mark if dragged too heavily over a softwood tabletop. A single

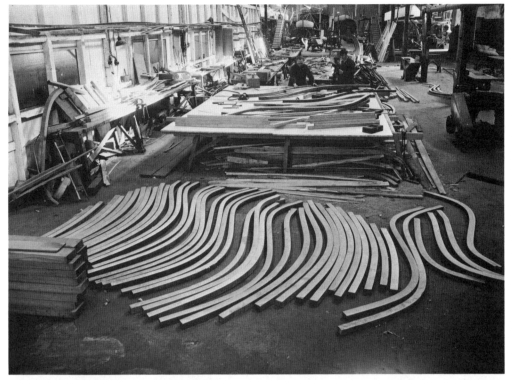

Concordia frames were originally steam-bent to shape (later they were laminated). Beveling the outboard and inboard frame faces for a proper fit against the hull planking and ceiling follows this step.

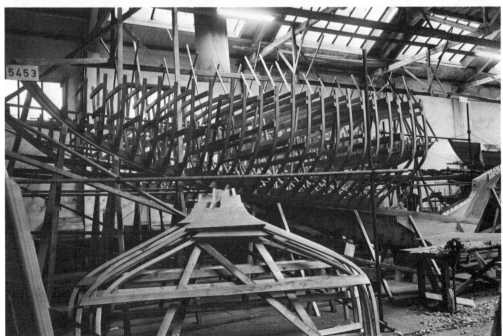

Frame units (made up of a pair of frames, a floor timber, and a deck-beam, along with temporary bracing) are being installed on a Concordia backbone. The pre-drilled floor timbers simply slip over their corresponding keelbolts.

strand of cotton wicking was placed in the void created by the facing grooves when one plank was set down against another.

Two planking crews of two men each worked on each side of the hull. One crew started from the keel up; the second started from about the waterline level, also working upward. This method left, at the turn of the bilge, one plank (the last, or so-called "shutter" plank) whose edges had to be treated differently. Here, the compressed grooves were made as usual in the plank edges, but then the wood on both sides of the groove was planed off flush. In this way the shutter plank could be driven tightly into place without any impeding threads of cotton. In time, and with the natural absorption of moisture, the depressed areas expanded to take the place of the missing strand of cotton. No glue was ever used in the German-built Concordia plank seams, only a light oil paint to seal them. Glue could be disastrous if the boat ever fully dried out; for if the glue held, the plank itself would have to split. And a split plank is almost impossible to repair.

After the 'midship frame unit has been leveled, plumbed, squared, and held in that position by over head bracing, every third frame unit forward and aft of amidships is likewise leveled, then braced. Full-length pre-marked battens are used to establish the correct frame spacing at the deck and bilge level, each frame head being brought to its mark on the battens and temporarily fastened. Stout ribbands next are screwed to the frames at the tuck and at the bilge to ensure a fair hull.

Even the layout of Abeking and Rasmussen's planking varied from what I was familiar with. There was no garboard plank as such running the full length of the keel. Rather, the planking commenced in a diagonal direction over the deadwood from sternpost to keel, where each plank died out to a point and each successive plank rapidly became longer and closer to level as the strakes climbed up the frames. Following this pattern, the planks required less shaping—a real advantage, because a straight plank tends to be a strong plank, with straight grain running parallel to it entire length. Of practical advantage, straight planks also lay up easily and create very little waste material.

I am sure that some excellent builders would argue their own system of planking in preference to that of Abeking and Rasmussen, but it is a matter of record that planking on these Concordia yawls has stood up very well—and actually has held the boat in shape when frames behind the planking were broken.

When planking was completed, topsides and bottom looked almost like a single piece of wood—abso-

Bilge stringers have been installed, and the sheer clamps are ready to be bolted to the frame heads, after which the sheer battens—having served their purpose— will be removed. Removal of the ribbands will take place as the hull is planked.

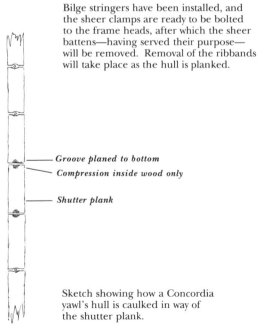

Groove planed to bottom
Compression inside wood only

Shutter plank

Sketch showing how a Concordia yawl's hull is caulked in way of the shutter plank.

Planking begins simultaneously (two crews working) upward from the keel rabbet and also from the turn of the bilge. On later boats, such as this one, the sterns were reinforced against increased backstay tension with a secondary sheer clamp.

lutely fair and smooth. The long planks coming from the same section of the same tree resulted in an almost perfect match as to color and grain. Since there were no conventional outside caulking seams, there was little likelihood that any seam would ever show.

The clamp-and-shelf assembly that Abeking and Rasmussen utilized was conventional and similar to that called for in Concordia's own construction plans. Abeking and Rasmussen followed Concordia's bilge stringer design as well, agreeing that the Concordia arrangement of several plank-like strakes fitted edge to edge was better than one narrower timber of greater thickness. The Concordia system spread support more evenly over the modest frame; fastenings could also be smaller and more numerous; and a flat, wide member interfered less with cabin furniture.

When installing Concordia chainplates, Abeking and Rasmussen avoided putting chainplate fastenings directly through the hull planking. Instead, the chainplates were through-bolted to filler blocks, which, when in place, bore against the structural clamp. The planks were in due course screw-fastened into the filler blocks.

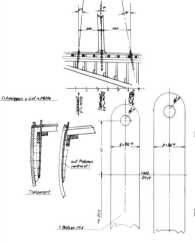

The chainplates are bolted to wooden blocks that are shouldered to bear against the sheer clamp and shaped to fit tightly against the hull planking, which in due course is screw-fastened to the blocks from the outside. No chainplate bolts go through the planking. (This is one of the many shop drawings Abeking and Rasmussen developed from those that Concordia furnished.)

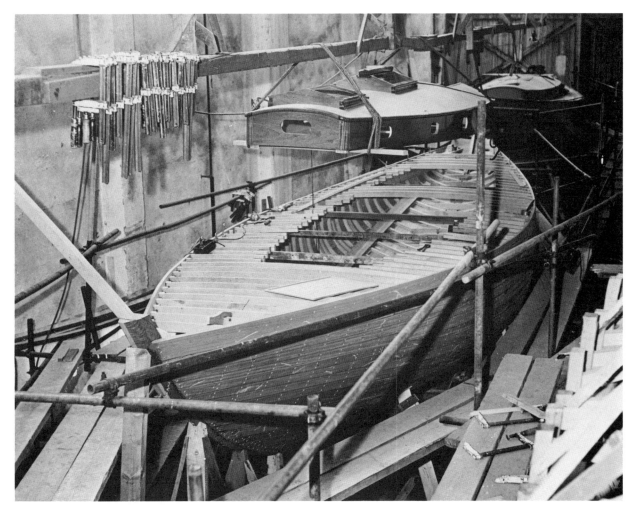

The cabinhouse, built in the yard's joinershop, was used to precisely mark the deckbeams for cutting and thus to establish the shape of the sill piece, which will be notched into the beam ends. Ultimately, the cabinhouse will sit directly on those sill pieces.

Firmly fastened chainplates are of critical importance. Not only do they assure support for the mast, but, when no chainplate motion is possible, deck leaks around them are less likely to develop.

Abeking and Rasmussen's method of framing the cabinhouse opening was again unique in my experience. Routine procedure at home was to install a heavy structural fore-and-aft carlin into which the ends of the deckbeams were either dovetailed or halved. The boats of Herreshoff, however, were an exception in that they had no carlins whatsoever, but simply depended on the cabinhouse side itself for fore-and-aft stiffness. Herreshoff cabinsides were merely through-bolted to the inboard ends of the deckbeams, with the decking itself

Hull planking is in the process of being planed fair and sanded smooth, the work being kept track of panel by panel with chalk markings. A number of Concordias were ordered with bright-finished topsides, a stunning alternative to paint made possible by the matched mahogany planking with its wood-to-wood seams. The teak deck, consisting of narrow planks sprung to the curve of the covering boards, is partly laid. This Concordia 41 was specially ordered without the usual bridge deck.

sandwiched between. This made a light, stiff construction, but relied rather much on the bolts.

The Abeking and Rasmussen system was a combination of the traditional carlin and the Herreshoff technique: Over the inboard upper ends of the deckbeams, a plank-like member 4 or 5 inches wide was let in so its upper surface came flush with the tops of the beams. The cabin rested directly on this sill piece where it was securely fastened. Adjacent decking, laid subsequently, did likewise.

For the decks of standard boats, Abeking and Rasmussen used African mahogany for the first fifty or so Concordia yawls, then shifted to special marine plywood for the next fifty. Canvas was laid over these decks as sheathing. In both cases, the covering boards were made from conventional planks, so that no edge-grained plywood was ever exposed to the weather. Abeking and Rasmussen would not have changed to plywood, except for the fact that the wide mahogany planks originally used tended to dent easily and on several boats showed their seams through the painted canvas sheathing that covered them.

All teak decks, on the special boats that had them, were traditional, with teak covering boards and narrow, caulked planks laid parallel whose ends were nibbed into a centerline kingplank. Deck canvas on the standard boats was laid in a special Abeking and Rasmussen paint mixture. The canvas terminated under the toerail outboard and, inboard, under a molding around the cabinhouse sides and cockpit coamings. This allowed for easy removal when the time came to replace the canvas.

Standard Concordia yawl decks and cabintops were sheathed with painted canvas whose raw edges were covered by the toerail or with appropriate trim molding.

8
Selling the Class

i

The business of selling Concordia yawls as a formal, ongoing proposition did not occur to me for several years, until the day Robin Langeman walked into our office. In addition to expressing a sincere and knowledgeable admiration for the yawls, this young boating enthusiast and advertising man pointed out earnestly and convincingly that conditions for promoting the class were exceptionally promising. Their size and type, as Robin pointed out, were ideal for family sailing. Their design was good and accepted. Their builder, Abeking and Rasmussen, was capable of producing the boats economically, in quality, and in quantity. And Concordia Company itself had excellent facilities for service and display. All that remained was to spread the good word among the sailing fraternity.

Robin's well-considered plan for accomplishing this promotion contained little that was actually new or surprising. But it thoughtfully outlined a practical, step-by-step, tasteful, low-key advertising program. My first reaction was favorable. Sure, why not? However, after sleeping on the idea for a night or two, I suddenly realized that success along these lines might well be the very worst thing that could happen.

In order to properly handle a volume of inquiries and correspondence, it would be almost imperative to enlarge and thus disturb our small, harmonious office team. To service an appreciable number of new boats simultaneously would involve a costly expansion of yard facilities — or at least a confusing partnership with individuals or organizations outside

The standard Concordia yawl, *Auda*, built in 1956, with Captain Hardy at the helm. Colonel Herrington ordered *Auda* by telephone.

Concordia. Merely building *x* number of boats at one time could result in an equal number of mistakes, which might be small or, on the other hand, might be very large. Then looking at the basic problem, supposing that one could build up an organization and successfully launch a popular fleet of first-class boats, the grave risk would still remain of that eventual slowdown of sales which almost inevitably occurs in boating promotions. At this point increased overhead swiftly deals its lethal blow before cutbacks can be made.

Rightly or wrongly, advertising programs as such were then and there permanently set aside, and Concordia sales were allowed to proceed at their own pace. To this day, I feel the decision was right. Our one-at-a-time methods made improvements possible on each boat as it came along, and also allowed me the continued experience and pleasure of working with each and every inquiry. Initial personal negotiations tended to weed out the undecided and to promote, among the convinced, bonds of understanding that became of inestimable satisfaction and value in extended dealings to follow.

ii

As every serious plugger in the boat game eventually discovers, no two customers are exactly alike. A boat means something different to each one of them. Happily, I can say that of those who bought Concordia yawls, at least ninety-eight percent were, in their own way, finest-kind.

Some intriguing few required little or no sales effort at all. In fact, one lady merely phoned long distance, introduced herself, and politely inquired if she could order one of the Concordia yawls as a birthday present for her husband. The giver had done her homework, and the receiver showed his appreciation by enjoying this timely gift for the remainder of his sailing days.

Another Chesapeake sailor, Colonel Arthur Herrington, made my selling job equally simple. He didn't even ask a preliminary question. "I wish to order a Concordia yawl," he said in his opening telephone statement. Somewhat caught off guard by this abrupt demand from a total stranger, I immediately asked, "How come?" The Colonel explained that our mutual friend Paul Hammond had recommended Concordia yawls and that this, in turn, had prompted him to look for promotional information. Finding no ads for Concordias in the boating magazines in spite of the reported sales, he concluded that the boats must indeed have some merit. That was that!

Then there was Parker ("Rip") Converse, ex-Commodore of the Beverly Yacht Club in nearby Marion. Rip was a friendly rival of ours, in that he carried on a yacht business in association with the John Alden office. On this particular Saturday morning, Rip showed up at South Wharf without previous notice for what I took to be a neighborly visit. The day being sunny and mild, we shoved off on a leisurely harbor tour in a yard skiff, chatting as we went. As we passed by one of the newest Concordia yawls I suggested that Rip might like to climb aboard and take a look. He nodded his assent, and graciously tolerated my brief guided tour, but ventured little comment and showed no obvious interest in the boat. Then, on the way back to South Wharf, he said simply, "I would like to buy one." He had known all the time what he had come for. I hadn't had a clue.

It would be a time-saver if all customers made up their own minds without advice or urging from the salesman. But I have always believed in giving honest opinions whenever I am asked—and, I admit, sometimes when not. However, even customers who are already sold usually enjoy putting up a front of uncertainty. Perhaps they just want to learn what sort of propaganda is forthcoming or to find out if any modifications of plan or price are possible. As an example of this approach, Alexander Macleod, his son Eldon, and a grandson arrived at South Wharf one day seeking information about Concordias. Eldon was the experienced sailor and asked most of the questions; Alexander Macleod and the grandson kept their own counsel. I answered Eldon's searching questions at length and according to convictions that had developed from my previous experience with Concordias. Although I understood and sympathized with this good sailor's wish to have me consider features that had worked well for him on previous boats, I stuck to my guns. It looked as if I would lose a sale I very much wanted to make.

But that is not the way it turned out. Walking toward the car in preparation for departure, Grandpa Macleod turned to his son and suggested, "Why don't we just take her the way she comes?" Alexander Macleod did not pretend to be a boat man, but he certainly was a kind, perceptive, and very capable businessman. We saw a great deal of him in days to come, and he was the only person other than my cousin George Howland that my brother and I ever asked to become a director of Concordia Company. Although he declined the invitation for reasons of health and age, he left us a legacy of friendship, loyal promotion, and valuable yearly business. His son, followed by three grandsons and, now, great-grandchildren, have made *Skye* a very special racing and cruising Concordia yawl.

Another sale of particular satisfaction to me required a bit more time and consideration. After a short correspondence, Dr. and Mrs. Raymond Curtis of Gibson Island, Maryland, made arrangements to pay us a weekend visit at South Wharf. At the conclusion of a most pleasant first

morning's discussion, I ventured the thought that the doctor really knew very little about boating. How, I asked, did it happen that he was so determined to buy a boat, and, more important, why had he chosen a Concordia yawl? The answer was interesting. Specializing in the remaking of misformed or damaged hands, Dr. Curtis was being overpressed by urgent calls, and felt that for his own health, he must get away from the phone for at least short periods. A sailboat, he thought, would be the answer. For several months, he researched different boats in every yachting magazine he could find. The good performance of Concordia yawls in Bermuda races had caught his attention, not because he ever planned to race, but just because he wanted proof that his boat would be safe and strong. His final question had now boiled down to whether to buy a new or used model. Mrs. Curtis made this decision for the family, pointing out that a new boat was affordable, but that her husband would then feel pushed to work harder than ever to earn the additional cost, and thus negate his whole purpose for having a boat.

If every buyer could have as clear an understanding of what type of boat he or she needed and could really use, there would be fewer disappointed sailors. The Curtises bought the third Abeking and Rasmussen-built Concordia as a secondhand boat. They then made arrangements to employ Wilton Butts for several weeks to help them with the fundamentals of sailing and cruising and to make the trip to Gibson Island. Dr. and Mrs. Curtis owned, sailed, and enjoyed *Rayanna* for twenty-six years.

Another Curtiss family presented a different type of sales opportunity. This experienced husband-and-wife crew had at the time sailed and cruised many a mile in their Casey-designed and -built 43-foot yawl, but were now finding her a bit of a handful for their changing needs. My suggestion was, of course, a Concordia yawl. In spite of my protestations to the contrary, they very understandably doubted that a boat only 3 feet shorter could solve their problem. They went on their way and discovered a much smaller boat that apparently achieved amenities they sought, plus full headroom, made possible by the ingenious use of a hollow keel. After a year's trial with this diminutive cruiser, they were back again. Very small boats are not too easy for grownups to get around on, especially on deck. The Curtisses proved this to themselves and then bought a Concordia in which they comfortably cruised until sailing was out of their picture.

With good lines, modest displacement and windage, simple rig, and workable deck space, a boat the size of a Concordia can be about the easiest and safest for any experienced man-and-wife crew. Others who have experimented will agree on this. The next step down for aging folks is a boat about 16 feet long on the waterline, worked out for cockpit comfort

Concordia #40, *Skye*, built in 1956 and for many years owned by the Macleod family of West Falmouth. The name comes from family connections in Scotland. Four generations of Macleods have enjoyed *Skye*.

and daysailing—something like a Herreshoff Fish-class boat, perhaps.

Two more individual sales stories, and I'll get on with a more general view of boat selling. Thanks to my friend John West, Moreau Brown and his wife, Alice, spent a weekend patiently listening to me explain and brag about the various virtues of our yawls—the bridge deck, the folding bunks, the coal heating stove, on and on. At the end of my inspired promotion, Mrs. Brown said with her charming smile, "Waldo, you know, there is really absolutely nothing I like about the Concordias."

This was fair enough; we now knew where we stood. I well appreciate that it is never easy to understand what makes for one's sailing pleasure. Within a few seasons the Browns were back again and initiated an order for one of our boats. Volumes of correspondence, which I still cherish, followed. To achieve more headroom (Moreau was 6 feet 2 inches tall), and special accommodation, they specified the modified Concordia Forty-one. To render access to the cabin less of a climb, and to bring the galley socially nearer to the cockpit, they eliminated the bridge deck. To enlarge the forward cabin, they lengthened the cabinhouse by several inches. These and other alterations, minor for the most part, took time and negotiations, but individual inches do count, and the well-thrashed-out modifications were well worth it to the Browns. When the 1954 hurricane badly damaged *Armata I,* they ordered a sistership which incorporated only one new change, and that was teak decks in place of canvas. Starting as kindly critics, Moreau and Alice became two of our most faithful customers and closest of friends.

In terms of time, I would guess that Dr. Edward Kline, from Cleveland, represented our greatest sales challenge. He took the pains and interest to educate himself as to just what boat would best fit his Lake Erie needs and his current pocketbook. Round number one of correspondence was a question-and-answer series about a Concordia yawl. Then came a silent interval of several months while he considered in depth a few other boats. Round number two was an analysis of a Concordia versus different types, and so it went for several years. I'm sure an advertising answering staff would have given up, but here was a fellow seriously considering his needs, and it was a rewarding and instructive experience to work with him. Once he made up his mind, he stayed right with his decisions through a Concordia yawl, then on to a powerboat with a Concordia cabin.

iii

Thinking back now to the sources of our yawl sales, it seems clear that enthusiastic owners were responsible for most of them. A significant majority of these good friends were key yacht club officers who, by their very example as well as their words of approval, carried telling weight among strong sailing fraternities.

Paid agents we might well have had, but we shied away from the agency system, feeling that confusion among persons involved, dilutions of purpose, increases in cost, etc., were all dangers too great to risk. Going it alone, we expected and experienced friendly rivalry, but happily were recipients of very little derogatory propaganda. Not only were we on the small side to be considered a threat by established competitors, but in those days yacht business in general was carried out on a happily constructive basis.

One exception to our direct-sales policy was with a yacht brokerage firm in far-distant California. At their instigation, Clark Sweet and his associate Fred Schenck not only sold five Concordia yawls for us but tended also to their off-loading and commissioning. I well remember flying out with our son Kinny, then eleven, to witness the christening at Newport Beach of the first California-owned Concordia yawl. She arrived after a long, drying trip on the hot deck of a freighter, and Clark, in preparation for her launching, had wisely assembled a battery of pumps, electric and manual. I unwisely bragged that I would drink all the water that she leaked. The test was a tough one for a wooden boat, and the Western launching party were understandably hopeful of at least a small Eastern embarrassment. The boat, God bless her, plucked me out of my own hot box, by leaking not a single drop.

Boatyards in general were often helpful Concordia promoters. For them there was no immediate monetary gain, only a strong potential for a valuable storage customer. I don't know exactly how it happens, but it does seem that the owner of a respected and loved family auxiliary tends to make the most satisfactory of boatyard and insurance company customers. Chester Crosby of the famous old Cape Cod catboat family was a particularly successful advocate of Concordia yawls, and built up a small but strong fleet of them at his Osterville yard. Chet seemed to have a sort of progressive program going. Many of his young customers started their sailing in Crosby Wianno Juniors, then went to Wianno Senior sloops and, as a third step, to Concordia yawls. To a lesser degree similar patterns developed in other harbors and helped substantially in building up our class.

Boating editors and writers also helped. Boris Lauer-Leonardi, editor of *The Rudder*, had, as I've said, worked with my father on many articles, and I myself had been shipmates with Herbert Stone and his right-hand man, Bill Taylor of *Yachting*. Further, we had special friends at *The Skipper*, that all too short-lived but excellent Chesapeake magazine, of which Colonel Herrington was a financial backer. Overlooking the lack of advertising

Chester Crosby in the wheelhouse of his own towboat.

Mason Smith's first *Javelin* was a Herreshoff H-23 that we accepted as partial payment on his new Concordia yawl of the same name. Other yawl buyers, whose families had outgrown their similar small-but-good boats yet still wanted a boat that sailed well, chose this trade-in approach.

support from us, all these magazines approved of the Concordia yawls and published their plans along with suitable editorial material.

Or perhaps I should say they largely overlooked our lack of advertising support. At New York Motorboat Show time I regularly received a formal request from *Yachting* for current information on Concordia products. Although I spent hours organizing this material and returned it promptly, it never appeared in the magazine. Meeting my good friend Herb Stone at the show one year, I said that I understood well enough why he did not use the material, since Concordia did not participate in the show, but wondered why he wasted my time by asking for stuff he never intended to use.

Herb, who usually had a good answer to every question, uttered a loud and amazed "What?" In years to come Concordia material always appeared in *Yachting* in good shape.

As we proceeded on past rows of shiny boat exhibits I had another question for Herb, this time about a little stock sloop that was being highly touted that year. Herb took one look at it and said, "She has just enough ballast to sink her when she capsizes." Maybe it's a golden memory, but it seemed in those days before corporate mergers that boating magazines had a truer understanding of yachting as a sport, even a feeling of obligation to contribute positively to its welfare. In this Herb Stone and others like him set a worthy and successful example.

In addition to our somewhat unconventional stand in regard to formal advertising, we offered no suggestions about financing. Without need for giving the matter a great deal of thought, it just seemed to me that if any owner could not comfortably afford a boat, he would eventually be unhappy with his purchase.

An understandable and recurring sales obstacle we faced with our yawls was their apparent or actual lack of accommodation. In a 40-foot boat, people were becoming accustomed to having six berths and certain land-type luxuries. I remember one special couple who arrived at South Wharf for an inspection visit. The sailor himself obviously admired our boat and its sailing record, but his girlfriend was interested only in cabins. She explored below decks in several non-Concordia craft to make her own comparisons, and came up with a special liking for the fine layout in Percy Chubb's 45-footer *Antilles*. Her simple compromise suggestion: to install an *Antilles* cabin in a Concordia yawl. If only things were that easy!

There was an occasion when I burst my heart out to sell a Concordia to a certain good friend who held firmly to his desire for accommodations for six, full headroom throughout, and other amenities that our boats failed to include. In the end he bought a more modern type, not a bad boat at all, except that she was a bit tender. He requested us to supply a couple of hundred pounds of lead ballast for him, but on looking into the situation, even he could find no suitable place to stow it: built-in water and fuel tanks occupied the entire bilge.

There is only so much space in any hull, and if extra berths or whatever are added, then space is lost for features that may well be more essential. You can, of course, always push the sides of the boat out, the bottom down, or the top up, but then you risk sacrificing fundamental sailing qualities. Perhaps there are times when such a sacrifice makes sense. But, please, I urge you, consider the overall picture well before you consider major compromises.

Front cover of a 1960s sales brochure.

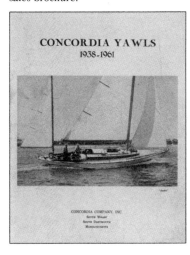

111

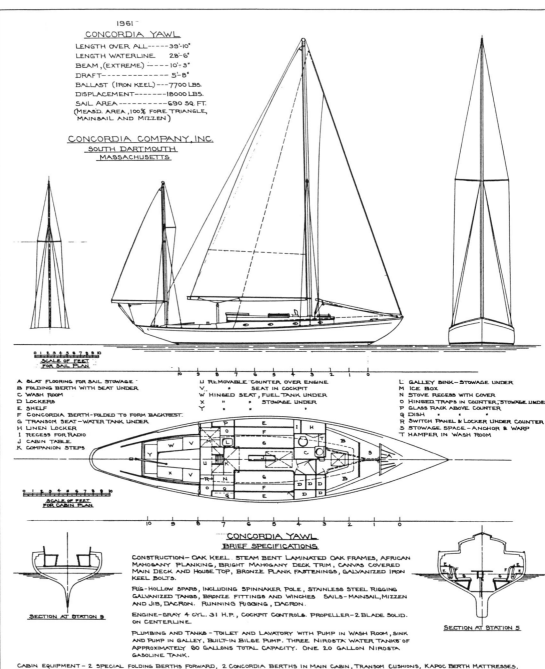

1961

CONCORDIA YAWL

LENGTH OVER ALL-----39'-10"
LENGTH WATERLINE   28'-6"
BEAM, (EXTREME) -----10'-3"
DRAFT------------- 5'-8"
BALLAST (IRON KEEL)---7700 LBS.
DISPLACEMENT-------18000 LBS.
SAIL AREA---------690 SQ. FT.
(MEASD. AREA, 100% FORE TRIANGLE,
MAINSAIL AND MIZZEN)

CONCORDIA COMPANY, INC.
SOUTH DARTMOUTH
MASSACHUSETTS

0 1 2 3 4 5 6 7 8 9 10
SCALE OF FEET
FOR SAIL PLAN

10 9 8 7 6 5 4 3 2 1 0

A SLAT FLOORING FOR SAIL STOWAGE
B FOLDING BERTH WITH SEAT UNDER
C WASH ROOM
D LOCKERS
E SHELF
F CONCORDIA BERTH-FOLDED TO FORM BACKREST
G TRANSOM SEAT-WATER TANK UNDER
H LINEN LOCKER
I RECESS FOR RADIO
J CABIN TABLE
K COMPANION STEPS

U REMOVABLE COUNTER OVER ENGINE
V "   "   SEAT IN COCKPIT
W HINGED SEAT, FUEL TANK UNDER
X "   "   STOWAGE UNDER
Y "   "   "   "

L GALLEY SINK- STOWAGE UNDER
M ICE BOX
N STOVE RECESS WITH COVER
O HINGED TRAPS IN COUNTER, STOWAGE UNDER
P GLASS RACK ABOVE COUNTER
Q DISH
R SWITCH PANEL & LOCKER UNDER COUNTER
S STOWAGE SPACE - ANCHOR & WARP
T HAMPER IN WASH ROOM

0 1 2 3 4 5 6 7 8 9 10
SCALE OF FEET
FOR CABIN PLAN

10 9 8 7 6 5 4 3 2 1 0

CONCORDIA YAWL
BRIEF SPECIFICATIONS

CONSTRUCTION— OAK KEEL. STEAM BENT LAMINATED OAK FRAMES, AFRICAN
MAHOGANY PLANKING, BRIGHT MAHOGANY DECK TRIM, CANVAS COVERED
MAIN DECK AND HOUSE TOP, BRONZE PLANK FASTENINGS, GALVANIZED IRON
KEEL BOLTS.

RIG-HOLLOW SPARS, INCLUDING SPINNAKER POLE, STAINLESS STEEL RIGGING
GALVANIZED TANGS, BRONZE FITTINGS AND WINCHES. SAILS-MAINSAIL, MIZZEN
AND JIB, DACRON. RUNNING RIGGING, DACRON.

ENGINE-GRAY 4 CYL. 31 H.P., COCKPIT CONTROLS. PROPELLER-2 BLADE SOLID.
ON CENTERLINE.

PLUMBING AND TANKS - TOILET AND LAVATORY WITH PUMP IN WASH ROOM, SINK
AND PUMP IN GALLEY, BUILT-IN BILGE PUMP. THREE NIROSTA WATER TANKS OF
APPROXIMATELY 80 GALLONS TOTAL CAPACITY. ONE 20 GALLON NIROSTA
GASOLINE TANK.

CABIN EQUIPMENT- 2 SPECIAL FOLDING BERTHS FORWARD, 2 CONCORDIA BERTHS IN MAIN CABIN, TRANSOM CUSHIONS, KAPOC BERTH MATTRESSES,
CABIN TABLE, ICE BOX OF 75 LBS CAPACITY, ALCOHOL STOVE 7 ELECTRIC LIGHTS, 1 KEROSENE LAMP, PANELLED PINE BULKHEADS, LOCUST TRIM.

OTHER EQUIPM'T-ELEC. RUNNING AND RIDING LIGHTS, ANCHOR AND WARP, BOAT HOOK, FLAG STAFF, CANVAS BUCKET, MOP, FEW TOOLS, FENDERS, LIFE RING,
DOCK LINES, COMPASS AND BINNACLE, LIFE LINES, PULPIT, DINGHY CHOCKS, HATCH & SKYLIGHT COVERS.

SECTION AT STATION 9

SECTION AT STATION 5

9
Specifications and Fenwick Williams

The Concordia philosophy of no formal advertising or promotion campaign for volume sales made good sense, but the word-of-mouth recommendations of enthusiastic friends and the very attractive value of the boats themselves nevertheless generated new orders faster than we expected. It became more and more urgent for us to develop new procedures for handling these orders efficiently. If only Concordia's prewar designer-draftsman Bill Harris had been available, all would have been well, but by now Bill was far away, pursuing his profession in Alabama.

To help with special drawings for the first two postwar Concordias (which were built locally at the Casey yard), we were fortunate in having temporary part-time help from several excellent designer-draftsmen, especially H. Miller Nichols. It was Nichols's excellent, updated version of Bill Harris's original drawings that Abeking and Rasmussen followed in making their metric drawings and in building their first three Concordia yawls in 1950–1951. However, Miller Nichols was working full-time elsewhere as a mechanical engineer when, in 1951, it became obvious that our standard plans should once more be revised.

Good fortune again came to our rescue, thanks primarily to my prewar partner, Ray Hunt (see *A Life in Boats: The Years Before the War*). During conversations with him about rig and racing matters, Ray introduced us to Fenwick Williams, who was working with Ray at the time as an independent architect on several important designs. One thing soon led to another, and before we realized it, Fenwick was a major factor in our Concordia yawl-building program.

Brief specification and sales sheet for the Concordia Standard Thirty-nine yawl, to accompany a current price. Drawn up by Fenwick C. Williams, 1961.

113

Standard specifications were made up in print form for both standard yawls and Concordia Forty-ones. In addition to being made up for the current sales price, they were to be modified for each buyer in such a way as to keep track of any changes or additions and the cost or credit of same.

With his badly nearsighted eyes, Fenwick could not drive. So after our first introduction, and for some ten years that followed, scarcely a fall or winter month went by that did not find me making a pilgrimage or two in my 1941 Plymouth coupe (still mine today and built with a trunk long enough to accommodate 7-foot oars) to Fenwick in Marblehead.

Fenwick's first major undertaking for Concordia was the drawing up of a skeleton construction plan, including elevation and plan view, that would accurately outline the limits of space available for cabin, cockpit, and deck details. The plan had to agree precisely with Abeking and Rasmussen's metric drawings, albeit scaled in feet and inches.

The second step was to draw into this plan the latest version of a standard arrangement. This was a more taxing and complex assignment than it might at first appear. There were at least three factors to consider in approaching the project. They were all different, but each aimed toward the same goal: a good boat with a wide range of uses, and one of quality with an economical price tag. In the cause of building efficiency and, hence, economy, it was essential to coordinate wherever possible our arrangement detail with Abeking and Rasmussen construction detail. (To take just two of hundreds of examples: *our* cabin bulkhead locations were adjusted an inch or two either way the better to utilize *their* framing locations; then the dimensions of the floor timbers were adjusted in height so the timbers themselves supported the cabin sole without the need for any additional framing.)

While considering customer requests and needs, still a third category of useful modifications came to light and had to be worked out and tied into the standard plan. (For example, John West urged us to find ways and means of attaining a more commodious cockpit without sacrificing the virtues of the original arrangement on *Java*. As it worked out, some eighteen inches of the forward end of the stern deck was replaced by a watertight 'thwartship seat set at the same level as, and making a continuation of, the side seats.)

After Fenwick had developed a comprehensive and accurate standard arrangement plan (which he kept up-to-date from year to year), transparencies were run off. (These were a type of brown-line reproducible plan on which detail could be added, altered, or removed. Their trade name at the time was "Van Dyke Intermediates"; now they are generally known as sepias.) One of these was assigned to each new boat as it was ordered and was dated and labeled with the owner's name. On it were drawn all the approved modifications suggested by the owner in question. Although, as I have said, we discouraged any changes in basics, we could without complication alter details of galley or toilet room layout and the like. In fact, we kept on hand a list of practical alternatives and extras that a purchaser could study and order from.

Standard specifications were worked up to match the standard plans. Unlike conventional specifications, Concordia's specifications were brief and designed primarily to show all concerned what the current base price of a Concordia yawl was based on. Four blue-on-white sets of prints (one set each for customer, builder, Concordia, and Fenwick Williams) were assigned and labeled for each new yawl order. No wording on these standard specification prints was to be erased.

Where approved modifications were involved, appropriate standard wording was crossed out and the new wording was typed (using carbon paper) between the lines or on the back of the previous page. Where differences in cost were involved, a quotation for extra charge or credit was noted beside each change. This method of keeping track of what was standard and what was modification was helpful to all concerned, and it avoided misunderstandings.

As I have said, we never had any formal contracts with Abeking and Rasmussen. The first few boats were ordered and financed by Drayton Cochran. Then, as Concordia took over all negotiations, we merely sent Abeking and Rasmussen a letter ordering another boat; and they in turn merely confirmed the order in writing and noted the current base price and delivery date, closing: "Please send the necessary informations soonest." This procedure may appear to be a bit casual, but our relationship was entirely straightforward: we wanted more good boats, they wanted more good orders. Any inferior product from them or any bad check from us would have destroyed the relationship immediately.

The contract situation with a customer was a bit different. The customer not only had to trust us but also Abeking and Rasmussen. In many cases he knew very little about either of us. Our answer to this predicament again had to be simple: "You, the customer, have seen an Abeking and Rasmussen built Concordia yawl; do you wish to order one like it, with the understanding that the price is x dollars and the approximate delivery date is thus and so?" Our customers' lawyers often took a very dim view of this loose kind of arrangement. But under the circumstances we felt we could not, in all honesty, give any performance guarantee. All we could—and did—guarantee was that we would return the buyer's money in the event his boat was not up to standard or arrived too late—or did not arrive at all.

Looking at it practically and legally, there was no way Concordia could rebuild a faulty boat or force Abeking and Rasmussen to do so. Distances were too great. Other architectural firms with their different situations

Concordia yawl standard sail and arrangement plans (see endpapers) were so handled that each owner received the equivalent of custom plans, that showed his required modifications. Extra costs or credits were covered in the accompanying specification sheets.

followed a more usual procedure, and sent over their professional inspector to check progress and workmanship from time to time, but in no way did I feel qualified to do so, nor did our organization have the time or money to pursue this pattern.

Most of our yawl production problems seemed to work themselves out little by little, but there was one that every fall put my nervous system into high gear. In order for Abeking and Rasmussen to set up a substantial building program for us, we had to advise them by late summer of each year just how many boats we wanted for the following spring. Only with this number settled could they figure their most favorable base price and a satisfactory sequence of delivery dates.

For the most part our buyers understood this situation and were anxious to cooperate, but all too often they found it impossible to come to an early decision. Even when they could, they often as not were unable to decide on details quickly. Such delays interrupted an all-important schedule. It might seem reasonable to start a boat without complete plans at hand, but Abeking and Rasmussen were entirely correct in their conclusion that such a procedure was just asking for trouble.

We never could actually reach our goal of perfect planning, so in the

FENWICK WILLIAMS

Fenwick Williams at the wheel of the schooner *Keewatin*, which he helped design when at John Alden's office. With Fenwick is "Skip" Pope, son of Dr. Graham Pope, who bought Concordia yawl #14 in 1953 and still owns her.

Fenwick was born on 22 December 1901, in Cambridge, Massachusetts, and spent his boyhood summers in Center Sandwich, New Hampshire—a delightful rural community that well suited his early burning interest in birds, four-footed creatures, and all living things. But somewhere along the line, Fenwick's attention suddenly turned to boats.

"Due to bum eyes," he has written me, "I didn't finish high school. After hanging around a few years wondering what, if anything, I could do with my life, I obtained a drafting job. Like Titus Moody's father on the Fred Allen show, I was so ignorant, I not only didn't know anything, I didn't expect anything. Someone my father knew took me to see John Alden, who said, 'I was going to tell you I didn't have anything for you, but after seeing these sketches I've changed my mind.'" Soon after he got the job with John Alden, Fenwick and his mother moved to Marblehead, a town the writer Jo Anne Rowe has called "a natural habitat for yacht

end all concerned just did the best they could. By late summer there were usually four or five definite orders on the books, plus several likely prospects. Although we had very little spare capital in the bank, we drummed up a bit of spare courage on the cuff, and arbitrarily came up with an optimistic number of orders for the coming year. Often enough this meant three or four orders on speculation.

Of course, we kept Abeking and Rasmussen well advised on the actual situation, so they fully realized they were sharing the risks to some extent. On several occasions they were more than patient with us on overdue payments. In return we tried, wherever possible, to be ahead of time on other occasions.

The customer had to take his chances, too. It was first come, first served, and we stuck to this faithfully in spite of tempting contingencies. Any attempt to get in with an early order and then delay with special requests was out. All speculation orders were started as standard boats. If a buyer bought one of these after it was well along, he had to accept it as it was, being granted only those special requests that could be worked in without complication. As it turned out, very few chose to wait for a later delivery date just to gain a wanted modification or two.

---

designers." That same year, Fenwick bought his first boat, a 21-foot knockabout, for $250.

As is often the case in big architectural offices, Fenwick received but modest recognition for the work he did for Alden. Nonetheless, his considerable knowledge of cruising and workboat types did leave a strong impression on many an Alden design.

During the Depression, Fenwick lost his job. But he returned to the Alden office during World War II, at twenty-five dollars a week, to help with design work on fireboats, rescue craft, and other defense projects. After the war, he was for a short time associated with the very fine yacht designer Murray Peterson, but this happy arrangement had to come to an end when Murray moved to Maine. It wasn't long after this that Ray Hunt and then Concordia started knocking at his door.

This door was in fact a cellar door, picturesquely opening out onto a sunny garden at the rear of the little house at the top of Lee Street in Marblehead that Fenwick shared with his mother. His mother, with her fondness for old New England ways and furnishings, had charmingly remodeled the upstairs rooms. Fenwick, with an equally intense interest in boats and machinery, had cleverly remodeled the basement to suit his office and workshop needs.

Here was a man considered practically blind, without a high school diploma, working in the corner of a small Marblehead cellar, and yet coping with the lion's share of the essential drawings and calculations not only for his own yacht designs, but for those of two other boating professionals, one with little formal design training, the other with none.

Fenwick's work for Ray Hunt included details for the *America*'s Cup contender *Easterner*, Max Aitken's formidable 46-foot ocean racer *Drumbeat*, and several experimental powerboats that were to lead the way to a new and popular deep-V type. His work for Concordia was somewhat different but made equal demands upon him.

It was indeed a strange and unlikely setup—yet a lasting one that benefited all concerned.

THE MAIN CABIN OF A STANDARD CONCORDIA

The main cabin of a Concordia Standard Thirty-nine yawl, looking forward.

The seat backs are shaped for comfort and to form fold-down sleeping berths. The cushions (made in two sections for ease of handling and to give easy access to the lockers underneath) are filled with kapok and covered with light-green corduroy. Some owners preferred to cover the canvas berth bottom with similar material and to hang a drape behind the slats of the seat back.

The kerosene lamp is standard Abeking and Rasmussen equipment. Over the Concordia Cabin Heater is a brass-trimmed mantel shelf—a special feature for the boat as is the mirror, the latter (above the stove) visually lengthening and brightening the cabin. The seat fronts slope outboard at the bottom to give wider floor space; the table is offset to port to provide a passageway to starboard. All paneling is knotty pine, with the knots carefully balanced for decorative purposes.

The teak cabin sole is painted black, after which it is spattered with white and light green paint dots, then varnished. I have always liked the appearance of the spatters on the floor—not only do they add depth to the space, but they make the surface less slippery and easier to keep clean. The varnished surface will take the heavy wear, while the paint underneath will look well for years.

The cockpit porthole, essential for cabin ventilation, is just visible to the left of the companionway ladder. The ladder is made in two pieces so that the upper three steps can be removed, thereby improving the galley without seriously disrupting access to the cockpit. When the ladder, 'thwartships galley counter, and engine box are removed, the engine is totally accessible from the main cabin.

The main cabin of a Concordia Standard Thirty-nine yawl, looking aft. For additional details, see Appendix I.

119

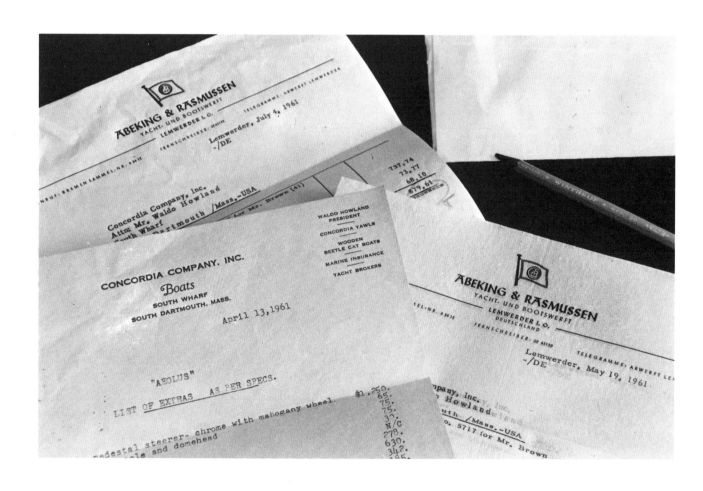

10
Paperwork

Believing strongly that every buyer of a worthwhile boat deserves a fair portion of pleasure for money spent, we always tried to be responsive to our customers' interests and concerns. This philosophy understandably involved us in a huge volume of correspondence. Fortunately, most of this correspondence was enjoyable—and all of it served a good purpose. A recent review of the complete files suggests an average count of about two hundred letters per boat; even more for a few, but many less for others.

Some half of the letters were between buyer and salesman—that is, between the customer and myself. As might be expected, most of these concerned details: deck and cabin modifications, rig and sail particulars, special equipment, and the like. Then there were business matters—costs, delivery dates, and so on. Usually sandwiched in toward the end of a file were a few letters expressing thinly veiled anxieties. But there were very few letters expressing serious complaints. The occasional disappointments, yes, but these were usually of a mutual nature. Exceptionally bad winter weather in Germany or a longshoreman's strike in Boston did several times delay a delivery. Once and only once did a customer firmly dispute his final bill.

Important as the correspondence with customers may have been, my most demanding correspondence was with Abeking and Rasmussen. For over fifteen years our letters flew steadily back and forth across the Atlantic. Literally, no important detail relating to the creation of each new German-built Concordia went unnoted in these files.

In fact, the extent of the correspondence with Abeking and Rasmussen was a blessing. For while it might seem that it would have been easier for us to do our business by telephone (an impossibility in this case, because of time and language differences, not to mention phone costs), frantic haste and a faulty memory can be a troublesome pair. But an even greater blessing was the fact that the yard manager, and the yard manager only, handled at least ninety-five percent of Abeking and Rasmussen's side of the correspondence. This remained true whether the subject concerned the length of a dish shelf, the technical aspects of building a mainmast, or our order for ten Concordia yawls. The yard manager was, until his death in 1952, our friend Elo Poulsen; after Elo, it was Horst Lehnert. I am sure these two very capable men had excellent help (both Herr Martins and Herr Ohlendorf filled in most efficiently at times), but it was a real bonus for us all that the top man in the yard personally followed through on all our transactions. There was no passing of the buck and no area left open for misunderstandings.

Horst Lehnert was undoubtedly a major reason why our yawls were so well and efficiently built. Although initially I knew very little about Horst, I liked and respected him from our very first meetings in Lemwerder. And while I never made a return trip to Germany, Horst did for some years make an annual trip to the United States. He well knew the importance of staying in personal touch with his American customers and of keeping up with American building activities and boating trends.

In planning his United States itinerary, Horst always reserved a day or two for my family and me in Padanaram. This welcome arrangement made possible the unhurried discussions that are so absolutely essential for planning and for the solving of important problems related to boats. Likewise, during leisurely tours through South Wharf, Horst had ample opportunity to observe Concordia at work and to understand its facilities and limitations. To our great benefit, he was ever eager to share his knowledge with our workers, many of whom had important questions about Abeking and Rasmussen construction methods, materials, and procedures. At our Smith Neck shop he was much interested in our Beetle Cat operation and announced in the presence of the crew that this was the best wooden boat production program he had seen in America.* I can tell you that praise from an expert like Horst did more than a little for the morale of Concordia's workers and owner alike. Just as Horst was departing from our home one year, he confided to our children that he would be missing them very much. At these words, our daughter Susie, aged five, ran to her room,

---

* As an experiment Abeking and Rasmussen did build one Beetle Cat Boat for us. They did a beautiful job of it, of course, but adding duty and freight, there was no way they could match our costs. More important, their mahogany-planked version represented a departure from what had become the Beetle standard, a standard of cedar and oak eminently suitable for the job intended.

grabbed her coat, and allowed that she would go back to Germany with him.

The Abeking and Rasmussen/Concordia files amply document the major trends that little by little influenced the Concordia yawls and helped make them an unusually long-lived class. One of the first of these trends was a move away from old-time European galvanized hardware toward newer American bronze hardware. This was a very early trend, because postwar buyers were generally not familiar with traditional galvanized types and because the quality of galvanized hardware had, at least in the United States, gone downhill perceptibly. We easily overcame this sales

HORST LEHNERT

Horst Lehnert in 1957, when construction of Concordia yawls was at its peak.

Horst was born in 1914, in Farge, a small village on the banks of the Weser River, not far from Bremen. In 1920 his family moved to nearby Delmenhorst, where Horst attended school. Instead of going on to college, for which he had been prepared, he spent the years 1934 through 1936 as a boat- and shipbuilding apprentice at Abeking and Rasmussen. In 1937 he worked for a season in Stamford, Connecticut, at the Luders yard, a well-known boatbuilding firm. During

this same period he also took the opportunity to visit the Herreshoff Manufacturing Company in Bristol and other American yacht yards, including several in Miami and on the Great Lakes.

Between 1938 and 1944 Horst held responsible positions at several German and Dutch yards that were working on destroyers, minesweepers, and E boat types. It was during this period that he earned a degree in naval architecture from the University of Bremen. In 1944 he returned to Abeking and Rasmussen as assistant managing engineer. After the death of Elo Poulsen in 1952, he was promoted to yard manager and put in charge of foreign yacht sales.

Not only is Horst an experienced marine engineer, he is an enthusiastic yachtsman. He began racing canoes and 14-foot dinghies at the age of twelve and began his active ocean-racing career six years later. For many years he has been an honorary member of the Weser yacht club. He became a member of the Cruising Club of America in 1957.

Horst remained at Abeking and Rasmussen as managing engineer during the changeover of the yard from yacht building to naval shipbuilding, exclusively, in 1973. (Among other changes, five slipways were replaced by a single, two-thousand-ton synchro-lift.) He retired in 1982.

123

Charles Child Howland enjoying his favorite hobby, the building of joinerwork, in our Padanaram workshop, about 1970. In 1963, toward the end of the Concordia yawl-building program, our son Charlie, then a sophomore at Harvard, accepted an invitation to spend the summer in Lemwerder with Mr. and Mrs. Lehnert and their two sons, aged ten and fourteen. He paid his way by working at Abeking and Rasmussen. In spite of his scant knowledge of German, Charlie enjoyed the experience and at the same time was exposed to the very best in wooden boatbuilding.

deterrent with a compromise that had advantages for all concerned. The Abeking and Rasmussen galvanized-steel masthead assemblies and spreader and tang fittings were retained. Beautifully designed and fabricated, they were reliable, light, yet very strong, and not too costly. Being aloft, they were largely unaffected by salt water and all but invisible to prejudiced eyes. Meanwhile, lower down—on booms and deck, where weight was less of a factor, but salt water was more—we changed the fittings to bronze. No complications resulted here, either, since Abeking and Rasmussen designed and built beautiful bronze hardware in their own shop—hardware that we subsequently stocked for general sale at Concordia.

In the matter of rigging, all of us agreed that the postwar European-manufactured galvanized wire was not as good as it should be, and used to be, and that the new American-made stainless-steel wire was far superior. Also, we had to accept the fact that the new American synthetics were an improvement over the excellent linen cordage originally supplied by Germany. As a result it soon became evident that Concordia, not Abeking and Rasmussen, should make up all the rigging, both standing and running.

As luck would have it, this revised procedure fitted beautifully into the overall Concordia picture. Our rigger, George Montigny, was one of the best in the trade, and during inclement winter weather had time to spare. From the start he had been anxious that we specify American stainless (the nonstretching 1-by-19 construction). More important, he kept pointing out the great advantages of making the final splices in place right on the boat.

As his standing-rigging system developed, George got the necessary plans as soon as they were available, and then cut his wire to the approximate length, spliced the upper eyes, and bundled the lot together in readiness for the time when the boat was under the derrick ready for final mast stepping. With all his partially finished rigging hanging from aloft and after marking all of its pieces for final length, he set up his vise on deck and spliced the lower ends right on the spot. There was thus no chance for misfits or mistakes in length. With the mast set at the desired rake, and absolutely plumb athwartships, every turnbuckle ended up with the exact takeup needed for fine adjustment,* and this, I might add, is essential for the proper tuning of any boat.

Many an experienced sailor understandably questioned why we continued to splice our standing-rigging eyes, when others had long since shifted to the modern swage fittings that were just pressed on to the wire ends. Actually we were convinced (with real proof) that our splices were more

* Even with costly hours of careful design measurements on paper and in the shop, slips can and often do occur, causing temporary trouble and complications for years to come.

reliable. First, they created no fixed flex point to fatigue the wire, as did the swage fitting. Second, the throat of the swage fitting tended to collect water and rust-swell the wire, which in turn started hairline cracks that led to ultimate failure.

It is a long story, but George, with his own system of special solid thimbles and soft wire servings, made our yard one of the few that could quickly and expertly accomplish the exacting task of making a good splice in 1-by-19 wire. In fact, his one-man routine achieved for us instant, trouble-free accuracy, reliability, and economy, along with a blessed freedom from outside swaging services that required scaled plans, difficult scheduling, added costs, confusions, and more. George's same general procedure worked equally well for the running rigging.

Another logical shift toward American-made products developed early on with winches and sails. Understandably, buyers had their own strong opinions in these areas and were therefore comfortably prepared to pay extra as necessary. For Concordia, it was no problem at all to supply and install any brand or appropriate size of winch that was wanted.

Although the original German cotton sails were excellent and beautifully made, the new American synthetic fabrics soon captured the market. Furthermore, sailors, especially racers, have always been partial to their own special sailmakers, and they like to discuss details face to face and not across the Atlantic. We continued to offer working sails as part of our standard package—first as made by Abeking and Rasmussen, later as made in South Dartmouth by our friend and sail loft tenant, Manchester Yacht Sails. In practice, Concordia made recommendations, the owner made his choice, the sailmakers cooperated, and we all lived comfortably together.

Below decks, the trend was similar. American plumbing and electrical equipment gradually took the place of the European equivalent. It wasn't that Abeking and Rasmussen's offerings were faulty. But availability of parts, convenience of servicing, and product loyalty all were factors leading to the change. Only the beautiful great galley pump remained German. For these lovely brass creations we kept spare parts; we even carried complete units in stock for installation in other boats. They must have been of prewar manufacture, because they, too, finally became unavailable, and we had to resort to manufacturing (at great expense) exact copies in our own shop. Even at that, they were well worth the cost, for a good galley pump is one of the few luxury items on a boat that is also an absolute necessity.

From the outset the engines for the Concordias were American made: first the small Gray 4–91; then, when available, the Gray 4–112. The Gray 4–112 (4 cylinders, 112 cubic inches) was the same size and weight as the

Gray 4–91, but, being bored out for bigger cylinders, had extra power that our boat could use going through places like Woods Hole against the tide. However, as in so many cases, the newer model was not all gain. Bigger cylinders meant thinner block walls and quicker rusting through—weaknesses we eventually worked to correct by equipping them with fresh-water cooling systems.

Gradually American engine instruments were also made standard for all installations, the aim being uniformity and easy replacements. The tanks and engine controls, however, were installed by Abeking and Rasmussen as original equipment on every German-built Concordia.

These shifts toward American equipment simplified future yawl maintenance, but greatly increased the workload for Concordia. Some of the work did, as I have suggested, fit in well with our regular yard routine. On the other hand, the assembling of all the American equipment, the coordination of information for Germany, the packing and final shipping with correctly prepared customs documents, etc., constituted a complex and major new responsibility. If it hadn't been for our indispensable man of all works, Alden Trull, we would have been in deep trouble.

In particular, we had to play a very sophisticated game of valuations and shipments in order to avoid unnecessary import duties. Uncle Sam had his own formulas for arriving at the dutiable value of an imported boat. If this final figure was under fifteen thousand dollars, the duty was six percent; if it was over fifteen thousand dollars, it was double that—twelve percent. Staying on the right side of the line was thus for us a matter of profit or loss.*

The formula was unclear to us at times and had a way of changing, at least in interpretation. Basically, the final valuation included German labor costs doubled, plus the cost of their materials, plus profit, plus shipping costs (labor and materials again). American equipment installed in the boat was figured into the final valuation, but was not in itself subject to duty. Another basic fact was that whatever came with the boat was part of the boat for valuation purposes.

At first the initial cost of the boats from Germany was low enough to cause us little concern, but as inflation took hold and as extras began to be called for, the figuring became more exacting, and more exciting. Here is where the trend away from German equipment started to work to our advantage. By specifying more and more American equipment we were able to hold import valuations within bounds, provided we installed the equipment after the boats arrived in Padanaram.

Even this required careful thought because certain equipment, espe-

* Toward the end the valuations were well above the fifteen-thousand-dollar mark, which was one of the factors that terminated our yawl program.

Alden Trull as a Fairhaven high school student, at the helm of Hugh Smyth's sailing dinghy. His love and understanding of boats and boating matters came early on and from the best of teachers.

ALDEN TRULL

Alden was born in Fairhaven, Massachusetts, in 1921, and grew up there as a neighbor and friend of Major William Smyth, the Major's brother, Hugh, and son, Bill, Jr., who was almost the same age as Alden. The Peirce and Kilburn Shipyard, where Hugh and the Major worked, was virtually a second home for him.

In 1938, the year Alden and Bill finished high school, the great hurricane wreaked its havoc and the Smyths moved to Noank, Connecticut, where Major Smyth took over management of the Mystic Shipyard in West Mystic. Alden, with boats firmly in his mind, determined to get a job at the Casey yard or the Scott yard. Finally, Palmer Scott hired him at twenty cents an hour, with a warning that he had better work hard, since the yard would be losing

money on him for at least a year. The work week was fifty-four hours; there was no overtime pay.

After a year spent studying civil engineering at Northeastern University in Boston, Alden returned to Scott's in the fall of 1941. He tried to get into the Transportation Corps (they delivered boats up and down the coast) and then the Air Force Rescue Service (which involved boats, too), but was turned down because of poor eyesight. In 1942 Scott won a contract to build 33-foot wooden bomb-carrier boats. Alden and Howard DeMoranville, brother of a long-time Concordia boatbuilder, were put in charge of this program and stayed with it until government orders ceased.

Alden's next assignment at Scott's was the

building a fleet of 31-foot short-ended auxiliary cutters designed by Crocker and known as the Amantha class. Palmer Scott's plan, which he successfully carried out, was to sell some of these boats to individuals and organize the balance of them into a charter fleet. This charter business flourished, and Alden (newly married) was in charge of the program, until he was recalled by the draft board and drafted (eye standards lowered) into the Army for a two-year hitch.

Alden and Rita Trull both came to work for Concordia in 1947. Now, some forty years later, they are still at the yard, Rita working there now and then after a long leave of absence for child-rearing. Successively (and sometimes simultaneously) carpenter, painter, stock room manager, bill preparer, office manager, and assistant treasurer—you name it, Alden has done it. The yard cry is the same as it always was: When in doubt, call Alden.

Hugh Smyth and his brother, Major William Smyth, two older friends who inspired Alden Trull to choose a career close to boats and who helped me all through my boating years. This photograph was taken about 1940.

"The senior fleet" at Mystic Shipyard, Inc. At upper left is Hugh Smyth's workboat *Dauntless*, whose hull shape was the inspiration for the Concordia-designed motorsailer *Hurricane*. Alden Trull and young Bill Smyth joined Hugh as crew on *Dauntless* on various towing and yacht-delivery operations that took them as far east as Boston and west to New York. The lapstrake sloop in the foreground is the converted lifeboat *Dawn*, Major Smyth's family cruising and fishing boat. At right is *Tyche*, Rodman Swift's 28' Alden schooner.

cially engines, had to be in operating condition in the event of trouble with our tugboat on the tow from Boston to Padanaram. With well-planned juggling we often could send the engine for a standard boat (the original 39-foot 10-inch yawl is considered standard) and hold the engine for a Concordia Forty-one (a more expensive version of the Concordia yawl), and then have the two boats shipped aboard the same freighter, thus keeping ourselves in a position of safety at sea and at the Customs office.

The ramifications seemed to be endless but were well worth studying. For example, when a dinghy was sent with a yawl it could, if entered correctly, be a separate boat, not part of the yawl unit. However, the duty was twice as much for a rowboat as for a sailboat, so we always saw to it that there was a hole in the forward thwart for a mast. Shipment of spare parts cost more in freight and duty if shipped separately, so whenever possible, spare parts or equipment were shipped aboard as part of a yawl unit. All this required coordination with Abeking and Rasmussen, typed declarations in triplicate made out in specified form, etc.

Although we tried to understand the duty regulations and play them to our best advantage, we also aimed to remain absolutely aboveboard with the Customs people. In return they were always fair and understanding with us. Before long they waived inspection at the Boston dock, and by appointment came to Concordia to do the job. Maintaining a reputation for scrupulous honesty in this sort of situation, was, is, and always should be essential.

Although the general direction of the duty figuring was on my shoulders, the detail was monitored and administered by Alden, and not a single Concordia came to this country with a duty liability larger than, or different from, what we had planned. We had Alden to thank for that.

11
From Lemwerder
to Boston
to Padanaram

i

With few exceptions (three early boats off-loaded in New York, five sent directly to California, and two delivered to their owners at Lemwerder) all Concordia yawls were shipped from Bremen to Boston. Good steamship service was, until the Vietnam war, available on this run, principally from the Holland-American and United States lines. Yawl completion dates normally determined which line we would use, but on occasion we made specific choices to emphasize our insistence on certain procedures that we felt were important. We had real leverage with the lines on this, because they valued our business. Also, when we had a choice, we designated a ship that was coming directly to Boston, rather than by way of New York. The less time the carrier spent at sea and the fewer cargo off-loading stops she had to make, the better were the chances for our boats to reach Boston in clean, undamaged condition.

For customs brokers, Abeking and Rasmussen employed the Bremen firm of J. A. Bachmann, and we at our end enjoyed excellent cooperation and guidance from Mr. Geddes of T. D. Downing Company. In an operation such as ours, it was critical that the import routine involve as few people as possible. We could ill afford bureaucratic delays and confusion.

Abeking and Rasmussen invariably did a superb loading job for us. Although their methods were time-consuming, these painstaking procedures certainly paid off. Of the ninety-nine yawls shipped from Germany, only one was damaged in transit. The damage: a broken tiller. Cause: a longshoreman sat on it.

Belvedere (#89), a standard Concordia yawl, is about to be loaded in Bremen aboard a freighter bound direct for Boston. Both the huge crane and the lifting bolts within the yawl made for a safe and chafe-free operation.

131

The off-loading in Boston and the trip to Padanaram were, of course, Concordia responsibilities. Our boatyard resources made these jobs straightforward enough, but they still required a special crew that knew the ropes, and a suitable towboat that could take a bit of weather. The former we already had in the persons of carpenter Wilton Butts and rigger Mark Foster, both excellent boatmen. The special boat Martin provided by buying an aging 39-foot Nova Scotia lobsterboat for seven hundred and fifty dollars. The purchase price was not really unusual, since these hardworking Novi boats had a reputation for being short-lived. For our purposes we strengthened up the limber hull with conventional wood floor timbers and replaced the old automobile engine with a new Graymarine motor. From the first day we owned her, she was known as *Fetcher*.

With her somber gray paint and her strange superstructure, *Fetcher* may have looked like a bit of a lash-up. With her 65-horsepower engine she might be considered underpowered. Nonetheless she was good—real good! Slow and easy is the way to tow a yacht, and low freeboard is finest kind for tying a low-sided yacht alongside. Although *Fetcher* was called upon to tow her charges from Boston in winter and summer for over ten years, she never damaged any of them—or herself.

Martin was in command of the first few towing expeditions and established a general operating procedure that, with variations, was followed thereafter. Simms Brothers boatyard in Dorchester, a fine builder of wooden boats with a snug basin for a layover, encouraged us to use their yard as a base. This luxury allowed our skipper to load his gear ahead of time, pick his day, make his run up through the Cape Cod Canal and across Massachusetts Bay, and know on arrival that he would always find a convenient berth awaiting him not too far from the steamer docks.

On off-loading days, Concordia went into high gear at an early hour. Head mechanic Len Tripp, tools and equipment packed, arrived around four o'clock in his beautifully maintained old Cadillac, a smooth rider we knew as the "Luxury Liner." Martin, Mark Foster, Butsy, and I, and sometimes an extra hand or two, climbed aboard the car, and we were off to Dorchester. We generally pulled into the Simms yard before daylight.

After Len checked out *Fetcher*'s engine, he and I drove over to one of the old East Boston docks and climbed the long ladder to the freighter deck to discuss entry details with our customs broker, Mr. Geddes. The most urgent project was to confirm a deal with the longshoreman boss whereby the longshoremen would get paid, but would stay absolutely clear of our boats. Hard-soled shoes, dirty hands, and rough talk did us little good. And besides, the ship's crew had, by agreement, already removed the canvas covers and lashings.

By eight o'clock the ship's cargo hatches were being cleared and her winches began to pant and rattle. But we had eyes only for *Fetcher* and McKie's lighter, as they came alongside. This accomplished, our friend "Slim," the lighter boss, took center stage. It truly was a stirring sight to see the sling gradually tauten, and the yawl with a tiny quake rise from her cradle into the air, swing over the ship's rail, and float gently down into her intended element right next to *Fetcher*.

After hooking up each yawl's new engine and checking it out, Len Tripp was finished with his mission and was ready to drive Martin and me back to Padanaram. *Fetcher*, too, was usually on her way before noon, headed for Scituate, a good, protected harbor a few miles down the line.

Usually these off-loading operations went smooth as a smelt, but not always. Once we forgot the sling and faced the horrendous prospect of not only delaying a steamer schedule but also of paying a lighter long hours of overtime. Slim worked us out of that one, but we never forgot our sling again.

Another off-loading delay was caused by severe weather. It was December and the temperature had dropped to ten above zero. Most of us had to wait overnight aboard *Fetcher*. As we were feeling our way in the dark up one of the narrow, channel-like reaches, searching for a suitable set of pilings to tie to, one of our crew lost his footing on the icy deck and slipped overboard. We couldn't see him, but could hear the sounds of struggle in the water, and finally we got back to him and pulled him aboard before the air entrapped in his oilskins leaked out. It was after this near-tragedy that we begged Abeking and Rasmussen to send new boats before December or (a real inconvenience to them) hold the boats until March or April.

ii

Regardless of what time of year a new boat reached Concordia, it was always best to complete our part of the final work as soon as possible. No two situations were ever exactly the same, but a general system evolved that we tried to follow.

My own most pressing assignment was to get from the government agencies concerned the required registration numbers for each new boat. This step-by-step operation was straightforward enough if you knew how to do it, but it could cause most unfortunate delays if you did not. Over time we developed a procedure that saved four mailings and at least four times that many days of headaches. This entailed my driving to the somber little ground-floor office of the Massachusetts Motor Boat Section at 445 Commercial Street in downtown Boston. Here Miss Walsh who *was* the Section, took from me a completed and endorsed Certificate of Award for Num-

The McKie Lighter Co. off-loaded Concordia yawls in Boston for our account. Their crane had a long boom that could gently lift a boat straight up. Although the freighters' booms were adequately strong for the job, they were too short for a delicate straight-up lift. Dragging a Concordia along a ship's deck, with a wire down through the skylight, could have done major damage.

With a natural grace of his own, Slim rode the great derrick hook to the new yawl as she sat, cradled on the freighter's deck, whistling instructions to his man down below at the controls. It seldom took him more than a minute or two to run the sling legs down through the skylight and shackle them to their eyebolts. With Slim there were no shouts or panics, just a slight motion now and then with his hand and a high-pitched whistle from his lips. Concordia owes Slim and his partner great credit for their flawless work.

bers from the Coast Guard and most kindly typed up for my signature the resale papers required if the ultimate owner of the Concordia yawl was a Massachusetts resident. Within an hour, I could be on my way back to Padanaram in time for our sign painter to do an evening number-painting job for us.

Looking back at this routine, I find myself feeling very sympathetic toward and grateful to Miss Walsh and her helper. Instead of being red-tape government monsters, they were in fact two human beings who appreciated being treated as such.

The yard had its own well-understood routines to carry out on a new yawl. Weather permitting, the painters gave all brightwork on a new boat, especially the spars, an extra coat of varnish. It wasn't that the builders had done a skimpy job, it was just that new work is especially vulnerable to chafe, scratches, and the like. Any final paint touch-up operations were greatly simplified by the fact that Abeking and Rasmussen sent with every boat a small can of each of the various paints they had used on her. Just before delivery to an owner, each new boat was hauled by Concordia for a fresh coat of bottom paint.

Our engine department faced an increasing amount of work when new boats began to arrive without engines, batteries, or instruments.

Fetcher at Boston with Concordia yawl #64, *Live Yankee*. So that she might safely carry the long Concordia spars, we fastened crosswise to *Fetcher's* foredeck several feet of strong blocking and placed a rugged sawhorse-type frame aft in her cockpit, onto which the spars could be lowered. *Fetcher's* shelter house was cut fore-and-aft down the middle, the port half being hinged open or shut as needed. For towing, *Fetcher* was equipped with a big bitt strongly braced by knees and the aft deck. The location was pretty much directly over her big propeller, so that the rudder remained effective even with a heavy tow astern. A towboat cannot be steered if the towing bitts are too far aft— or forward, for that matter.

However, Abeking and Rasmussen had a spare engine, and duplicate instruments and electrical fixtures to use as patterns, so our re-installation work was very simple. Not always so simple was the process of installing and hooking up electronic equipment. As I have already mentioned, newly minted electronic devices did not fit in with my stubborn, old-fashioned thinking, and I tried in every way to discourage owners from installing telephones, direction finders, wind indicators, and the like. I even forbade them to go to boat shows. But my efforts were usually in vain. In the end, Concordia was induced to order the troublesome instruments and have the local electronics man install them. Then, when the owners had trouble with these new inventions, they would get cross with Concordia and perhaps even withhold payment until the situation was, shall we say, reviewed.

Electronics in those years were a proper headache, as Captain Hardy was the first to agree. When, after Father's death, Captain Hardy went with Colonel Herrington aboard Herrington's Concordia yawl, *Auda*, the Colonel installed an electronic wind indicator. "See how much this helps, Captain?" boasted Colonel Herrington one afternoon, hand on helm, eyes on the instrument. "Yes," said the Captain, "I can see all right. Our wake looks like a snake was pushing us."

The plumber's job changed very little in the years we were preparing Concordias for delivery. At first it was merely checking things out. Later it involved hooking up toilets, lavatories, etc. But this wasn't any real problem, either, as identical equipment had already been installed and then removed from each boat by Abeking and Rasmussen.

For the carpenters, on the other hand, the new-boat workload seemed to increase constantly. Earlier Concordias gradually acquired new and useful refinements, which, as I have already said, later owners saw and requested. Although we stuck to the premise that our standard layout was the best for most families, we could sympathize with a customer's special needs. In making any modifications, however, we tried to do them in such a way that, with little trouble, they could be undone and converted back to standard. This approach often proved its worth when the customer came to sell his boat.

For families with young children we suggested small canvas berths, shaped to hang forward over the foot of the fo'c's'le berths. These merely required leather or metal brackets outboard and lanyards from above, inboard. They were comfortable, airy, and out of the way, as well as being easily removable.

In the main cabin there was an easy-enough solution for bedding one extra full-sized body. It involved a pipe berth that by day stowed under (and partially outboard of) the seat cushions. The in-use, nighttime position was fore-and-aft, partly over the stove area, partly over the foot area of the starboard Concordia berth.

A final extra berth possibility involved the cockpit, and awning, and, again, two pipe berths or a lash-up of boards that filled the space between the seats. Length here was no problem in most cases because the cockpit was designed to be at least 6 feet 6 inches long between bridge deck and stern deck.

The best type of cabin table was often a topic of discussion, as was the arrangement of the ladder and engine box area. Custom anchor and dinghy chocks, locust paper towel holders and towel racks, special fathometer brackets, and extra flag sticks were just a few of the long list of special items that we could and did make up ahead of time, thus saving precious time as we prepared a new boat for its first summer of sailing.

The main elements of the rigger's completion work I have already touched upon, but there were many smaller jobs of considerable importance: lifelines to install, chafe rollers to go on the main shrouds, gilguys to be made up; together with the making up of reefing gear, anchor warps, docklines, flag halyards, fender lines, dinghy painters, and more. As with other departments, the riggers understood our aim to have work as completely finished as possible before actual delivery took place.

The work was sometimes fussy, the details endless. But there were rewards that went with it. On 4 October 1957 Dr. Clarke Staples ordered

Concordia yawl #58 (Abeking and Rasmussen's hull #5329), *Off Call*, one of several Concordias that we had originally ordered built on speculation. *Off Call*'s construction was too far along to allow us to install the teak decks that Clarke had hoped for, but we incorporated other extras and modifications without problems.

Clarke expressed a wish to have *Off Call* delivered in Marblehead on May 1, 1958. He explained that his son was due back from a long cruise aboard Irving Johnson's *Yankee*, and that if *Yankee* and *Off Call* could meet at sea, it would be a great thrill for both of them. This was certainly a long chance, but Clarke's oft-repeated account confirms that Concordia was able to deliver. *Off Call* did tie up at his Marblehead mooring a few hours before the time agreed upon and, furthermore, was fully equipped and provisioned for the big day.

Fetcher with Concordia yawls #49 and #52, *Moonfleet* and *Banda I*, coming through the Cape Cod Canal on the way to Padanaram in 1957.

LOADING IN GERMANY

Leaving nothing to others, the crew at Abeking and Rasmussen, like our own Concordia crew, stayed right with the yawls and performed or directly supervised all operations related to shipment.

On the appointed day Abeking and Rasmussen fired up the small yard tug (complete with round stern, padded bow, and guardrail all around) and towed the yawls up the Weser River to Bremen. In this picture, workers are covering *Dusky IV*'s decks with canvas to protect her from dirt and damage and to keep her black topsides from drying out.

The Concordia Forty-one *Melinda*, #54, headed for California delivery. No lifting straps are needed, as slings go down through skylight and shackle into big eyebolts in the keel.

Concordia Standard Thirty-nine yawl #103, *Irene,* as seen from the bow. This photo, and the one of *Live Yankee* below, shows the unusually hard bilges that are such a distinctive feature of the Concordia design. (If *Irene* seems to have two bow pulpits, she does. This was just a way of shipping an extra one for our use on one of the earlier boats.)

In place of strap-type slings, the Concordia sling was just a short pair of cables hung from a ring at the top. The two legs led down through the skylight, where they shackled into specially placed main keelbolts with temporary eye nuts threaded onto them. This inside sling system was simple, safe, and non-damaging to the hull. Abeking and Rasmussen kept one sling, we kept another; thus, there was no need for the shipping of extra slings, which would have entailed an additional freight or duty charge.

Once in shipping position, the hulls were given a thorough dusting and washing. Next, their gear, together with any special equipment, was carefully checked and stowed according to a fixed system that would not upset the balance of the boat when she was being off-loaded. Then the affected deck areas—bow, stern, shipping mast-stub, and cockpit winch bases—were padded to accept tie-down lashings. Finally, boats were successively wrapped in three covers: a light, soft one to prevent chafe, and two heavier ones to protect against dirt and weather.

Small spars were stowed in the boats' cabins. The longer spars were wrapped with burlap, then encased and bound in long, narrow mahogany or teak edgings. These spar bundles were handled with rope slings and in due course lashed alongside the cradles. The shipping cradles had to be handled somewhat differently. Abeking and Rasmussen made up four or five, so that more than one yawl could be shipped at a time. Regardless of the quantity, the cradles, along with the covers, always remained with the freighter and went back to Abeking and Rasmussen for reuse.

141

12
Ill Winds

So far the Concordia story seems to read like a fine-weather cruise with nothing but fair winds and sunny skies. But in 1954 all hell broke loose, and for a spell the rosy glow gave way to some really bad going. In fact, had it not been for our understanding friends and our full boatyard facilities, it is doubtful that the yawl program would have continued at all.

The first adversity was not brought on by human error. Mother Nature just blew it down upon us in the form of yet another hurricane—one that caused much devastation along the entire New England coast. I was not in Padanaram when Hurricane Carol hit there, so I will let my father tell part of that story:

"On the afternoon of August 30th," Father wrote a friend on 8 September, "there was a good, stiff southeasterly breeze—just such as I'd been waiting for all summer in which to give *Java* and her new rig a good testing. Although I was still a bit shaky, we started out under whole sail and gave her the works. It was a very wet but most satisfying afternoon, except for the ominous looks of the weather—a feature which had driven a number of strangers into Padanaram Harbor under short sail.

"By 7:45 next morning it was blowing hard from the northeast, and the weather report only confirmed this, with the further statement that the same would continue throughout the day. My barometer stood at 29.2. This was not an alarming drop from the evening before, and I was not greatly concerned as long as the wind remained in the northeast. Nor was Captain Hardy concerned when, at around eight o'clock, he rowed out to *Java* in company with my seventeen-year-old grandson and namesake, who

The height of Hurricane Carol is approaching, wind still in the southeast, barometer at 28.8. Already several boats have gone adrift from the basin, and Tom Waddington's schooner *Olad II* is about to part her lines (although she received no serious damage). The winter cradles in the foreground are hopelessly scrambled. Note the black-hulled converted PT boat looming in the middle distance; she ended up against the sail loft building.

The basin at South Wharf, as it appeared in the late spring of 1954.

was paid hand aboard Otis Stanton's New Bedford 35 *Tropic Bird*, moored close to *Java*. However, as these two neared their respective charges, the gusts coming off the land increased in strength to such a degree that they had a hard pull to come alongside. Already Captain Hardy had made up his mind that, when the time came to go ashore after seeing everything snug aboard *Java*, he would make for the beach on the west side of the harbor and walk home across the bridge.

"With the help of their engines, the Captain and Louie succeeded in getting out extra anchors. But within an hour, both their tenders had filled, parted their painters, and disappeared. The two had no choice other than to ride it out aboard their boats. In the meantime, the glass at my house had suddenly dropped to 28.8, and as I watched Hope's Garden disintegrate I realized that Hurricane Carol—none other—had arrived.

"A little lull came at about 10:40 A.M., as the wind shifted to east and

Martin Jackson preparing for a northeast gale some months before the 1954 hurricane. It's getting dark, and there isn't much more that Martin can do.

then southeast. Then it blew harder and harder, with frequent boomings as of great guns, until it seemed that no tree, nor hedge, nor window could withstand the pressure. A half hour later the glass had risen a tenth and the wind was south and not long after southwest, and here at the house the air was so full of spray and wreckage that one hardly knew whether one was earth- or airborne.

"At about four o'clock that afternoon, young Louie...came into the house in shreds and tatters, his face and eyes scored deep with sand, salt, and mud.... His description of how he and the Captain had maneuvered to keep their boats from breaking adrift and free from collision was both graphic and moving. The picture he gave of what had happened to the fleet of strangers and homers in the harbor was appalling....

"Tuesday night, there was no word from Waldo and the boys on *Fetcher*; Wednesday night, no word; then Thursday noon, at last, when the tension was like a steady toothache, came a word-of-mouth message from a stranger who had seen *Fetcher* and her crew all in good case after the gale and on their way home...."

This was Father's version of the story of Hurricane Carol. Let me now continue the account from *Fetcher*'s point of view.

My three sons and I were snugly anchored in Quitsa Pond, south of Menemsha, and were having a good breakfast, all unconcerned about any serious storm. Captain Rodman Swift aboard his little schooner *Tyche* was secured nearby to his own heavy mooring. One other small motorboat lay anchored somewhat farther away.

The wind, which had been strong during the night, suddenly came on with gusty determination, and *Fetcher*, with her high bow, began to tack back and forth, lessening any chance for even her big 75-pound fisherman anchor to hold. An old sea story that Father had read to me years before jumped into mind: about a square-rigger seaman who had saved his ship by the expedient of climbing partway up the mizzen rigging. Apparently the force of the gale against the seaman's body was just enough to tip the balance and bring the ship's head up to a favorable angle toward wind and wave. *Fetcher* obviously needed sail aft, and I lashed a small bit of canvas to the spar-carrying sawhorse rig in the cockpit. Tiny as it was, this makeshift stormsail steadied things down.

Next I set an extra anchor, which, however, never really took hold. In hopes of standing our ground, I started the engine and stayed at the helm and throttle for the next four hours. The boys, all wearing their life jackets, tied themselves together down below. Tommy, aged six, wisely went to sleep. Charlie and Kinny helped me wait and wonder.

What with rain, spray, debris, and roiled-up, soil-yellowed water, there was no telling whether we were afloat or ashore. At long last afternoon did arrive, the wind did taper off, and we were still afloat not far from where we started. Captain Swift launched his little dory and sculled over to have supper with us, and talk over the day's events. He apparently had listened to the radio but had failed to get any helpful hurricane warnings. His greatest worry had been that *Fetcher* might drag down on him. He had not realized it at the time, but he too was at times slicing across the wind on his mooring line just like a trout when first it feels the hook.

Next morning there still were so many broken branches, pieces of houses, and other odd wanderers floating about that I dared not leave for fear of propeller damage. Not wishing the boys to develop any permanent fear or dislike of the water, I made as little of the situation as possible, merely mentioning that when cruising, little blows like this do come up, and you just have to wait the situation out. To stretch our legs and pass the

time, we rowed ashore and took a little look around. The storm-driven sea had broken right through the south beach. The bridge was impassable, and sections of the road to Gay Head were all but gone. Car tops and roofs of buildings formed weird little islands here and there.

Of course, there were no communications open to us, and this we knew was dreadfully worrisome for the folks at home. On the plus side, the sun shone, the bunks dried out, and there was plenty of food in the larder.

On the second day, and in spite of waterborne hazards, we weighed anchor and gingerly wound our way out of Quitsa, across Menemsha Pond, and down channel to Vineyard Sound. Passing the tiny harbor of Menemsha Bight we had our first glimpse of real disaster. Not a whole boat did we see. Pete Culler's 53-foot charter schooner was head down underwater, with a big piling up through her stern, obviously a total loss. We later learned that her crew did get ashore, but Pete, without insurance, had lost his charter business with his boat.

Crossing Vineyard Sound was not so dismal. Sunlight, sparkling water, rocky beaches, all seemed natural and unchanged; only the bobbing flotsam and jetsam reminded us of Carol's wrath. In Buzzards Bay it was much

At 10:00 A.M. the tide is some 3' above normal and still rising. Yacht club floats have already started going adrift, although Concordia's spar sheds, along with the power line poles and fence, are still standing.

147

At extreme high water, the still-high wind is in the process of backing into the northwest. The ebb tide has become strong enough to influence the boats at the head of the harbor, in spite of the wind direction. South Wharf has been swept clean.

the same, but the run in from Dumpling Rock to the breakwater presented a totally new and tragic panorama. No boats were sailing or even floating. All lay wounded on the beach. Padanaram Harbor was even worse, and an eerie numbness came over us. It seemed as if some great, angry giant had wreaked his vengeance on everything. Of a large fleet of boats, only three or four remained at their moorings. The west shore was piled high with every kind of slanting mast and gruesome wreck.

On South Wharf itself nothing but the derrick remained. Spar sheds, fish shed, all the usual clutter, everything, had just disappeared. Farther shoreward, all was an unnatural, almost unrecognizable scene of shambles. Sodden wreckage and broken boats were piled against damaged buildings. Nowhere did anything look familiar. *Fetcher* and her crew seemed to be the only living creatures left.

After tying up at the end of South Wharf, we made our way to the yard gate, where a National Guardsman stopped us and ordered us to go to the Town Hall and procure an identification tag. Standing in a woebegone line waiting for a permit, I was brought back to reality by my friend Percy Chubb. "This is pretty bad, Waldo," Percy said. "What can we do for you?" Having just seen the wharf and knowing without a look the condition of

Concordia's bank account, I answered without hesitation, "Perhaps ten thousand dollars would help." Before we even got back to the yard, I had not only Percy's personal check, but also the welcome news that salvage equipment was already on the scene.

Having authority to proceed immediately with salvage operations on Chubb and Son's behalf, and with the equipment to carry it out, Concordia could collect and safely store Chubb's insured risks at the yard, before further weather problems, looting, or other misadventures added to a yacht's damage or the concerns of her owner. From this, you can understand why I was so happy to see Percy Chubb standing in line at Dartmouth Town Hall that desolate September afternoon.

ii

To explain how the Chubb and Son/W. & L. Howland Insurance Company arrangement worked in practice, let me offer a brief explanation and then two case histories.

The position of W. & L. Howland Insurance in the insurance business was unique and, under hurricane conditions, offered unbelievable assistance to all concerned.

As far back as 1934, when Ray Hunt and I were still operating as partners out of 53 State Street, Father engineered for me a sound connection with both the Boston Insurance Company and its president, Henry Hedge. I was soon turned over to the manager of the company's Marine Division, Mr. Veasey, who saw to it that I acquired an insurance broker's license. With the expert and friendly guidance of this wonderful gentleman, I gradually developed a little business. (As it worked in practice, I found the customers, and Mr. Veasey's department wrote up the policies.)

When Concordia moved to Padanaram, my association with the Boston Insurance Company continued until Mr. Veasey retired, and by that time I had, thanks to Percy Chubb and his marine manager, Walter Gherardi, established the beginnings of a very fine working arrangement with Chubb and Son, managers of the Federal Insurance Company.

As I have earlier explained, the scope and orderliness of Concordia's insurance activity improved considerably when my brother, Louie, entered the picture and together we formed the brokerage partnership of W. & L. Howland Insurance. Soon thereafter we progressed to the status of a Chubb agent (in the yacht field), and entered into survey and adjusting work, in addition to sales. With Concordia's expertise and facilities, we also gradually acquired actual salvage and repair assignments from Chubb and others.

With self-imposed limitations as to size and type, W. & L. Howland slowly developed a complete marine insurance service, in which Concordia yawls played an important part. From the moment the new yawls were loaded aboard ship in Germany until they were legally transferred to their final owners, they were automatically insured by an open Chubb policy and for Concordia Company's account. This arrangement prevented any possibility of an unintended omission or worry about coverage. At the time of delivery to the customer, we as agents were prepared (and anxious) to explain about and then furnish a suitable policy for their account.

In case of a claim, we were in a position to adjust same, usually without charge to the owner or to Chubb. Following this, Concordia, at going rates, often did the actual work that was decided upon.

All this would certainly appear to represent a real conflict-of-interest situation, but by working very closely with the Chubb heads of departments, we were able to make the claim settlements very smoothly and economically.

Chubb appreciated our yacht business mainly for the simple reason that good, family-owned auxiliaries had proved to be the finest of yacht risks. There were two worries that they did have, however, about most of our accounts. The first was fire. There being as many as sixty Concordia yawls plus other auxiliaries in one yard, a real hazard existed with too many eggs in one basket. This unavoidable risk could only be lessened by well-thought-out safety precautions, and in this connection Chubb monitored our facilities quite regularly.

The second serious worry was hurricane potential. In preparation for our particular vulnerability in Buzzards Bay, Chubb worked out a carefully considered procedure. Early on they made a standing arrangement with a major rigging firm in Hartford, whereby the latter would reserve certain mobile cranes, flatbeds, and other salvage equipment for Chubb/Concordia use in case of a hurricane.

Our friend Jack Parkinson was not inclined to carry any insurance on his Concordia yawl *Winnie of Bourne*, except for liability. My brother, however, persuaded him that Chubb, in addition to paying for damages, would also assist him with salvage at a time when salvage might be difficult or impossible for an individual boat owner to obtain on his own account. So when Carol washed up *Winnie* on Jack's front lawn, he was gratified to learn that help would soon be on its way.

I remember so clearly leading the great yellow mobile crane down the Cape road to Bourne, and then watching the big Irish operator gently set the undamaged *Winnie* back in her native element. Even more clearly I visualize my shouted discussion with Jack about hauling *Winnie* out to deep water. He wanted to use his little Seagull outboard; I felt that a line out to a mooring would be safer. With the great crane roaring impatiently between us, I finally hollered to Jack, "Do you want to do it your way or my way?" After a bit of a pause the answer roared back, "Oh, goddamn it, Waldo, do it your way." Any further procedural discussions I had with the crane operator invariably began with his question: "Hey, Captain Seaweed, you want to do it my way or your way?"

The salvage of Johnny West's Concordia *Gamecock* had another twist to it. When I went to inspect her, she was in Newport, perched partway up the cliff on the south side of Brentons Cove. It was easy enough to inspect her masthead, because that fitting was leaning up against the terrace wall of one of those beautiful shoreside mansions. It was impossible to inspect her bottom closely, but it was obvious, even from above, that one side was totally chewed away. I contacted the local lighter man who was, needless to say, over-busy. He didn't want any bother with a little yacht job right now because, he said, insurance pay on these was "too damn slow." I told

Some boats, like *Djinn*, were stopped by the bridge; others landed on it. Still others, like Dan Strohmeier's *Malay* (shown here, stern-to), jumped the bridge altogether.

After being patched, *Djinn* was lifted by crane onto a low-bed and moved along the bridge from her original shoal-water resting point to a launching site over the deep-water channel. In the course of launching *Djinn* the crane came within seconds of capsizing and following *Djinn* into Padanaram Harbor, but saved itself by dropping rather than gently lowering *Djinn* into the water—an exciting moment that I watched in horror.

him he could have a certified check for $1,500 the moment he landed the wreck at a designated Newport dock. With wired money from Chubb, with help from our own riggers, and with the facilities of the Hartford salvage team, *Gamecock* was back inside Concordia's main shed in quick order.

That was not the end of the story. *Gamecock* was very badly damaged, and means for getting her back to her "original condition" appeared to be difficult to impossible. John agreed to accept a total loss from Chubb and Son, which took care of him. Chubb agreed to accept a negotiated purchase price from Concordia for the wreck, and that cleared them of further liability. In due course Concordia rebuilt and re-equipped the boat according to their own specifications. When offered for resale, the buyer could see what he was getting for what price, so there were no gray areas for argument anywhere.

Although Hurricane Carol treated Concordia with great severity, our ability to settle claims promptly, as well as to undertake repairs and salvage with efficiency, allowed us to carry on our normal business. Indeed, having a sound insurance business was a critical factor in Concordia's long-term solvency and success, and, in marginal times, no doubt saved us from serious financial complications.

iii

Hurricane Carol was the first calamity that befell us in those years. It was not the last.

During Carol, Concordia #12, *Kahala*, landed on a stone wall at the north end of Edgartown Harbor. In spite of this rough treatment, she appeared to have no damage beyond a broken bottom plank, the repair of which was covered by insurance. *Kahala* was sailed hard the following summer, still without showing any signs of trouble. That fall, however, somewhat by chance, the owner discovered two broken frames amidships and just above the waterline.

Considering the beating *Kahala* had taken in Hurricane Carol, the two broken frames were no cause for alarm. Nonetheless, a further investigation was in order, and in the course of it we made the shocking discovery that practically every frame in the boat was broken or cracked. From an insurance point of view, the hurricane could have accounted for the breaks, and Chubb again paid the costs of repair. We installed steam-bent sister frames in the middle of each frame bay. We made no attempt to bolt them to the original frames (more holes, more weakness), but merely screw-fastened the new frames through the planking from the outside.

But the fact that a majority of the breaks had occurred along the hard turn of the bilge (at about the waterline) suggested a distinct weakness in that area. This, in turn, raised a horrible suspicion in my mind and instigated an immediate series of letters back and forth with Abeking and Rasmussen, whose first reaction was one of complete surprise that such a series of breaks could occur. I personally felt that the European oak was perhaps not as good stock for bending as some of our New England white oak. Abeking and Rasmussen, however, felt that it was. Both of us realized that the African mahogany* planking stock was harder, less compressible, and less forgiving than woods like pine, cedar, or even the Mexican mahogany that Casey had used in planking *Java*.

The absence of a caulking seam at the edge of each plank might further have aggravated the tensions built up on the frames by swelling planks. In the end, we agreed that a basic problem in materials and construction was augmented by the shape of our boat. Her very hard bilges caused an initial severe bending stress on the frames at about waterline level. The unforgiving planking exerted its cumulative forces in the same critical area. The two together formed the straw that broke the camel's back. There was no doubt that something had to be done about this situation. Quickly.

---

* When the Quincy Adams yard started building Herreshoff Twelves and used mahogany rather than cedar for planking, the boats developed broken frames. Likewise, the Yankee One-Design boats planked with hard mahogany at the same yard had considerable frame breakage.

We considered strapping all new boats, Herreshoff fashion, but this would have added to complications and expense. In the end, we opted for additional reinforcing frames to be located in the critical area. The detailed decision was to install laminated frames in the middle of every second frame bay, except well forward and aft. These were to extend above and below the waterline, and thus span about six planks and be about 3 feet long. They were to be fastened with screws in the normal way, but given an added rivet at each end. This strengthening specification was put into effect on new boats as soon as was practical, which happened to occur on Concordia #35, a boat built in the winter of 1955–1956.

The auxiliary frames were an excellent solution for all future boats, but unfortunately did nothing to solve the probable breaks in the existing Abeking and Rasmussen-built Concordias. It was a staggering thought to consider; the reframing, at our own expense, of perhaps as many as thirty

PERCY CHUBB

Percy Chubb II and fellow members of the *America*'s Cup Selection Committee of the New York Yacht Club, 1964. Left to right: Henry Sears, Julian K. Roosevelt, Henry S. Morgan (Chairman), Percy Chubb, George Hinman, DeCoursey Fales, and W. Mahlon Dickerson.

boats. However, there was just no other positive way to go. So whenever a pre-1956, German-built boat was in our yard, we scheduled a time, suitable to the owner, for installing the reinforcing frames.

In attacking the project we felt certain that frame breakage was all part of a chain reaction, which in general started amidships. A broken frame in that area put added tension (the frames broke right across and not in long slivers) on the next frame forward and aft. Keeping this in mind, every boat received auxiliary frames from cockpit to mast, but the process was not necessarily continued into the bow and stern except as seemed advisable.

Most fortunately, several factors worked in our favor. Abeking and Rasmussen's construction was such that from the outside no unfairness of hull or opening of the plank seams ever took place. The planking, in fact, always looked perfect and actually held the hull together, as the line of the

To his contemporaries within the business world, Percy Chubb II was an outstanding third-generation representative of the illustrious family which most successfully founded, managed, expanded, and diversified the great marine insurance company long known as Chubb and Son. He was an East Orange, New Jersey, native, a graduate of St. Paul's School and of Yale University (Class of 1931).

After graduation, he immediately went to work in the hull department of the family firm and soon thereafter married Corinne Alsop. During World War II, and living in Washington, D. C., he served the government with great distinction, first in matters of insurance policy and then as a director of the War Shipping Administration.

The year 1945 saw him back at Chubb and Son, where, as one of his associates so aptly states, he guided the company with wit and wisdom as department head, President, and Chairman of the Board. His directorships in countless outside activities, both business and otherwise, extended his already far horizons to the benefit of those concerned.

In the yachting world Percy again followed in the steps of his father, Hendon, and Uncle Percy by being involved in yachting, both here and abroad. After racing his Herreshoff S-class boat in Padanaram, he became owner of a series of Sparkman and Stephens-designed family cruising and racing auxiliaries, namely: the 35-foot Lawley Weekender-class *Topgallant* in 1939, the 44-foot keel yawl *Laughing Gull* in 1949, the 46-foot keel/centerboard yawl *Antilles* in 1958, and finally in 1974 the 48-foot Norwegian-type trawler with auxiliary sails that he named *Bird of Passage*. A very active member of the New York Yacht Club, he became its Commodore for the years 1967 and 1968.

To me personally, he was a wonderful and most generous friend. Not only did he make possible our special insurance business, but he and his wife opened the way for Katy and me to enjoy many of the finest experiences that boating has to offer. Our cruises aboard Chubb boats started in Buzzards Bay, but annually went farther afield to Nova Scotia, Newfoundland, the Caribbean, and even to Ireland, Scotland, Norway, and finally a voyage for me back from the Canary Islands to the absolutely unique Chubb domain on Peter Island in the British Virgin Islands.

155

WALTER GHERARDI

Walter Gherardi aboard
his friend Burr Bartram's
ketch, about 1937.

I met Walter through Percy Chubb in the early 1930s. He was then living in Greenwich, Connecticut, and working in New York City with Chubb and Son in their yacht and hull department. Before long he became manager of the department, as well as a partner in the firm.

Walter's father and grandfather were both admirals in the U. S. Navy, which meant that as a boy he saw many parts of the world. Walter attended St. George's School in Newport, Rhode Island, and Harvard University. His hobby was boating, which he came fully to understand from sailing and racing with many keen yachtsmen.

Before the war, I saw a great deal of Walter. He and his wife cruised with me aboard my old Norwegian pilot-boat *Escape,* and he included me in many a gala family gathering at his parents' quarters in the Boston Navy Yard. His own home was always open to me on any trips I made to New York.

Walter was a very special friend. During our years of business together he helped W. & L. Howland Insurance Company and Concordia Company in every way. At one stage, Chubb insured about seventy-five percent of the Concordia yawl fleet.

planks generally crossed the line of the breaks, rather than paralleling it.

Another favorable factor was that with only a screwdriver all sheathing and joinerwork (furniture, bunks, galley, etc.) could readily, and without damage, be removed and then replaced again. This was true even in the cockpit area. This fortunate situation left us clear to work from the inside of the boat, with no need to disturb the beautiful planking. (New bungs for new fastenings did require a new paint job on topsides, and, in this, most owners were happy to pay their share.)

The actual reinforcing partial frames were made up during spare time and on a production basis. Starting with an individual mold for each frame, we found it economical to make up several pairs of frames at one gluing. With extra frames in stock, all carefully numbered, it became simple enough to install them neatly and in a relatively short time.

Frame problems are seldom consistent, but with the Concordia yawls, certain interesting facts came to light. The Abeking and Rasmussen practice of strapping the lower two or three feet of the full-length frames (those aft and amidships) did discourage any breaking in that lower area where the frame's curve reverses to form the so-called tuck.

The Casey-built Concordias seemed to prove that if especially good stock were used for bending the oak frames, plus planking that would compress to some degree, and the seams were caulked, the frames could withstand the upper hard bilge turn. This conclusion seems to be backed up by yawls #6 and #7. Although built in Germany, these two never had serious frame problems. The only difference in them from the others was that, as an economy measure, they had been planked with larch. Larch, like cedar, tends to have little knots, and is perhaps less susceptible to taking a smooth, hard, racing finish, but it is a good, tough planking material and is definitely more compressible and therefore more forgiving than African mahogany.

The happy conclusion to this frame nightmare was that Concordia (or, in a few cases, another yard) did add the necessary reinforcing frames to the pre-1956 Concordia yawls and that this did satisfactorily solve the particular problem. Starting in 1959 with yawl #70, all frames, main as well as reinforcing, were laminated. If only this had been the last of our problems. It was not.

iv

Concordia's third storm didn't come in as suddenly as did Hurricane Carol. Rather it developed slowly, and was preceded by little gray clouds that were hardly noticed.

During the winter of 1959–1960 while we were getting *Winnie of Bourne*

(Concordia #11) in shape for her transatlantic crossing,* we had occasion to question the composition of her screw fastenings, and sent several samples to Germany for analysis.

Just a few weeks later, in early spring, we received a telephone call from Bertram Lippincott, whose *Wild Swan* (yawl #25) was stored at the Newport Shipyard. It was not at all a happy call. Mr. Lippincott had already organized his plans for the upcoming Bermuda Race and now, at this late date, had suddenly been told by his yard that planking was falling off the bottom of his boat.

Our survey team immediately rushed over to Newport and found that *Wild Swan*'s plank fastenings were even worse than we had thought possible. Complicating matters further, the yard had already removed several planks in an effort to reinforce newly discovered broken frames.

This was truly a lowest of low points, and after a sleepless night, I put in the only telephone call I ever made to Germany. I knew in my heart that there was nothing Abeking and Rasmussen could do about the problem, but I just had to pour out my desperation on someone. I even discussed getting a new boat over in time for Mr. Lippincott to race her to Bermuda. This was impossible, but Mr. Lippincott did agree to have his yard replace the removed planks so that we could bring his boat back to Padanaram.

Concordia well knew the frame routine and went right to work installing partial frames throughout. (This in itself added reinforcing fastenings in critical areas.) The removal of faulty fastenings is always a trying job, but our carpenters devised their own version of a special "easy-out" drill that bored into a bad screw, all the while twisting counterclockwise, thus helping to back it out.

The condition of the old screws seemed spotty. In general, those in the topsides were still good; those in the bottom were poor or worse; those in the area of the mast, where special strains develop, were very bad. Those along the garboard, where moisture can collect, were equally bad. Those in the deadwood (an area of relative repose) were so-so. Where screws were good they usually backed out well enough; when bad, their heads broke off, and all we could do was drill out the remains as best we could.

Good, bad, or indifferent, all fastenings in the bottom and topsides were replaced. Although it had been deemed impossible at first, the *Wild Swan* repairs were completed in time for her to start her third Bermuda Race, and to the great benefit of her owner's and my own morale, she fared better than most of the other Concordias.

While the *Wild Swan* repairs were in progress, correspondence with

---

* To be on the safe side, we refastened topsides and bottom as well as adding reinforcing frames throughout.

Abeking and Rasmussen revealed that their yawls built prior to mid-1954 were fastened with what I will call brass screws. They were of a composition that seemed to stand up satisfactorily in the Baltic, where water is less salty than ours. It was now becoming clear, however, that they were not adequate for our use, especially in underwater portions of the boats.

Thus, for a second go-round, Concordia was faced with a serious problem, this time involving some eighteen boats. Again, our only solution was to get on with a correction as soon as possible. We checked all boats in question, as soon as we could get them in our yard, and refastened them with a good grade of bronze, as seemed necessary. For reasons often unknown to me, some boats showed fastening troubles more quickly than did others, but in the end all the original brass screws had to be replaced. Although Concordia absorbed the cost of actual refastening,* owners again cooperated by paying a share of the necessary topside refinishing.

After mid-1954, new Concordias were fastened with a German grade of bronze which we were amply convinced was equal to the American Everdur, and in this way, thank goodness, the plank-fastening storm drifted gradually out into the past.

To be sure, Concordia yawls had other lesser problems here and there, but due to the Abeking and Rasmussen construction methods, and to Concordia yard facilities, most of them could be overcome without causing too much inconvenience or any cost to the owners. On the whole, those modifications that were called for from time to time were mainly directed at improving a design feature and not correcting a construction weakness. After all, a boat is not a boat if it has no problems, and I remain deeply beholden to Abeking and Rasmussen for their major part in making the Concordia class a long-lived one.

---

* Abeking and Rasmussen readily agreed to pay the cost of repairing *Wild Swan*, but on the other boats it seemed more important to build new Concordias at a favorable price than to discuss who should do what on the existing ones.

13
Good Boatkeeping

i

It is interesting to speculate on why so many of Nature's creations get along so well when left alone, while man-made structures deteriorate rapidly in the absence of regular and understanding care. Considering boats by themselves, a few small examples have been known to survive usefully with little maintenance, but most types benefit greatly from almost daily attention. This attention really should be, and often is, a part of the pleasure and satisfaction of owning a boat. Just the same, it behooves the novice buyer to find out in advance what sort of maintenance demands he is getting into, before he chooses a boat.

Charlie York, who is now in charge of Beetle Cat construction at Concordia, recently told me about a lapstrake pram which its Norwegian owner claimed had been built by his great-grandfather and which had already served four generations of the family. At one hundred and fifty years of age it was still in shipshape and useful condition. When questioned about maintenance, the pram's owner said that it got only scheduled applications of light tar. Neither tar nor its dark color is for everyone's taste or every use. The truth remains, however, that the more closely wood is treated the way it likes to be treated, the easier, the better, and the longer it will serve.

Looking at an opposite extreme, many of us have admired a classic mahogany launch, resplendent with varnished topsides, polished brass fittings, gilt lettering, and all. Her beautiful appearance is just as important to our senses as is her special design to her performance. However, only the unwary would choose such a boat for normal family use, unless he

In the days of wooden-boats-only at the Concordia yard, spring painting created the greatest problem in getting boats commissioned on schedule. Here Nick Demers and George Burns are sanding the topsides of a Concordia yawl while snow is still on the ground.

161

could afford a professional crew or was himself a very dedicated lover of boat work.

The maintenance needs of a Concordia yawl lie somewhere in between all tar and all varnish, and the intent of this chapter is to describe the annual upkeep procedures that our yard came gradually to follow, and to emphasize again the importance of individual men and women in making any system work successfully. Almost from the start, good boatkeeping became a number-one requisite of the Concordia system, and for some forty years it has been Arthur Correia, with his meticulous attention to detail, who has made the Concordia boatkeeping system work so rewardingly well for customers and yard personnel alike.

As each boat arrived for winter layup, Arthur or his helper removed all gear, listed it, labeled it, tended to its special needs, then stored it in one of our large walk-in lockers, each of which was numbered and decorated with the boat's name. These lockers were built into special dust-free and lockable sheds, and for easy viewing and good ventilation all had wire mesh doors and partitions.

Some owners preferred to strip their own boats, which was all to the good. But, even then, forgotten oddments were bound to show up during Arthur's shipkeeping chores, which took him into every nook and cranny of a boat. It was during these inspections that Arthur made a visual survey of the physical condition of the boat, noting things that needed further investigation or correction. The problem might be as minor as a pocket of water that ought to be sponged out, or it could be a telltale stain on the paint that suggested a serious leak. Whatever the result, this fall boatkeeping, far from being a costly waste of time, actually saved time, lots of it. Every job that followed went along more quickly, meaning fewer hours in the final bill.

Sails and canvas gear required a slightly more elaborate routine. However, the necessary moves were greatly simplified by the fact that early on, Concordia acquired what might be called a "captive" sail loft.

This followed the death of a major Padanaram waterfront landowner, Henry L. Tiffany, in 1946, when my brother's wife, Sally, bought from Tiffany's estate the vacant lot that lay directly north of South Wharf, on the west side of Elm Street. If wishes had been money, Sally, Louie, and I would have bought all the other Tiffany waterfront rental property that came on the market that year. But while the magnitude of such a purchase was well beyond our reach, there was one building that did present a possibility. This was an 85-by-55-foot, one-story wooden dine-and-dance hall known as the Lobster Grille. The hall boasted a splendid rift-sawn fir floor, the center section of which was uncluttered by posts or partitions. With

The basin at South Wharf in spring
of 1957. Concordia yawls came to
represent an ever-increasing percentage of our boat storage business.
Eight are shown here, four with sails
bent on and ready for an early-season
sail. The yard boat *Gracie* is tied to
the float at lower left.

	Materials	Work	Hours	Cost
Boat _____ **Owner** _____ **Date** _____		**Suggested Work**		CONCORDIA CO. South Dartmouth

Suggested Work — CONCORDIA CO. South Dartmouth

	Materials	Work	Our Best Guess	
			Hours	**Cost**
Bottom	Bottom paint and sandpaper Boottop paint Red lead	Sand and paint, 2 coats Sand and paint boottop, 1 coat Red-lead keel prior to painting	28	
Topsides	2 qts. flat 2 qts. gloss Sign painter	Sand and paint, 2 coats	25	
Brightwork	2 qts. varnish and sandpaper	Sand and varnish, 2 coats Sand and varnish blocks, locker gear, etc.	55	
Deck	2 qts. deck paint	Sand and paint, 1 coat	12	
Cockpit	Cleaning supplies	Scrub teak seats and cockpit sole	4	
Cabin	1 qt. red lead	Clean and paint bilges	3	
Spars	2 qts. varnish and sandpaper	Sand and varnish, 2 coats	25	
Sails	Services	Check and make minor repairs		
Standing Rigging		Minor maintenance	3	
Running Rigging		Minor maintenance, also grease winches, oil turnbuckles	6	

Engine	Parts as needed	Winterize engine, overhaul starter,
		   distributor, generator, etc., and
		   paint all
		Commission engine, change oil, etc.
		·Check lights
			17	

Plumbing	Parts as needed	Disconnect for winter, check toilet pumps; hook up in spring	10	
Tender	Varnish, etc.	"Dyer"-sand, varnish bright- work 2 coats, scrub topsides	3	
Step Spars and Rig	As needed	Unrig boat in fall Fit out boat in spring	12 12	

Misc. Repairs	Storage, locker
	Misc. sandpaper, gas,
	   alcohol, etc.
		Haul, store, cover, uncover, launch
		Misc. free hardware, check fire ext., etc.
		Store gear in fall, load gear in spring
		Electronics; remove masthead gear,
		   etc., reinstall
			25
			8
			9
			
			5	

TOTAL			262	

This suggested work sheet is made out to show about how long each task will take in the annual care of an average Concordia yawl. Although hourly rates and materials have risen dramatically (from \$1.75/hr. to \$28/hr.) over the past 45 years, it still takes about the same amount of time (approximately 300 hours), and materials still come to about 25 percent of the labor cost.

164

almost continuous windows on all sides, it had excellent light. Around the dance floor perimeter was ample open space that would be ideal for sewing machines and overhead shelves.

The 1944 hurricane had badly damaged the building and, adding insult to injury, had left it partially out on Bridge Street, obstructing bridge traffic. Now closed as a going concern, repositioned, and jacked up on temporary blocks, it was for sale, with or without the property on which it stood. For Tiffany's trustees it was a proper headache. For Concordia Company it was a godsend.

Louie put together a deal whereby our friend and mechanic for some years, Len Tripp (with his partner, Mr. Davis) bought the property for a gas station, and Concordia acquired the building for a sail loft. Along with the purchase came permission to do some minor land filling, so that we could easily roll our bulky prize across a slightly extended beach directly onto our newly acquired lot. There at our new northern boundary we jacked up the whole show onto high cement-block walls, thus automatically gaining yard protection from northerly winds, additional (and much needed) covered storage for boats, and—the main windfall—a ready-made sail loft.

Having woefully inadequate funds for this (to us) large project, it was more than convenient that the New Bedford sailmaker Tom Manchester was not only willing but anxious to supply much of the needed capital. The simple understanding was that Tom would have the use of the sail loft, free of charge, for *x* number of years. As further good luck, Uncle Sam was so puzzled about the deal that at the time he couldn't think up a ready law for taxing its dividends. To put the final frosting on the cake, Old Tom, in making his move to Padanaram, brought along his nephew, Ike Manchester, who was in due course to inherit and continue the business until 1982, when his family sold out to Concordia.

No sooner was the new enterprise in operation than it became part of our storage routine to take all sails and canvaswork directly over there to be washed and repaired as necessary, before they were carefully folded and stored in the owner's locker. A torn jib is but a forgotten nuisance in late November, but becomes a real panic if discovered on a Friday afternoon in June.

ii

Probably there was little that was new or uniquely efficient about Concordia's early methods of boat maintenance. We just did what had to be done that day. However, as the Concordia yawls increased in number and came to represent perhaps eighty percent or more of our storage business, then the advantage of more specialized procedures became quite obvious.

Holding to our original conviction that good boats fare best with first-class and regular upkeep, and realizing that for Concordia to survive, our yard staff would have to do the "upkeeping," we soon came to know in advance roughly what a boat's winter work and spring bills would look like. To let the owners in on this vital information we developed the suggested work sheet shown on page 164 that listed the individual projects and estimated hours and dollars. Although never precisely accurate as filled out and presented, these sheets served as a most useful guide to all concerned. The customer, especially a new one, could fully understand what he was getting into, before leaving his treasured boat to our tender mercies. At

MECHANICAL WORK

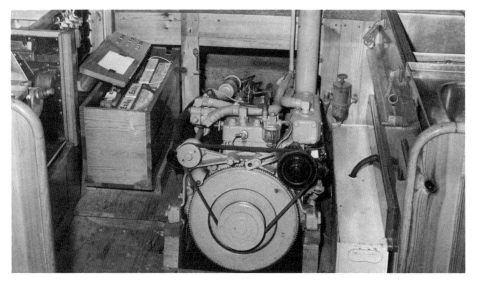

The engine compartment of a Concordia yawl with the engine box removed and the cover off the battery box. The long tank at right is the icebox sump. The front of the electrical panel is open, and the panel itself is in a dry and easy-to-get-at place right next to the battery terminals.

Concordia engines were given extra loving care—partly because, being out in the open, they were easy to see around and work on. For all our engine and electrical work Jimmy Archer was for many years the head man. (In fact, Jimmy was so expert in his field that he was often called on by other yacht yards and designers to draw up electrical systems for them.) As each boat arrived for storage, he ran its engine and made his own check for mechanical problems. In due course, one of his helpers laid up the engine, drained the water from the block, etc., then disconnected and brought to the shop the batteries, generator, starter, and carburetor. During the winter each of these accessories was tested, overhauled, and stored in a dry place. The procedures were simple enough, but done in a systematic way that saved time and helped to forestall trouble on reassembly day or during the sailing season.

the same time, our own staff had at hand a clear picture of what was to be done, and our bill maker was put on the alert for any hours or materials that varied widely from the norm.

Once the new work sheets were understood and in force, it became practical for the yard to get on with a planned routine that, if all went well, utilized the best weather conditions for each job, required the fewest man-hours, and, at the same time, considered seriously the owner's spring delivery requirements.

In a further quest for efficiency we soon learned to rely ever more heavily on our five or six division heads. In those happy days of the 1940s through the 1960s, these capable and dedicated artisans not only knew their jobs thoroughly, but had both the authority and the obligation to

LAYING UP AND FITTING OUT

Robert Bacon has borrowed Concordia's "banana wagon" to tote his gear from his yawl *Phantom* (#93) back to his winter storage locker.

Come spring, as Martin slipped the boats one by one under the derrick for re-masting, Mark Foster had only to back our old two-wheel banana wagon up to one of the locker doors, collect the desired rigging gear, and trundle the lot down to the end of the dock. There, in a surprisingly short time, he and George Montigny would methodically complete the fit-out: clear sail tracks of varnish with a special tool; alert the mechanic to check mast light and instrument wiring; raise and plumb the mast and establish its correct rake; set up the rigging at the right tension; lash in lifelines and life rings, etc. It was all part of a well-practiced routine. A follow-up from the office added little.

undertake routine repairs on the spot. Naturally, when a serious situation arose, we consulted with the boat owner. I vividly remember one instance when the problem was an engine that needed to be replaced. The estimated cost of replacement came as a shock to the boat's owner, who made his own investigations and found that at a company elsewhere he could obtain the same engine at a discount and have it installed free of charge. "By all means get the engine installed by the other concern," I told the owner, "and be sure to make arrangements to store the boat with them on a permanent basis—because all we have to sell is labor and material, and if we can't make a profit on these two items, we are out of business." After a moment's hesitation, the owner asked Concordia to buy and install the new engine. For over thirty years this owner has remained a top Concordia

PLUMBING AND OTHER SYSTEMS

Concordia's plumber followed a routine very similar to that of the mechanic. Getting a good head start in the fall was the main thing. He checked, freed up, and repaired as needed all pumps, pipes, and seacocks; then disconnected each throne and took it ashore to the plumbing shop to be worked on during those winter days when he had time to make complete overhauls. The overhauls involved the renewal of all wearable parts (which came in kit form from the manufacturer). Some owners questioned this annual overhaul, and indeed the kit label itself

Four types of Concordia stock equipment: heater, cabin lamp, smoke head, and galley pump (based on Abeking and Rasmussen design).

suggested that a replacement every other year would suffice. However, our thinking was that, since we took the toilet apart each winter to check things out, then this was the efficient time to install new parts, rather than risk a possible need for them in midsummer during an extended cruise.

owner and friend. Mutual understanding is surely a major part of the whole boat-maintenance operation—and that includes an understanding of the economics of the boat business.

Concordia's storage arrangements and procedures were important in attracting more Concordia yawl owners to store their boats with us in the winter, which, in turn, seemed to encourage the purchase of more Concordia yawls. This was not only good for business, but a matter of pleasant associations and friendly memories for all concerned.

RIGGING WORK

From early on, George Montigny was in charge of Concordia's rigging department. From long and wide experience George not only knew the problems and the answers, but, with his own hands (kept soft as a baby's from constant applications of tallow on marlin seizings and lanyards), was more than able to do the work skillfully and expeditiously.

As soon as a boat arrived for winter lay-up, George went aboard to look aloft and alow and check over all the rigging, noting those special repairs, renewals, or adjustments that he found necessary. As storage plans dictated, the spars were removed, examined, and set on sawhorses handy to the spar shed and handy for the painters.

Under George's supervision, running rigging was unrove and washed off as needed, its shackles freed up and oiled. After being coiled, it was stored, along with spreaders, boom crotch, lifelines, boathook, flag sticks, etc., in that boat's individual gear locker. The standing rigging, tied together for easy handling, stayed with the spars, all turnbuckles having been freed up and oiled.

George's careful planning was not only good for yard and owner, but for himself. By thoroughly checking the rigging on a pleasant autumn day, he spared himself a rush job in the chill of a spring morning.

Concordia yawl evolution resulted in some boats having single spreaders while others had two sets, as shown. There were masthead rigs and those whose headstays terminated at jumper struts seven-eighths up the mast. All were understood and carefully cared for. Rigging failures were rare.

PAINTING AT CONCORDIA
(also see Appendix IV)

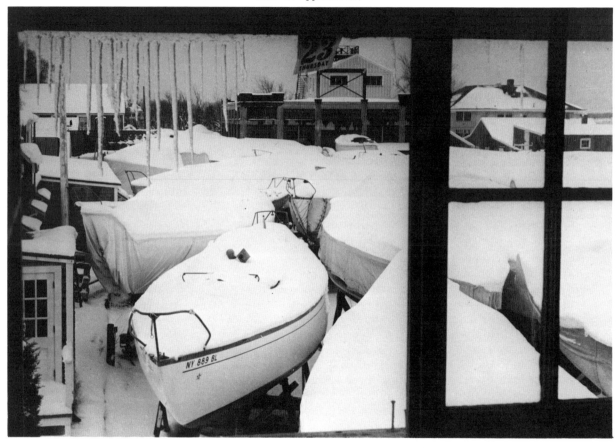

The storage yard at South Wharf as seen from the sail loft. The calendar page reads "March 23." We sent this photograph to a customer who "was counting" on having his boat ready on April 1.

The Concordia yard was a good summer stop for visitors desiring off-season maintenance work. The weather was better than in the spring, the water and air were clean in Padanaram, and good moorings and the yacht club were handy by. Repeat visitors kept Concordia busy right through to September, when winter regulars returned.

Painting was a big time-consumer in my day, and Nick Demers, our boss painter, had a big department to match. His basic principle for all boats was methodically to keep the paint work up in good condition and, if possible, avoid that situation where a total stripping job became necessary all in one year. This system spaced out the cost of painting and made it easier for a customer to plan on about the same annual budget year after year.

To prevent bottoms from opening up in the cold, dry days of winter, they were given a coat of bottom paint in the fall. Although this special paint was expensive and didn't do a very good protective job, we never found a suitable substitute. As most bottom paints lose their antifouling properties in the air, a second and final coat had to go on just before spring launching. Fortunately, bottom painting can be done even on a damp day.

The topsides paint jobs were the ones that really got us into some time pinches. It didn't seem to make sense to do any of this work in the fall or winter, so the recommended two coats —one flat, one semigloss—had to be taken care of in the spring. Although there are some 120 days between the end of February and the beginning of July, many a New England spring granted us fewer than twenty painting days, and, from where we sat, a lot of these fell on weekends. We often absorbed time-and-a-half pay on Saturdays, but Sundays were for the Lord alone.

Katy kept a spring calendar at home on which she glued yellow dots over good painting days, black dots over impossible ones. These gloomy charts helped counter owners' complaints. Even so, we would have been in serious trouble on occasion were it not for the simple fact that spring sailing weather in Buzzards Bay is no better than spring painting weather.

Tom Waddington's Crosby-designed and -built schooner *Olad II* gets a midsummer coat of paint on her topsides. Left to right: Nick Demers, George Burns (on raft), and Martin Jackson and Mark Foster (in yard skiff). The skiff was a gift from the gods that stayed with us, soaking away in the water both summer and winter for thirty years.

iii

Even with a good understanding of yard procedures, many an owner at one time or another wanted to satisfy himself that Concordia charges (and services) were competitive. It was fairly late one summer when our good friends and customers Moreau and Alice Brown confided to me that they had relatives in the boat business whose yard was closer to home than ours. Much as they hated to leave us, they felt that family bonds dictated the move.

Moreau was a very successful banker, one of the family leaders in the private banking firm of Brown Brothers, Harriman. Home for the Browns was on the Main Line in Haverford, Pennsylvania, and, certainly, the logistics of his weekend cruising out of Padanaram were far from simple. Losing such customers as the Browns would have been a very sad loss for us, but as events turned out, the Browns were back with Concordia after a single winter's absence. This substantially confirmed my sense that it would be difficult, if not nearly impossible, for most other yards to offer either the monetary savings or the camaraderie provided by Concordia's unique one-design service facilities.

For reasons I don't fully understand, these built-in advantages we offered had the effect of making the Concordia boatyard and its crew more and more anxious to please, rather than motivating us to seek any special advantage from our customers. With good customers relying on us, it seems that we felt compelled to return the confidence. Perhaps this sequel to the story of Moreau and Alice Brown may help explain what I am trying to get across.

Having already met the Browns as cautious buyers and satisfied owners, we now got to know them as steady customers whose cruising routine endured for some twenty years, until Moreau could sail no more.

On Wednesdays from May through Columbus Day, Alice would call Mrs. Hathaway of our office to get an update on the gossip at Concordia and to remind Martin to have *Armata* in at the float at South Wharf on Friday morning. Thursday was her day to phone Eddy Lincoln at the village market and give him her basic grocery order. The order was made up and put aboard *Armata* Friday noon.

Arthur Correia's *Armata* routine was equally predictable. First thing Friday he would toss the ice tongs into a yard skiff and scull standing up (to save getting the seat of his pants wet from the heavy morning dew) across to the fish market, where Forest Waite would chop him off an *Armata*-sized chunk of ice. Once ice was aboard *Armata*, he would top off all tanks and cans: water, gas, lamp kerosene, and stove alcohol.

Alice herself would arrive at about noon on Friday, usually by taxi from

Some of Concordia's yard crew during an off-season party in Captain Hardy's shed. Hamilton Stiles, owner of Concordia yawl #33, *Phoebe S*, organized the party as a way of thanking the men for their friendly treatment. Back row, left to right: Martin Jackson, George Montigny, Jimmy Archer, Mark Foster, Vincent Jackson (Martin's nephew), Ben Thurston, Bill MacKenzie, Arthur Correia, Joe Viera, Pete Bourassa. Front row: Joe Sylvia, George Burns, Nick Demers, Red Fontaine, Axel Gulliksen. Part of Captain Hardy's picture gallery shows on the wall.

the Providence airport, or, early in the season, in her own fully laden station wagon. Either vehicle could be parked right at *Armata*'s float ramp, making it an easy courtesy for a passing worker or friend to lend her a hand in getting things aboard. For the rest of the afternoon, Alice had plenty of housekeeping chores on the boat to keep her busy.

By now it might be getting on for six o'clock, and Alice and I were ready for refreshment and food. Whenever possible, we made it together up to my house, where Katy, God bless her, and the children played hosts for a lovely family evening of it, until the time came for some of us to be back on the boat to share a nightcap with Moreau. He held a standing plane reservation on the flight from Philadelphia to Providence and had a charter arrangement from Providence to New Bedford. So assuming all went well, the Browns were off on a good little cruise by half past nine

173

every Friday evening, with Katy and me sharing the fringe benefits.

By necessity or choice, many Concordia owners spent one or more spring weekends right there in the basin at South Wharf. From the westward came an early spring contingent who did their summer sailing out of Norwalk, Connecticut. My friend and benefactor Addison Taylor was one of these. As a partner in Chubb and Son, he was an ever-available guide to us in insurance matters; as Commodore of the Norwalk Yacht Club and longtime secretary of the Cruising Club of America, he carried the Concordia banner with grace and telling effectiveness. Add and several other yawl owners usually showed up a week or two in advance of commissioning day to bring gear from home and get things squared away for the final overnight push to the westward.

Then there were three crews from near Port Washington who had a way of livening up Concordia's basin; likewise, a group from Southport. Few of the Oyster Bay owners stored with us; they had their own unique winter facilities at the Seawanhaka Corinthian Yacht Club. But there were other Long Island Sound and Narrangansett Bay friends who annually favored us with single or joint commissioning visits. And it was much the same pattern with Concordia owners like Frank Soule, John Robinson, and Alida Camp, whose summer home ports were in Maine.

I haven't mentioned our many local customers, who, whether or not their boats were in commission, were apt to wander into the yard on weekends to catch up on the boat news or greet old friends. Brand-new Concordia yawls, and owners, added further to the general air of festivity on a spring weekend. And while all this activity might have caused the yard some trouble, it almost never did. For newcomers, the long-time owners were more reassuring and persuasive than any salesman. Besides, Concordia old-timers knew the gospel by heart.

So far this account reads as if these busy commissioning months from March through June were mostly good fun. For boat owners, they mostly were—and we meant that they should be. However, for the yard management, the last four or five weeks of spring were frantic to the point of distraction.

Martin had to start by sunrise if he was to get out his quota of moorings, move his boats into position for rigging or measuring, and line up work for the yard crew when they arrived at seven. My own day began somewhat later than Martin's but often ended after dark. Always hovering over me in those final days of May was a vision of the already overworked owner's wife who had finally arranged for the babysitter, organized the food, canceled conflicting engagements, and was at long last ready to head for Padanaram, to meet a husband who himself had spent weeks rescheduling business commitments, who had left the office early, and who even now was racing for the airport.

Whether we at Concordia were ready, or not quite, it's always seemed that anything that would help valued owners enjoy their well-earned weekends was well worth the doing. And so I played the night shift to Arthur Correia's day shift, fussing with last-minute ice, coal, blankets, and even the odd flower freshly cut from Hope's Garden.

Although it seemed we would never survive the peak pressure before Memorial Day, we always did, and likewise our own Independence Day, when the perennial last of the storage boats was turned over to its owner, Mr. Shapleigh. Every year Mr. Shapleigh gave us until July 4th to get the boat ready, and every year we just made it, if you call noon in a slightly leaking condition making it.

To be sure, yachting is a service business, as well as a seasonal one. And even if we at Concordia had been content to do the bare minimum required to make our customers feel welcome during those stressful weeks of late spring, our days would have been longer, our tempers shorter than we might have wished.

But if we worked extra hard for our customers, so, more often than not, our customers worked extra hard to repay our courtesies in kind. For Katy and me and our children, a high point of every winter was our annual visit in late February to Moreau and Alice Brown in Haverford, when the Browns overwhelmed us with hospitality and good cheer. In fact, it was almost like being a member of a particularly congenial club. Throughout the year, for Martin, Alden, and the rest of us, we found our own efforts being reciprocated by Concordia's loyal customers in acts of kindness both large and small.

Certainly Concordia was a profit-making business. My brother and I wouldn't have had it any other way. But the real gains, in business as in life, can never be measured in dollars alone. We all felt that the work we did at Concordia was worth doing. That our customers agreed with us was a reward of a very special kind.

Seven Concordias rafted with the sloop *Gesture* (third from left) and the schooner *Integrity* (fourth from left) in Hadley Harbor during the 1966 NYYC Cruise. From the left, the boats are *Winnie of Bourne, Ballerina, Gesture, Integrity, Sagola, Absinthe, Skye, Astra,* and *Dame of Sark.* (The white boat, far right, is not a Concordia and is probably not part of the raft.) The Concordias with single spreaders are Thirty-nines; those with double spreaders are Forty-ones. *Sagola, Absinthe,* and *Winnie of Bourne,* rigged as sloops, took first, second, and third in Class III for this event in which all seven Concordias participated. The Howland schooner *Integrity,* with my sons Kinny and Tommy as skipper and cook, had been chartered by Jack Parkinson as mother ship for his *Winnie of Bourne.*

Part III

THE FLEET IN BEING

14
Variations on the Cruising Club Rule

i

Each period of yachting history has witnessed its own special glamour and also its particular limitations. The Gay Nineties and the years before World War I were glorified by beautiful yachts of a size and grandeur unknown before or since. Their sailing and racing exploits and their lavish cruising adventures were spectacular indeed, but actual participation was confined to only a few wealthy owners and their professional crews.

Following World War I came the boom-and-bust years of the Twenties and Thirties, with top-notch open-class racing under various measurement rules: the Universal Rule that produced the letter-designated M, O, P, Q, R, and S boats and the mammoth and famous J's; the International Rule that led to the phenomenally successful Six-Meters, the Eights, the Tens, and the Twelves. In addition, many small but excellent and long-lived one-design classes came into being: Internationals, Atlantics, and Stars (which date from 1911), to mention just three.

During these same years ocean racing for amateurs became increasingly popular. Starting out with traditional seagoing types, the ocean competition quickly intensified to a point where the need became apparent for an equitable measurement rule that would recognize potential speed as well as seagoing performance. Thus, in 1934 the Cruising Club of America Rule came into being. Substantially guided by this CCA Rule and its subsequent modifications, the racing in the three decades following World War II was some of the most rewarding and wholesome that cruising-class yachtsmen have ever known.

Dusky III, one of the first **Concordia yawls** to be built by Abeking and Rasmussen. With her diamond-stayed double spreaders, split-legged permanent backstay, and inboard toerail, she is nearly identical to *Java* as originally rigged.

179

Before going into detail about Concordia's participation in ocean racing, it is worth taking at least a layman's glance at the CCA Rule itself. (The technically minded reader can follow the detailed evolution of the rule by studying the yearbooks of the CCA.) Various design trends and achievements that followed will then appear more logical.

History has shown that it is all too easy to work around any simple rule and take advantage of it. Therefore, the CCA Rule was drawn up with restrictions that are both voluminous and complicated. The basic idea, however, was straightforward enough: to penalize extreme hull forms and to encourage good, seaworthy designs. Most important, the Rule provided for changes as needed to assure that the spirit of the Rule would be upheld even when the letter of the Rule was being circumvented.

It is an accepted fact that with displacment (non-planing) hulls, potential speed varies according to the square root of waterline length. The CCA Rule, based on this fact, is substantially a waterline rule. It aims to take into account other basic factors that influence speed in order to arrive at a fair rated length. Stating it another way, those factors that result in potential speed are taxed, and those that tend to limit speed receive a credit.

To list these basic factors, the formula does the following:

1) Encourages moderate *overhangs*. Longer overhangs are penalized; shorter ones receive a credit.

2) Encourages a normal *beam*. Wider boats receive a credit; narrower boats are taxed.

3) Encourages normal *draft*. Shoal draft receives a credit; deep draft is taxed.

4) Encourages normal *displacement* (total weight of boat). Heavy displacement receives a credit; light displacement is taxed.

5) Encourages normal *sail area*. Lesser sail area receives a credit; larger area is taxed.

6) Encourages normal *freeboard*. Higher freeboard receives a credit; lower feeboard is taxed.

7) Encourages normal ratio between ballast weight and hull weight. Light ballast keel, heavy construction receives a credit; heavy keel, light construction is taxed.

8) *Propeller* allowance. The bigger the propeller, the greater the credit.

Originally worked out for ocean sailing events, the CCA Rule gradually came into general acceptance for local racing as well. Racing enthusiasts and designers quite understandably concentrated their talents on boats that would involve the *fewest penalties and greatest credits without materially sacrificing speed*. These departures from what the Rule considered the de-

Mustang (ex-*Revonoc*), Rod Stephens's **New York Thirty-two** sloop. Designed by Sparkman and Stephens and built by Henry B. Nevins in 1936, this fine one-design cruiser-racer was a consistent winner for Rod Stephens between 1947 and 1967, especially in long-distance races. Like the Concordias, the New York Thirty-twos were good all-around boats that remained competitive, especially in ocean racing, in spite of subsequent rule changes.

Mischief, one of the three **Newport Twenty-nine** sloops designed and built by Herreshoff in 1914 and for many years an outstanding competitor in Buzzards Bay cruising-class racing. She is shown here with her original gaff rig. A sistership, *Dolphin*, and the 1953 Seth Persson-built near-sister, *Rogue*, with modern seven-eighths rigs, generally raced in the same class with the Concordias and took more than their share of silver. The Newport Twenty-nines and most other Herreshoff boats were developed for local racing, rather than for offshore competition or ocean cruising, having lightly constructed hulls and a high percentage of outside lead ballast. *Mischief* and *Dolphin* are still going strong (the third boat, *Comet*, was lost in a hurricane). They are among my all-time favorite designs.

sired norm usually produced lower ratings all right, but not necessarily better boats in an absolute sense.

In prewar days, classes of family boats for daysailing, cruising, and racing had developed without over-much consideration of specific rules. Out-and-out racing was for out-and-out racing classes. All-around good boats like Herreshoff's Newport Twenty-nines appeared in 1914, the Fishers Island Thirty-ones in 1927, Paine's 36-footers and Stephens's New York Thirty-twos in 1936. Concordia yawls, Lawley Weekenders, Alden Off Soundings, Rhodes Bountys, and others also appeared in the late 1930s. All were good, sound boats for general use and rated at about their natural waterline length as it came to be visualized by the CCA Rule.

After World War II there emerged a new emphasis on racing, both local and ocean, in family-sized cruising boats, particularly those in the 27- to 30-foot waterline length sizes. Design approach became more clearly focused on winning races. New boats in one way or another soon reflected the influence of the CCA Rule.

ii

One of the first and most successful of postwar classes was the Owens Cutter. First produced in 1946 by the Owens Yacht Company of Baltimore, Maryland, they were of normal sound design, but their construction throughout was new for this type of boat. Especially different was their planking, which was a combination of thin planks on the outside over a plywood-type layer on the inside. The overall aim was to produce a light, fine-lined hull that would accommodate a heavy ballast keel, and thus foster good sail-carrying ability. These Owens Cutters performed beautifully from the start and materialized into a very popular class during the years 1946–1949, and they remained competitive over a much longer period. In spite of their light construction, which did cause some maintenance problems, and really terrified me, they survived hard local competition and, in several cases, years of ocean racing.

In the skillful hands of her owner, Robert Coulson, the Owens Cutter *Finn MacCumhaill* was year after year the friendly scourge of Long Island Sound. With limited gear, sparse accommodation, and an outwardly unkempt appearance, *Finn* consistently saved her time against most of her competitors. Another Owens, *Prim,* weathered countless Bermuda and other offshore races under the ownership of Morton Gibbons-Neff of Philadelphia and always put on a good show. (She, however, was much modified over the years.)

Locally, and on several New York Yacht Club cruises, we in the Concordia yawls had experienced difficulty in keeping pace with the Owens Cutter *Departure,* owned by our good friend Edmund Kelley. We fully realized that Ed was a brilliant racing skipper, but we couldn't help wondering why the Owens class rated below the Concordias.

In due course we had a chance to observe *Departure*'s underbody as she sat hauled out in our yard alongside a Concordia yawl. Ray Hunt with his keen eye came to the conclusion that the Owens just couldn't have the displacement recorded in their rating certificates. Ed was naturally surprised at this conclusion, and he took steps to have the whole matter thoroughly checked through. As it turned out, an error had indeed been made in the actual weights. Ed, a thorough sportsman, forthwith ordered a new Owens Cutter built of conventional double-planked construction at the Henry Hinckley yard in Maine. Owens Cutter ratings went up as corrected, and the competition evened out.

In the late 1940s Harry Sears, then Rear Commodore of the New York Yacht Club, informed me that the club was planning to sponsor a new one-design class, one that was to feature a boat smaller than the successful New York Thirty-twos. He encouraged me to stir my stumps, come to New York,

Finn MacCumhaill, an **Owens Cutter** owned by Robert Coulson. One of the first and most successful of the post-war cruising class boats, the Owens Cutters—except for the first five boats—were built by the Owens Yacht Company of Baltimore, Maryland. Unusually light construction coupled with the increasingly popular masthead rig gave these boats some distinct racing advantages. Hoisted to the top of the mast as shown here, for example, the spinnaker can be larger and flies clear of the mainsail's wind shadow.

and make an active effort to promote the Concordia yawls as the one-design of choice. Although Harry owned a Concordia yawl at the time (in all he owned three Concordias), I never did follow through on his suggestion, partly through inertia and partly because I have never had a strong belief in the long-term advantages of yacht club sponsorship. Shortly thereafter, the Sparkman and Stephens-designed Loki yawls were selected as the class of choice by the New York Yacht Club.

The Lokis were a normal, good CCA Rule type and displayed their racing intention mainly through their efficient and currently popular and rate-saving yawl rig. These yawls had already been thoroughly proved out

Porter Buck's **Loki-class** yawl *Nugget*, built by Tore Holm, Gamleby, Sweden, 1953. Note that the mizzen staysail and low-cut jib are doing their share as well as the mainsail and mizzen. The Loki yawls were a normal and good CCA Rule type and displayed their racing intentions mainly through their efficient rate-saving rig. The design had been thoroughly proven out by the experienced sailor and seaman Gifford Pinchot, owner of the original *Loki*, which was beautifully built in 1948 by Albert Lemos of Riverside, Rhode Island. Heidtman Werft in Hamburg, Germany, built additional boats for the class in 1953.

by the experienced sailor and seaman Gifford Pinchot, owner of the original *Loki* built in 1948. Others of the class followed shortly and in 1953 an additional small fleet was built by Heidtman Werft in Hamburg, Germany. I always had the feeling that the Lokis could have been improved for building and practical use by a little more waterline length and beam. Be that as it may, the Lokis won their share of prizes.

It must have been in 1949 when Ray Hunt asked me if I would like to promote with him a class of boats that would be highly competitive in that they would not only sail well, but also rate exceptionally low. The plan that he had worked out after consultation with Frank Paine showed a centerboarder that would receive rule credits for short overhangs, ample beam, shoal draft, and high freeboard. With deep, modified V-sections she would have good displacement, yet with structural weight innovations for centerboard and trunk, etc., she would not require a heavy keel and therefore have a favorable ballast ratio as viewed by the Rule. With her very modest wetted surface and given a modest, efficient rig, she would sail faster than her rating would indicate under most conditions. In addition to these very important racing advantages, the shape of the boat promised great possibilities for excellent accommodations and shoal-water sailing.

In spite of the appeal of the proposal, I remained hesitant to place bets on a Rule situation, and in the end abstained. Ray, however, did build this boat, which he named *Shoaler*. In 1950 he won most, if not all the races he entered with her. With a 30-foot waterline, a phenomenally low rating of some 25 feet, and with Ray's racing skill, there was just no easy way to beat *Shoaler*.

Before selling his *Shoaler*, Ray proved his design by chartering her to other skippers. They, too, consistently won with her. This interesting, if not altogether beautiful, raised-deck boat found her way some years later to Padanaram, where as *Reaper*, and in the able hands of top-racing skipper Phil Benson, she easily continued on for years with her winning ways. Only when thrashing to windward in rough conditions did a Concordia yawl show a degree of superiority over her.

As in other design explorations, Ray was the first to demonstrate how much a heavy centerboard and centerboard trunk could reduce a boat's rating under the CCA Rule. Others had approached the subject in different ways. Carleton Mitchell's home waters were in Chesapeake Bay, where shoal draft is often a great advantage. For some years he had owned and raced with success the shoal-draft 58-foot Rhodes-designed centerboard yawl *Caribbee*. Before he switched to a smaller boat, he came to Ray Hunt to discuss the various elements of *Shoaler*'s design.

When, in 1953, Mitchell got together with Olin Stephens for the de-

Shoaler (later renamed *Reaper*), a 38' LOA sloop drawing less than 3', designed in 1950 by Ray Hunt, led the way to a ten-year reign of keel/centerboard racers.

signing of his now-legendary, family-sized, shoal-draft *Finisterre*, the collaboration fell heir to a most favorable keel/centerboard development. With an aim toward attaining extra strength in a normally weak area they worked out a heavy bronze centerboard trunk/maststep unit. A considerable weight was thereby automatically added, which for stability, acted as ballast but, for the Rule, was counted as structure. With good beam and freeboard, shoal draft, ample displacement, relatively light ballast keel and yawl rig, *Finisterre* rated rewardingly low for her actual size and speed potential. Add to this Mitchell's racing skill and the boat's nice lines, and there is no wonder that *Finisterre*'s early racing achievements were spectacular. By 1955 a fleet of modified sisterships came out as Nevins Forties, named so after their builder, Henry B. Nevins. These boats were not cheap or easy to build but were beautifully constructed, had fine accommodations, and for cruising had all the advantages of shoal draft. They were good performers and attracted numerous able sailors over the next few years. Several of them, such as Colin Ratsey's *Golliwogg* and Wellman Cleveland's *Indigo*, were raced hard, often, and successfully.

The rating reduction and other advantages of this keel/centerboard yawl combination soon became apparent, and many new boats, large and small, joined the bandwagon and appeared in increasing numbers at the starting lines. One of our own good Concordia yawl owners, Miss Rose Dolan, asked us to design and build for her one of these "up-to-date" (this wording hurt my feelings) types. She listened attentively to my reasons for not going to a modern keel/centerboarder, but, as Fenwick Williams taught me, "a person convinced against their will, remains of the same opinion still." She made a good choice of designers and went to Aage Nielsen, who worked out for her a most successful 39-foot keel/centerboard yawl, which she named *Pellegrina*.

iii

In addition to these various new classes of boats that achieved advantages within the CCA Rule, there were some individual experiments that more glaringly focused attention on other Rule loopholes. I didn't keep up with all of them by any means, but a local race-minded customer brought to our yard a very radical yawl named *Hoot Mon*. Designed and built by several well-known Star Boat racers in Miami in 1952, she had been outstanding in her first winter's racing on Florida's Southern Ocean Racing Circuit (SORC).

As I viewed her, *Hoot Mon* was basically a light-displacement, shoal-bodied hull with a kind of fin keel. She was, however, equipped with numerous carefully placed water tanks. For measuring purposes these

Colin Ratsey's **Nevins Forty** yawl *Golliwogg.* A near-sistership of the prodigious *Finisterre*, she was built by Henry B. Nevins, Inc. in 1955 and, like other boats in the class, had an excellent sailing record and did much to extend the popularity of the keel/centerboard type. Nevins Forties were rated with a ballast weight of only 5,100 pounds, a distinct advantage as compared to the Concordia's 7,700 pounds.

tanks were filled, and with this added weight *Hoot Mon* floated low and became a displacement boat. For racing, the tanks were emptied and *Hoot Mon* floated higher and had all the speed advantages of a light hull with planing potential. Tricks of this type obviously required modifications to the rule. In 1954 the Rules Committee had to spell out what equipment was, or was not, to be aboard at the time of measuring, and what the status of the tanks should be.

Another form of this weight complication resulted for the Rules Committee when Ralph Wiley, well-known designer and builder from Oxford, Maryland, built (I think with tongue in cheek) a boat with a structural keel made of lead, rather than wood. As far as I know, the construction was sound and practical enough, albeit expensive. However, it made possible an unusually light ballast keel, which in turn gave the boat a low rating.

All of these weight innovations, some more obvious than others, which produced boats that rated below the true spirit of the rule length led to a further rule change in 1957 that lessened the advantages of centerboards, light keels, etc. This was accomplished by allowing less credit for ballast-ratio factors, and this again brought competition back to a more even basis, at least for the moment.

To add to all these complications, another innovation was fast taking hold in the boatbuilding business. This was the use of fiberglass and, to a lesser extent, aluminum. These materials permitted a redistribution of weight in a hull in ways that would be impractical with wood. With the new materials, it was easier to create a boat with lighter topsides and decks and heavier structure below. As early as 1948, Sparkman and Stephens designed a very nice 28-foot sloop (waterline length) to be built of aluminum by Jakobsen of Oyster Bay. Only three were built, I believe, but in increasing numbers larger custom designs came to be built of this same light, strong metal. Not all of these boats had racing in mind, but many of them did.

In 1957 Philip Rhodes promoted a class of 28-foot (waterline) sloops that were built of the then-new fiberglass material. These were attractive Cruising Club-type boats and presented no obvious problems to the CCA Rules Committee. However, the following year, 1958, a relatively new name in the design field came into the limelight. William Tripp of Long Island, who had worked with both Rhodes and Sparkman and Stephens, but was now on his own, came out with an extremely successful class of fiberglass boats with a 27-foot 6-inch waterline.

The first of these were known as Vitesse yawls and were built by my one-time New Bedford neighbor Carl Beetle. He was one of the earliest users and promoters of fiberglass and had recently moved his Beetle Boat Com-

Yawl **Hoot Mon**, scourge of the 1952 SORC.
She was designed and built in 1952 by Worth
Brown (of Miami, Florida), a well-known racing
skipper of Star-class fame. This 38'9" LOA
essentially light-displacement boat was built
with a series of water tanks that within the
current Rule could be full for measuring
purposes and empty for competitive racing.

Swamp Yankee, Van Alan Clark, Jr.'s Tripp-designed 1958 **Vitesse-class** yawl, built of fiberglass by Beetle Boat Company, East Greenwich, Rhode Island. This very successful keel/centerboard design was also the basis for the Block Island Forty class and, later still, for the Bermuda Forty class, built by Hinckley of Southwest Harbor, Maine. *Swamp Yankee*'s big mizzen staysail shows clearly in this picture.

pany to East Greenwich, Rhode Island. After the first year, the name of the class was changed to Block Island Forty, and the builders became American Boatbuilding, also of East Greenwich.

Besides being a good design, these Tripp boats incorporated many elements—some new, others used before—that combined to achieve very low ratings. The fiberglass material itself favored a rounding off of the bow leading edge and stern trailing edge, so that the hulls had, in effect, a longer sailing length than actual waterline measurements indicated. The boats had the advantages of the beamy, shoal-draft centerboard type, the higher freeboard, and they also featured a big foretriangle and a stern that was wide enough for the proper trimming of a long-footed genoa.

Block Island Forties like Van Alan Clark's *Swamp Yankee* and Benjamin du Pont's *Rhubarb* were for years a serious threat in any NYYC Cruise or ocean racing event. The same basic design was later used by Hinckley in creating the beautifully built class of Bermuda Forties, used mainly for cruising.

iv

The rating advantage of having a big, long-footed genoa paired with a high, narrow mainsail became more and more apparent. Sail area in the mainsail was figured at one hundred percent, whereas the area in the measured foretriangle was rated at only eighty-five percent. The overlapping portion of headsails went unmeasured. The same general considerations favored a yawl rig. Although the mizzen area itself was figured like mainsails at one hundred percent, the bigger mizzen staysail, carried in light weather downwind, was substantially free.

By 1960 this rating advantage of the yawl or ketch with big foretriangle/small mainsail was brought into full focus, when the well-known Connecticut designer Bill Luders with his Luders Twenty-seven (27 feet long on the waterline) *Storm* won on corrected time the Stamford–Vineyard Race. Although measured for only a tiny mainsail, *Storm*—rigged that year as a ketch—actually used no mainsail at all, just a big genoa and spinnaker plus the mizzen. Even the racers who knowingly or not had been taking advantage of the big genoa loophole protested *Storm* loudly as a Rule-beater. The Rules Committee soon made another Rule modification to tax more heavily the large foretriangle, and to block the huge-jib-no-mainsail ploy. After 1960 all headsails themselves had to be measured, and their actual square footage was henceforth worked into the formula.

During all this sail experimentation, Ted Hood, Marblehead sailmaker and yacht designer, became a very important factor in racing results. He and his father developed and actually manufactured excellent specialized synthetic (Dacron) sailcloth, that made practical new sail shapes. On top of this, Ted designed and campaigned his own boats and, with them, proved the merits of his revolutionary sails. Combining his great sailing skill, his centerboard racers, and his ingenious and top-notch sails, he gradually became a dominant prizewinner as well as recipient of many sail orders. My first introduction to Hood came after the 1954 hurricane, when, as I remember, he came to Padanaram in connection with the buying of a badly damaged boat. Even before that, Ray Hunt carried Ted's name on the Hunt business letterhead as an associate. That temporary association led to several experimental sails for Harry Sears's Concordia sloop *Actaea* in 1953.

v

With sail-area measurement problems at least partially under control, the biggest remaining weakness in the Rule appeared to be with ballast-displacement ratios. In other words, by using various ploys and new materials, boats could be designed and built with good stability, well able to carry big rigs, and yet at the same time be advantageously rated as though they were boats with heavy construction and modest ballast.

To correct this inequity, the Committee soon undertook a method for actually measuring stability. By 1963 all boats had to be "inclined," which gave the CCA measurers the tedious job of heeling the boats with known weights at stated distances from the boats' centerlines. Although this was a complicated process, it was a big move in the right direction: it definitely determined the stiffness of a hull. Even here, however, ingenious designers soon came up with a hull shape that would initially heel easily within the range of heeling angles that were to be measured, but would then stiffen up as the wind came on and she heeled just a bit further in actual sailing.

In spite of all these difficulties the Rules Committee was doing a very fine job in keeping competition on a sensible course, when a California designer dropped a new type of bomb into the racing arena. I feel it is fair to say that Bill Lapworth was a light-displacement advocate, who came at the right time in an ever-recurring racing cycle to popularize shoal-bodied, fin-keeled boats, and prove once again that this hull form sails fast.

After producing a number of successful individual racing boats of this general type, Lapworth came out in 1963 with his now famous Cal (for California) Forties. These were nice-looking, well-designed boats with moderate beam, overhangs, draft, freeboard, and ample sail area. They were only off the CCA norm in that they were of relatively light displacement, had fin keels and separate spade rudders. With this underwater configuration they had a very low wetted surface (no deep forefoot or aft deadwood). Low wetted surface favors high speed in light winds, while light displacement favors a high maximum speed when the wind blows harder.

The aim of this Lapworth design—to go fast and sail above her initial

Storm, designed, built, owned, and sailed by A. E. Luders, Jr. One of the handsome **Luders Twenty-seven class** (39' LOA), *Storm* was built in 1955 and is shown here with her original and quite conventional sloop rig. It was when she was rigged as a ketch and raced with only a tiny mainsail that the fur began to fly. As might be expected from such a flush-decked, cabinless craft, cruising accommodations were minimal—deliberately sacrificed for good visibility and working space for racing.

30.5 rating—appeals to me as being fair enough. For racing purposes the Cal Forties were excellent. Of fiberglass construction, and being of light overall weight, they were relatively inexpensive to build. It is not at all surprising that for a time they attracted a strong following among racing enthusiasts—especially in California, where racing fits in with the coastline better than cruising does. They certainly led the way toward a light-displacement trend that has both good features and bad. The boats sail fast and often well, but they don't tolerate the extra weights of provisions and equipment sometimes wanted for ocean work or cruising.

During the following few years, a rash of light-displacement boats appeared on the market. Determining the exact displacement (weight) of each boat had always been a problem for the Rules Committee, so in a continual attempt to plug loopholes the Committee ruled in 1965 that after 1 January 1966, designer displacement calculation figures would no longer be accepted, and each yacht would have to be actually weighed. Practical implementation of this weighing was difficult for the boatyards, but it meant that the weight (displacement) of each boat was at last pinned down. When it finally happened, the rating of the Cal Forty jumped from 32+ feet to 35+ feet.

Following the brief but remarkable racing reign of Lapworth-type boats with fin keels and spade rudders, there came a realization that factors giving an indication of wetted surface should also be incorporated into the CCA Rule. If one considers wetted surface as causing skin friction, it is easy to see that the less wetted surface a boat has, the more easily she can be propelled through the water at low speeds, when her wave-making resistance is not a major consideration.

A complete study of this new problem by the Rules Committee was interrupted by the advent of an entirely new rule—the IOR (for International Offshore Rating)—which was accepted in 1970 by the Cruising Club of America, as well as by most other sailing organizations in the Western world.*

Here, then, in brief was the ever-changing racing atmosphere in which Concordia yawls participated for twenty and more postwar years. As ably controlled by the CCA Rule, the rivalry remained keen and enjoyable. The The very same brains that sought to make fast boats within the rule were often the very ones that worked on the Rules Committee to plug unhealthy loopholes. All in all, it was a sporting era.

Ed Kelley's **Cal Forty** *Destination* on a beam reach. With fin keel and spade rudder, the Lapworth-designed Cal Forty marked the beginning of the end for boats of a conventional underwater configuration. The Cal Forty class came into being in 1963 and were leaders in a general move toward light displacement that led in 1970 to adoption of the IOR Rule. Cal Forties were built of fiberglass by Jensen Marine of Costa Mesa, California.

* Wholesome cruising boats that had been racing competitively, like the Nevins Forties, Loki yawls, and Concordias, became instantly obsolete for racing under this new rule. Almost overnight the racing fleets became completely monopolized by light-displacement, high-sided racing "machines" with short, deep fin keels and spade rudders, far more extreme than Cal-Forties.

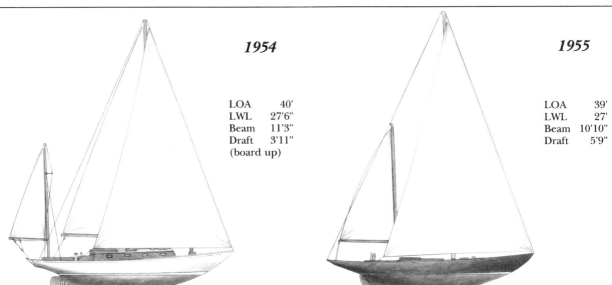

1936

LOA	45'
LWL	32'
Beam	10'7"
Draft	6'6"

New York Thirty-Two Class
Designed by Sparkman and Stephens

A fine, conventional keel sloop designed by Sparkman and
Stephens, with full knowledge of the then-new (1934) CCA Rule

1938

LOA	39'10"
LWL	28'6"
Beam	10'3"
Draft	5'8"

Concordia Yawl
Designed by Concordia Company

Hull lines by C. Raymond Hunt with full awareness
of the CCA Rule

1954

LOA	40'
LWL	27'6"
Beam	11'3"
Draft	3'11"
(board up)	

Nevins Forty Class
Designed by Sparkman and Stephens

An early class to recognize the rating advantages of the
keel/centerboard configuration and masthead rig

1955

LOA	39'
LWL	27'
Beam	10'10"
Draft	5'9"

Luders Twenty-Seven Class *Storm*
Designed by A.E. Luders, Jr.

A nicely shaped conventional keel sloop which demonstrate
shortcomings in the way the CCA Rule rated sail area

REVIEW:

ampling of classes
t raced under
CCA Rules
4–1970)

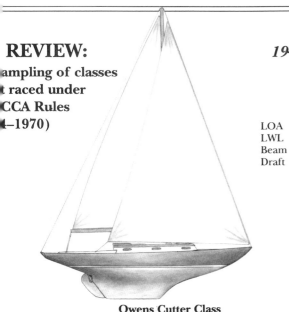

1946

LOA	40'6"
LWL	28'
Beam	10'5"
Draft	5'10"

Owens Cutter Class
Designed by Owens Yacht Company

First class racing under the CCA Rule to carry a masthead
rig and be built with special construction for lightness and
of weight above the waterline

1948

LOA	38'
LWL	26'
Beam	9'7"
Draft	5'8"

Loki Yawl Class
Designed by Sparkman and Stephens

One of the last of the conventional keelboat classes
designed with CCA rating in mind

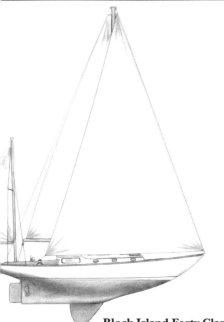

1958

LOA	40'8"
LWL	27'6"
Beam	11'9"
Draft	3'11"
(board up)	

Block Island Forty Class
Designed by William Tripp

First class to utilize fiberglass construction with its advantageous design and weight-distribution properties

1963

LOA	39'3"
LWL	30'6"
Beam	11'
Draft	5"

Cal Forty Class
Designed by William Lapworth

An excellent light-displacement flyer that for a time raced
with unusual success under the CCA Rule

EVERS BURTNER

Professor Evers Burtner and his wife, Mary, about 1965. Burtner measured boats from Maine to New York, including almost all of the Concordia yawls.

By long custom, the race committees of recognized yacht clubs designated a qualified measurer for their members to call upon. The individual selected for this important task generally had technical training in the yacht design field, but, to avoid conflicts of interest, was usually not a yacht designer by profession. Until quite recently the Cruising Club of America, because of its large and widespread membership, made it a policy to recognize a number of approved measurers, in order to conveniently cover the country as a whole. Official measurers are now designated by the United States Yacht Racing Union, located in Newport, Rhode Island.

Living only two hours away from Padanaram, in Wakefield, Massachusetts, Evers Burtner, who was official measurer for all three Marblehead yacht clubs, conveniently became Concordia's measurer, as well, and praise be for that! No more cooperative or capable man could have been found, and of this we had ample time to learn, because our association with him lasted for more than thirty years.

Evers always seemed much younger than he actually was. But I learned that he was born in Hagers-

town, Maryland, in 1893. Much of his early youth was spent with his grandfather Abraham Evers, who, although a preacher by profession, owned two working farms in the area. Young Evers's father, Daniel Emory Burtner, was likewise a preacher, but early on his duties took the family out of Maryland to parishes first in Massachusetts, then to Pennsylvania, then finally back for good to Massachusetts.

For three years Evers attended Lynn Classical High School,* from which he graduated with top grades in mathematics and physics. During school vacations, the odd jobs he fell heir to almost invariably involved boats. It was during this period, too, that Evers developed his lifelong passion for steam engines.

Along with five or six other Lynn classmates, Evers enrolled at M.I.T. (Class of 1915), where he took the four-year marine engineering course. He stayed on as an assistant instructor, initially making the munificent salary of $500 a year (tuition was then $250). His associates at M.I.T. included George Owen, a well-known naval architect and yacht designer and one-time employee of the Herreshoff Manufacturing Company; Cecil Peabody, author of some eight important books in the field of naval architecture; and, later, James Robertson Jack, a self-educated Scottish naval architect of wide practical experience.

Especially in his early days at M.I.T., Burtner's assignments were far from routine. Several involved work at Herreshoff Manufacturing Company in Bristol, Rhode Island. On one occasion Clinton Crane asked Evers to develop some sail-carrying calculations on the old and successful Herreshoff-designed Cup sloop *Resolute*. Crane needed these figures for the new Cup contender *Weetamoe*, which he was then designing. Evers told me that Herreshoff's four available drafting rooms were some busy in those weeks in 1930. Sidney Herreshoff presided in the main room, which housed the files and blueprint machines. Separate general yard work was churning along in a second room. Crane had his secret

---

* The great yacht designer Charles D. Mower was also a graduate.

designs underway in the third, and Starling Burgess, who was designing the rival Cup contender *Enterprise*, occupied the fourth.

So life went on for Evers: special projects and routine teaching. It continued this way right up until his retirement, about 1970.

It was in 1916 that Evers took over from Harold Everett the measuring duties for the Eastern, Corinthian, and Boston yacht clubs of Marblehead. Branching out from there, and continuing over a period of more than fifty years, he measured yachts in small coves and large yachting centers from City Island, New York, to Bar Harbor, Maine, and to the west as far as the Great Lakes. His fees were low indeed—a mere twenty to twenty-five dollars per boat to begin with—but Evers found compensation in the fact that boat owners as a group were wonderful folks and that rating rules were interesting and exacting.

When the Concordia class was growing fast, our need for measuring increased, and Evers, who had measured the first Concordia yawl for my father in 1940, saw a lot of us at Padanaram. This was especially true in the months of May and June, when boats were being commissioned for the coming season.

The Professor would, weather permitting, arrive at our yard early on the designated morning. His uniform, most suitable for the task ahead, was always the same: dark, baggy trousers, precariously held up with a slim and venerable leather belt, a gray work shirt, and an old jacket that drooped long from his shoulders due to constant use of its side pockets. His well-worn gray-blue cap sat low on his head, promising not to blow off. (The visor could be—often was, in fact—twisted to the side or back to suit the requirements of the sun, the wind, or the project that occupied Evers.)

Clutched in one hand was his working partner of many years, a small leather bag (like a doctor's) that, when set down, flopped open easily at the top and revealed a few stubs of pencil, scraps of paper already partially covered with figures, CCA measurement forms, a few well-used and sharpened awls with

wood handles (so they wouldn't sink), several homemade plumb bobs (each with 10 feet of fine string), and at least two 50-foot tape measures with a bit of string attached to the tape ends. Under his arm he carried his long, self-made, floatable waterline measuring stick, 4 inches wide, painted white, with big black markings. The stick was hinged in the middle to save carrying space.

The actual steps taken to measure a boat for a CCA rating certificate became more and more time-consuming and complicated as the years went by. Meanwhile, the general physical conditions required for accurate measurement were never less than strict. It was essential for accuracy to work in a sheltered area, free of wash or wake of any sort, and also to take some of the vital measurements at a time when there was little or no wind. Evers told me that he seldom measured a boat in Marblehead Harbor for these reasons. Rather, he preferred to have his boats taken over to Salem, where he could work in the quiet lee of historic Derby Wharf.

Concordia's basin had good protection behind its own L-shaped wharf, but by mid-morning a breeze so often sprang up that an early start was the rule.

For fair and accurate results, the boat to be measured had to be fully rigged, with sails bent, normal equipment and gear stowed, tanks filled (later rules specified that tanks be empty), and the boat correctly trimmed to float on her designed waterline. Because most owners were far away, and possibly asleep, on the appointed day and hour, the final details of getting the boats ready for the Professor usually fell to me. In the spring rush all this additional work was (to put it mildly) inconvenient, but we all very much wanted to give every owner as fair a racing potential as possible.

The first measuring step was to establish an accurate waterline length. To do this, the Professor, using his steel tape, established an overall length from extreme bow to extreme stern. Next he hung a plumb bob from bow and stern, allowing the bob itself to hang below the water surface, thus damping any motion and ensuring an accurate measurement of the boat's overhang. Then with his tools he clambered into an available skiff—preferably a wide, stable one, without too much water in it. Propelling himself by oar and hand, or perhaps with a yard helper, he positioned himself under the yacht's bow. Here is where his long, hinged, special measuring stick came into play. Floating it full length in the water, he allowed its brass-tipped end to just touch the bow and swung the calibrated edge over to just touch the string of the plumb bob. He went through this maneuver several times to arrive at an accurate average.

After the same procedure was carried out under the stern, the two overhang measurements were added together; the sum subtracted from the overall length; and the all-important waterline length figure arrived at. I write in all this detail because I wish the uninitiated reader to realize that a little slop on the water, or sloppiness on the part of the measurer, could create an appreciable error and an unfair rating.

It was less difficult to get the beam measurement, but the process was interesting to watch. It must be remembered that the extreme beam, not necessarily the beam at the deck, was needed, and on a Concordia yawl, with its topside tumblehome, this occurred not at deck level but a little aft of amidships and a foot or so above the water. After balancing the boat's spinnaker pole accurately crosswise on the cabintop, the Professor hung a plumb bob on each of the overhanging ends of the pole and by trial and error adjusted their loops to the point where each string just barely touched the side of the boat. By measuring the distance between the final loop positions, an accurate beam measurement was obtained. It was necessary, of course, to also make a trial fore-and-aft stationing of the pole to determine exactly where the greatest beam occurred longitudinally.

Freeboard measurements were even more simply attained from the top of the covering board to the water at the designated points directly above the waterline.

With these major* hull measurements at hand, the Professor applied them to the formula together with figures of displacement, weight of ballast keel,

and draft, these three vital statistics having been supplied and certified by the designer, who, in our case, was Fenwick Williams, whose cooperation and accuracy were always the very finest.

For the necessary sail area measurements, Evers could work alone to get his boom lengths, and his foretriangle base (mainmast to jibstay intersection with deck), but for hoist measurements, someone had to be hoisted aloft to find the exact location of the intersection of headstay and mast, and the measured peak positions of mainsail and mizzen. For accuracy, and because he said the view up there was just great, Professor Burtner always insisted on going aloft himself, and Martin always insisted that only special members of the yard crew be trusted to get him up there. The man usually designated as helper was Arthur Correia, and over the years the hoistee and his hoister gained considerable confidence in each other. A slip on the winch below or a falling tool from above could have had tragic results.

I have already suggested a few of the tricks that designers and owners used to get around the forty-six percent ballast ratio factor, and how as a result the CCA Rule was revised (in 1957) to call for the inclining of all boats, to arrive at their actual, rather than indirectly calculated stability. This somewhat delicate operation added a new element to the measuring process and created additional work for the measurer and his yard assistants.

Basically, it meant that Arthur and I had to appear earlier than usual at the yard, be accurately weighed by the Professor on the old platform scales inherited from Colonel Green, and then be taught the "inclination two-step." After slacking off the boat's lifelines so we could stand erect, we had to stand awkwardly with one foot directly in front of the other on the rail, about amidships, while Evers performed his act below. His equipment, all on the fore-and-aft centerline of the boat, consisted of a plumb bob hanging from the locking tongue of the hatch above, and its weight extending down into the center of a bucket full of water that sat on the cabin

* There was also a four-percent-waterline figure needed. This is somewhat difficult to explain, but it was a designed waterline, four percent of the actual waterline length, above the actual waterline. This was to discourage rule-cheating overhang shapes.

sole. With a ruler supported on the rim of the bucket, Evers could easily measure the degree of tilt of the boat from level to the inclination caused by Arthur's and my three hundred pounds of weight standing 5 feet out from the centerline. The process was all a bit puzzling to fellow yard workers and solicited some facetious remarks. However, the inclining requirement really was a positive step toward a much more accurate assessment of a boat's stability than earlier ballast ratio calculations had given.

Just as some eager beavers tried to shorten their waterline length for measurement purposes by trimming their boat down by the bow, they also tried to make their boat appear less stable by stowing heavy gear up as high as possible, even to the point of putting water in the dinghy lashed on the housetop with concealing cover in place. Rather small potatoes, as the saying goes, but similar tricks often won races, albeit rather ingloriously.

Such continuing Rule-beating attempts led to continuing Rule clarifications. To prevent, insofar as possible, rig and sail circumventions, an extra job for the measurer was eventually called for. In 1960 certain dimensions of big headsails and spinnakers had actually to be measured, and, if found oversize, the rating was increased accordingly. Evers and I usually ended up piling the designated sails into the commodious trunk of my faithful old '41 Plymouth coupe and toting them up to our house, where they could be stretched out, often with the help of one of our children, on the clean and level lawn. Afternoon was the time for this, as by this time the in-water measurements had been made and the dew on the grass had dried. Measuring the width of a jib was easy enough, but to get the maximum girth of a light, stretchy, and often temporarily wind-nervous parachute spinnaker was a bit more demanding. Even worse was the occasional revelation that some sail would have to be shipped back in haste to the sailmaker for modifications, in order to avoid a penalty on an important and imminent race.

The measuring feature that became most troublesome to the yard came in 1966 when the rules called for actual weighing* (rather than the use of the designer's calculations) to arrive at a boat's accurate displacement. Some yards had lifting facilities for weighing, but there were no such luxuries in our area, so at considerable expense to ourselves we purchased four individual truck scales. Upon these big, bucket-sized devices we could with our jacks lower cradle and boat and thereby get an accurate displacement figure by subtracting the predetermined weight of the cradle alone from the total.

Our part in measuring boats was something of a hindrance to our work schedule and a pain in our pocketbook, but we were truly fortunate to have a boatyard with the necessary facilities for accurate measurement. It was definitely in the overall interest of the Concordias as a class, and hence of our company, that all boats be measured by a single competent measurer in one location, giving all concerned fair and uniform ratings.

The Concordia yawls had not been designed to take advantage of measurement rule loopholes, and on occasion they did suffer in their ratings as a result. But over the years they received few drastic penalties and were therefore able to maintain a competitive position. In fact, I am told that the Concordia yawl design was sometimes used as a trial horse to predetermine the effects of a proposed rules change. I'm convinced it was the sincere wish of the CCA Rule Committee to encourage—not discourage—a good all-around cruising-racing boat. Certainly the Committee's rulings helped keep Concordias in the thick of the action for a very long time.

I've always felt that the verities of good yacht design are quite demanding, and that when you depart from them to favor a man-made racing rule, you may be getting into trouble fast.

Racing rules usually do lure racing folks away from the verities, and then the cruising and daysailing groups follow them—a cycle of errors and designs that are different (modern) but not necessarily good. In fact, although boat styles may change every twenty years or so, it is not necessarily progress.

---

* In the 1920s and during the time of the Universal Rule, R and Q boats were so competitive that actual weighing was required because displacement was such a vital factor in how the boats were handicapped.

15
Day Racing

i

I have already written about Father's *Java* and how she fared in local pre-war racing under the simple New Bedford Yacht Club rating rule. This level of competition continued after the war until, in 1947, Harry Sears introduced us into a bigger league by his purchase of a *Java* sistership. At the time Harry was an officer in the Indian Harbor Yacht Club of Greenwich, Connecticut, but he was soon to become Rear Commodore of the New York Yacht Club and to commence his climb up the traditional ladder to the highly responsible position of Commodore.

As delivered, Harry's first Concordia yawl—named *Actaea*, as were Sears-owned boats that preceded and followed her—was almost identical to *Java*. She was built by the same yard, Casey, had a lead keel from the same mold, the same deck and cabin plan, and also the same yawl rig with a 42-foot 8-inch hoist on the mainsail and a seven-eighths foretriangle. (This is an arbitrary designation for rigs where the headstay does not extend to the top of the mast. The Concordia headstay happened to be located about 8 feet down from the main truck.)

Once he started racing *Actaea* on Long Island Sound, Harry and his Greenwich "towel boys" (as friends called his usual amateur crew) made few changes. They did find the "damn mizzen" in the way, and after dubbing it and all its rigging a "tank trap," they tossed it ashore. But since all Concordia yawl mizzen masts were stepped on deck, their removal was not a problem. Also, Harry began to feel—and he was quite right—that *Actaea* was underrigged for Long Island Sound racing. In 1952, after consulting with Ray Hunt, he lengthened the boom by 1 foot 6 inches to bring it to 20

Add Taylor's Concordia Standard Thirty-nine yawl #16, *Sumatra* (ex-*Gamecock I*), winning a working sail-only race off Marion, about 1960. Add Taylor is at the helm; I am in the straw hat. Because Concordias don't rely on oversized genoas for speed in light air, they do especially well when reduced to working sails. This makes them good cruisers and favorable working-sail-only racers.

205

feet 6 inches and added a 3-foot bowsprit that permitted the use of a longer-footed genoa—and, more important, made possible a wider and therefore better-shaped spinnaker. (Under the CCA Rule, the width of a spinnaker was governed by the base measurement of the foretriangle from mast to jibstay at deck level.) These changes did appreciably increase *Actaea*'s speed without adding materially to her rating. The added foretriangle sail area was largely balanced by the reduction of the removed mizzen sail area.

Sailors then and now might well wonder why a racing-minded Concordia yawl owner went to a bowsprit when most cruising-class competitors did not. The main reason is that the quickly narrowing beam of a Concordia aft of amidships will not allow proper sheeting of a long-footed genoa. Thus, owners kept the genoa sheet blocks at the maximum beam and achieved the increased spread of sail by means of a bowsprit. The deck widths of other boats were purposely carried farther—sometimes a lot farther—aft just to create a suitably wide base for long-footed genoas. The gain was additional sail area, unmeasured by the CCA Rule.

By the time I joined *Actaea* for the 1952 NYYC Cruise, she was a proper sloop. I have good reason to remember the first get-together meeting that year in New London. In the course of it yacht designer John Alden sauntered up to our group and, after passing the time of day, put his arm on Harry's shoulder, congratulated him on having a "nice little cruising boat," and followed up with the fatherly suggestion that, in due course, it might be appropriate for Commodore Henry* Sears to acquire a larger boat of greater racing potential. Harry shrugged off the suggestion with a noncommittal smile. But I was, shall we say, a bit taken aback.

The next day we faced our first run—to Block Island. In our Class C of small sloops and yawls, the toughest competition appeared to be three Owens Cutters: *Finn MacCumhaill, Interlude,* and *Departure.* Before getting underway we had a serious decision to make. Should we bend on *Actaea*'s light Ratsey mainsail or a new, flatter Manchester-made sail? My experience on *Java,* added to the fact that I had lugged it all the way from Padanaram, prompted me to urge that we use the Manchester sail. The rest of the crew opted for the Ratsey sail. After reminding me of John Alden's comments of the previous evening, Harry finally said, "OK, Waldo, have it your way."

It was a lovely day, and once we got around Sarah's Ledge we were blessed with a combination of both fair and head winds mostly on the moderate side. The fleet separated widely—making it difficult to tell just how we were doing—until eventide, when all boats gradually converged

The catboat *Defiance,* the Race Committee boat for the Edgartown Yacht Club (photo taken about 1931), epitomizes the spirit of day racing as I like to remember it.

* This was his given name.

207

on Block Island. It seemed far too good to be true, but as we neared the finish line, we slid slowly by a larger Class B yawl, at the wheel of which sat a grim-faced John Alden.

We had certainly proved a personal point. More important, the evening race committee information sheet showed that *Actaea* had not only won the Navy Challenge Cup in her class, but also, as I remember, had the best corrected time in the entire fleet. This was the first really important Concordia victory.

Sad to relate, *Actaea*'s whole crew celebrated that evening to such an extent that the following day's run to Newport was a disaster. From then on, however, we reorganized with a more down-to-earth attitude, to give *Actaea* a chance to prove that, properly tuned up and sailed, she was now a serious racing contender as well as a "nice little cruising boat."

Harry had risen by this time to Vice Commodore of the New York Yacht Club, and was so intrigued with the ever-increasing racing potential of his little *Actaea* that, in the fall, he called for a strategy session with Ray Hunt, for the express purpose of discussing what advantageous modifications in shape or rating could be incorporated in a new Concordia.

Basically, Ray suggested keeping the same rig (even the same spars) but modifying the hull slightly to achieve a reduced rating without losing good sailing qualities. Current provisions in the CCA Rule made this possible, without going to any radical changes in either rig or hull shape. The first move in this new design was to raise the freeboard about 4 inches, which perforce made the boat about a foot longer on deck. Next, the hull was, on the drawing board, submerged about 2 inches deeper in the water, which did increase waterline length and draft but, more important, added displacement while still leaving the freeboard higher than on Sears's present *Actaea*. (Both displacement and freeboard, if increased, were credits within the rule.) Furthermore, heavier teak planking below the waterline and other structural modifications of similar nature combined to minimize the rating penalty that would have been involved in a materially heavier ballast keel. On paper anyway, this new Concordia *Actaea* would rate slightly lower than Harry's present one (28.2 versus 29.2) and with her added length would be a faster boat.

Harry approved Ray's suggestions, and this new *Actaea*, which arrived from Germany in the spring of 1953, became the original Concordia Forty-one model.

This first variant of the standard 39-foot 10-inch Concordia yawl was not without her faults, but she was for several years the most notable performer in a growing Concordia class and led the way to some important refinements. Almost as important, she became, in 1955, the flagship of the

Henry Sears, one of the first to buy a Concordia yawl after World War II, was Commodore of the Indian Harbor Yacht Club and later of the New York Yacht Club. He was also the one who led the Concordia class into big-league yacht racing.

New York Yacht Club—a revolutionary breakaway from precedence. In previous years and decades, flag officers of the Club had owned yachts of more impressive dimensions, such as Vincent Astor's 260-foot diesel yacht *Nourmahal* in 1928–1930, Junius Morgan's 70-foot commuter *Shuttle* in 1934, George Roosevelt's 60-foot schooner *Mistress* in 1942–1945, or John Nicholas Brown's 73-foot Sparkman and Stephens yawl *Bolero* in 1952–1954. As it happened, Harry Sears's small-boat approach became a significant trend in competitive CCA Rule racing—a trend that gave 40-footers an increasingly prominent position in major as well as minor yachting events.

With her sloop rig, a 2 1/2-foot bowsprit, and a rating of 28.2, *Actaea* joined the 1953 NYYC Cruise to Maine. During the night run from the Cape Cod Canal to Boothbay Harbor, I learned one thing for certain, and that was that Concordias behaved well and handled easily under rough conditions. Winds, according to reports, piped on from the northwest to forty knots. We were charging along, handling the big seas in good shape and keeping up with some of the larger boats. For five or six hours it looked as if we would definitely be in the money, but as the amateur fisherman and the small-boat racer so often explain, we had a bit of hard luck. The cringle in the clew of our brand-new genoa pulled out like a loose tooth, and we lost valuable time getting squared away with a smaller jib, which, I might add, we should have been using right along. Concordias do not sail any faster by being overpressed. On a subsequent reach and run to Tenants Harbor, *Actaea* really proved her potential by taking a first in fleet.

For the following two years she continued on with this fine caliber of racing, and this, needless to say, did nothing to discourage other Concordia yawls, both standards and Forty-ones, from joining the fun. In fact, on the 1954 NYYC Cruise there were five Concordias in addition to *Actaea*. All of them showed up well. On the first four runs *Actaea* won two firsts and a third. Johnny West and Arthur Weekes with *Gamecock* (standard hull, sloop-rigged with bowsprit) took a third. Drayton Cochran with his usual one or two-man crew sailed his brand-new *Sly Mongoose* (41-foot hull, yawl rig with bowsprit) to a big-margin first place for the Navy Alumni Cup. Standish Bourne with his now two-year-old standard yawl *Rusta IV* confused the issue of the big foretriangle by winning, without a bowsprit, the Rear Commodore's Cup.

Perhaps the biggest thrill for me on that cruise came with the results of one of the last runs; the Commodore's Cup Race from Edgartown to Mattapoisett. *Actaea* did not enter this race. Harry and several of his crew had left the cruise for other engagements. So just my Padanaram friend Joe Frothingham and I remained aboard, and we decided not to take the responsibility of racing another man's boat short-handed. Instead we opted to set *Actaea*'s main and loose-footed working jib and, for a spell after the start, to jog along as spectators to leeward of our C class. Much to everyone's surprise, *Actaea*, close on the wind, not only kept up with the class but in the fresh breeze actually gained on it, pointing higher and footing faster than all of those boats that were lugging big genoas.

We did not see the finish of the race, but when the final tally was figured, *Rusta IV*, captained by Mrs. Standish Bourne and with a young Padanaram crew, not only took the Commodore's Cup in class, but had the best corrected time in the fleet. To put the frosting on the cake and to

Concordia yawl #4, *Actaea I*, with mizzen removed, single spreaders, boom lengthened, and bowsprit added, and with a bateka dinghy carried on her cabinhouse top. A high-cut balloon jib would be a better sail for reaching this far off the wind, but just the same, the boat seems well balanced with her helm right amidships. This boat was built by Casey in 1947.

211

Concordia Forty-one sloop *Harrier*

JESSE BONTECOU AND HARRIER

Jesse Bontecou raced with his uncle Ray Hunt during the two seasons Ray owned *Harrier*, and he became her owner in the fall of 1956. Since then, and retaining the 1957 masthead sloop rig with short bowsprit, Jesse and *Harrier* have done about as much successful racing and cruising together as any team in the Concordia class. Their impressive thirty-year record shows some dozen or more Bermuda Races, four Annapolis Races, and many of the yearly local events. Racing under different rules as time has passed they have won more than their share of prizes. Among their triumphs: first in the 1957 Annapolis Race, second in class in the 1963 Annapolis Race; first in class in the New Bedford Whalers Race; second in class in the 1977 Marion-to-Bermuda Race.

show what ladies can do in a man's weather, the new *Crisette*, sailed by the ageless Rose Dolan, took second, and Moreau and Alice Brown in their new 41-foot Concordia *Armata* took third. No one could now doubt that my father's wish to create a boat that old folks could sail to windward in Buzzards Bay had been granted.

In 1955 *Actaea* was still the New York Yacht Club flagship, and, again, she was the outstanding Concordia (there were now seven others) on the NYYC Cruise. By this time she was sharing top honors in the fleet with Carleton Mitchell's new *Finisterre*, rather than with previous rivals *Finn MacCumhaill* and *Departure* of the Owens Cutter class. New centerboard types were already showing their speed and at the same time reaping their low rating advantages.

In 1956, although Harry remained Commodore of the New York Yacht Club, his interests and energies were increasingly taken up by his leading part in reviving the *America*'s Cup competition. Although he campaigned *Actaea* that year and part of the next season, he did so with a relatively high rating and with diminishing success. By 1958 he had sold *Actaea* and was principal owner of the Twelve-Meter *Columbia*.

ii

While working with Harry Sears on *Actaea* details, Ray Hunt was prompted to create a special Concordia Forty-one for himself. In 1955 he took delivery of *Harrier* at the Abeking and Rasmussen yard in Lemwerder. Although I had no part in designing *Harrier*'s rig (or her excellent cabin arrangement, for that matter), I do know that she was rigged as a sloop with a seven-eighths foretriangle and that her larger-than-usual mainsail had a hoist of 44 feet and a foot of 22 feet. Her jibs were tacked to a 5-foot-long bowsprit. (The first two or three bowsprits that we worked out were conventional wooden ones, and designed to fit over the standard Concordia stem fitting—including anchor chock—in case of future removal. Our later bowsprits were, like *Harrier*'s, of metal A-frame construction. Cross braces and canvas webbing made them a safe platform to work on.)

Harrier's other nonstandard rig details included a mainsheet trimmed to the afterdeck and running backstays anchored at chainplates. (In a way, these runners were more efficient in achieving a taut headstay than were slides on tracks. *Actaea* was one of several other Concordias using this system. However, they involved extra winches. In the end we reverted to standard rig backstay slides on the track.)

After brief sailing trials in Germany, Ray and his crew—his wife, daughter, and two sons—sailed *Harrier* directly to England to take part in the famous Cowes Week Regatta. There he proceeded to upset the racing as thoroughly as had the schooner *America* some one hundred years earlier. Out of six starts, Ray won six races. To the competition it seemed as if something were amiss with *Harrier*'s rating. However, a remeasurement only resulted in a lower, not a higher figure.

Back in the United States for the 1956 season, *Harrier* performed well with her big rig, as did her sister 41-footer *Gamecock*, which had a shorter bowsprit but a similar sail plan otherwise. By now, however, her rating was 29.6—a foot higher than for the Owens Cutters and over 3 feet higher than for *Finisterre* and the Block Island Forty types. With this adverse rating, her season's record was good, but not by any means outstanding.

Something obviously had to be done, and during the fall Ray rerigged *Harrier*, shortening her mainsail hoist to 40 feet and its foot to 20 feet, cutting her bowsprit from 5 feet to 2 1/2 feet. Of perhaps greater importance, he carried her headstay all the way to the top of the mast. This change to masthead rig was not a first for competing classes, but it was a first for the Concordias. Gradually over the next couple of years it affected the planning of all Concordia rigs, new and old.

With her rating down to 28.7 and the rating of many of her competitors up a foot and more to reflect new rules changes, *Harrier*'s 1957 record was absolutely tops. On the NYYC Cruise she won four firsts (including the Astor Cup) and a fourth. For this exceptional performance the Race Committee awarded her the Cygnet Cup.* This was a real feather in Ray's cap both as a skipper and as a designer. Needless to say, it was a significant boost for the whole Concordia class, as well.

iii

The year 1958 brought a summer of Twelve-Meter competition for the *America*'s Cup, in which both Harry Sears and Ray Hunt were deeply involved. Fortunately for us, Eugene W. ("Bill") Stetson was by this time an active participant in Concordia's racing progress. Through a series of rig experiments with two Concordia 41-foot sloops, each named *Banda*,** Bill not only enhanced our competitive position, but, more important, led us to some final determinations for mast and sail measurements.

---

* "In its discretion," reads the Cygnet Cup resolution of 1947, "the Race Committee of the New York Yacht Club may determine the outstanding performance of any yacht enrolled and taking part in an annual cruise of the club, and for such outstanding performance award a prize to be known as the Cygnet Cup."

** A Far Eastern place name to follow *Java, Malay, Suva, Moorea*, etc. Bill named his first two Concordia Forty-ones *Banda*. No Concordia actually had a *I, II,* or *III* painted on its stern; I have used these numerals in this book for the purpose of helping the reader understand which boat I am referring to. There were two boats named *Banda* one after the other; there were three boats named *Gamecock* one after the other. Yet at any given time, there was only one *Banda* and one *Gamecock*.

Bill Stetson at the wheel of *Snow Goose*, going through New York's East River on the way to Florida for the SORC.

E.W. (BILL) STETSON, JR.

In 1953 my friends Bikie (Mrs. John) Brooks and Drayton Cochran, then both Southport, Connecticut, neighbors of Bill Stetson, formally introduced him to us as an excellent sailor vitally interested in boats. I was soon to learn the validity of this introduction. In fact, I have over the years come to the conclusion that Bill should have become a yacht designer after graduating from Yale, instead of following in his banking father's footsteps.

From an early start, Bill successfully raced class boats such as Alden O boats, Stars, one-design R boats, Atlantics, and Thistles. As a youthful member of Southport's Pequot Yacht Club he won a junior sailing championship in a top league of Long Island sailors. By 1952 he was winning races in his new Owens Cutter, *Interlude*.

During the summer of 1956 Bill was, without our realizing it, chartering *Sly Mongoose* from Draytie Cochran, and it was later that season that he paid us a business visit to check over our standard Concordia yawl specifications. (As of that time we had no standard specifications for the Concordia Forty-one.)

From the very beginning Bill had design ideas of his own. Although he quickly settled on a 41-foot hull, he specified as extras: a lead keel, a new (to us) bright topside finish, and a mast stepped 7 inches aft of the standard position. He had in mind bigger headsails to take advantage of the eighty-five-percent foretriangle sail area provision of the CCA Rule.

After waiting for favorable word from Ray Hunt about Ray's rig experiments on *Harrier*, Bill settled on a masthead rig. However, he modified the actual *Harrier* rig dimensions. Instead of a 40-foot hoist on the main, he went to 43 feet. He shortened the boom measurement from 20 feet to 19 feet because of the aft position of his mast. And he eliminated the 2 1/2-foot bowsprit for the same reason.

Being the first Concordia to be ordered with a masthead rig, *Banda* required a new spar-and-rigging plan. As well as considering Ray's conclusions on the subject, we sought and received most helpful engineering assistance from Abeking and Rasmussen. Feeling it best that all shrouds come to the deck for easy adjustment without going aloft, we kept double spreaders but eliminated the diamond shrouds. Instead of figuring on a *Harrier*-type single forward strut for upper mast support, we followed Bill's suggestion of strengthening this area by using a mast with less taper.

Banda I arrived on schedule from Germany on 3 May 1957. After commissioning and being measured out at a rating of 30.3 (the same as *Actaea*), she raced her first season with only modest success—this in spite of the fact that Bill had a very competitive and good crew, which included such sailors as Jack Keeshan, Pete Gref, and Phil Snyder.

Right from the start at the New York Yacht Club's annual spring regatta at Oyster Bay, Bill found his new boat a bit tender. He therefore shortened his mainsail hoist to 40 feet and thus lowered his rating by nearly a foot. But on the August NYYC Cruise he did not fare nearly as well as did *Harrier*, with her 40-by-20-foot mainsail and 2 1/2-foot bowsprit. Although *Banda I* did win almost every local Buzzards Bay race she entered, Bill fully realized that improvements could and should be made to her rig and thereby enhance her rating. He immediately set several changes in motion. Bill had an interest in Hard Sails and received special help from their master sailmaker, Wally Ross. Together these two, sailor and sailmaker, worked out sails of the best shape and size for *Banda I*—and as it turned out for other Concordias to follow.

Now, with more sail area and yet a lower rating (29.5), Bill again entered *Banda I* in the 1958 NYYC Spring Regatta. In this he took first place, but subsequently withdrew to avoid a protest controversy. On that year's NYYC Cruise no Cygnet Cup was given, but *Banda I*'s overall record was as good as that of any other boat in the fleet. She defeated old rivals

like *Finn MacCumhaill* (rating 28.7 feet) and *Golliwogg* (rating 27.1 feet), and, with a record of one first and three seconds, she tied for top honors with *Finisterre* (rating 26.8 feet).

Concordia Forty-one sloop #52, *Banda I* (built in 1957) became flagship of the New York Yacht Club, as *Sagola*. *Banda II* (built in 1959) was finished bright like *Banda I*, but had teak decks.

George Hinman was, as a charterer, racing the Nevins Forty *Golliwogg* that summer and had an ideal opportunity to observe *Banda I*'s comparative performance. That he should approach his friend Stetson that fall to discuss buying *Banda I* was of particular significance. Not only was George one of America's best and most enthusiastic racing skippers, he was also slated to become Commodore of the New York Yacht Club for the following two years. He chose not to buy a new boat at this point, but rather to obtain one to his liking that was already well tuned up. Bill most generously told George that he was welcome to *Banda I* and that he himself would buy a new Concordia Forty-one. And that was that.

217

Before giving up *Banda I*, however, Bill tried an interesting experiment. Having originally sailed her without a bowsprit and then having added one, he now tacked his number-two genoa to the stemhead instead of to the 2 1/2-foot bowsprit and found that the boat seemed to go just as well this way as with the bigger number-one genoa at the end of the bowsprit. With this evidence before him, he removed the bowsprit completely.

Bill's planning for *Banda II* commenced immediately and, of course, was based on his experience with *Banda I*. About this time, Bill bought a delightful old Padanaram house situated right across the street from South Wharf. For some weeks it seemed as if we had an ideal setup for real in-depth new-boat planning. But Mother Luck saw fit to interrupt us. Early in that fall of 1958, my doctors started me on a series of operations that kept me out of the office for a number of months.

While "the cat was away," Bill got out his designer pencil and drew up a clipper-bowed version of a Concordia Forty-one which included a number of hull and rig modifications. When I got back, however, with my stubborn determination to retain a basically standard boat, I quickly drew up a long opposing dissertation for Bill. In essence, I argued: Radical changes can be for worse as well as for better; variations in a production model are costly for all concerned, much more so than people realize; modifications can, and often do, ruin a good class by making older boats obsolete and therefore less valuable. Bill, God bless him, understood me as well as my theories, and without delay he ordered *Banda II* as a standard Forty-one sloop, mast in standard position, and with no cost-affecting major changes.

Arriving on schedule in May of 1959 and in the usual good order, *Banda II* looked very much like *Banda I*, except for her teak decks. Although she rated a reasonable 28.6 feet (just one foot under her actual waterline length), she did not fare especially well in the NYYC Spring Regatta. The perennial team of *Finn MacCumhaill* and her owner, Bobby Coulson, again took the fleet. John West and Arthur Weekes with *Gamecock* took third, however. Bill was down the line with a seventh. On that year's NYYC Cruise *Banda II* entered only the New London–Newport run, which, happily, she won. Interestingly, *Banda I*, now named *Sagola*, beat *Banda II* to the finish line, but lost on corrected time. Back in Padanaram for the summer Buzzards Bay racing, *Banda II* continued Stetson's reign as local menace par excellence.

Come 1960, *Banda II* was beaten at the NYYC Spring Regatta by designer/builder Bill Luders's controversial and slippery *Storm*. Nonetheless, *Banda II* fared better than did her sisters *Sagola*, *Baroda*, and *Gamecock*.

That summer's NYYC Cruise was probably typical of the decade, but I remember it as being especially good fun. In addition to *Banda II* (sailing without bowsprit and rating 28.0 feet), there were three other Concordia Forty-one sloops: *Sagola* (without bowsprit), *Baroda*, and *Magic* (both with bowsprits); and two 41-foot yawls, *Windsong* and *Starsight*. There were also three standard Concordia yawls: *Ballerina*, *Racquet II*, and *Westray*. If we include *Malay*, which raced only on Astor Cup day and won her class, the Concordias were ten in number and represented more than half of Class III.

In fact, there were so many of us that old rivals *Finn MacCumhaill*, *Swamp Yankee*, and *Finisterre* never had a chance to get to the top. All the 41-foot sloops picked up top silverware, but to everyone's delight the forty-six-year-old Herreshoff sloop *Dolphin*, beautifully sailed by her loyal and skillful owners, the Lockwoods, had the best record of us all. That was something to think about.

In local racing, *Banda II* remained an almost impossible boat to beat. She won all of the races run by the New Bedford Yacht Club, as I remember, and then won both days at the Edgartown Regatta, giving her a chance at the coveted Osborn Trophy. On and on it went, and at least a few of the local sailors began to feel the loss of the regular trophies that they used to share before the arrival of the bandit *Banda*s.

At this point Bill decided to swing over to another tack. He traded *Banda II* to Weekes and West, who wanted to try their luck with the up-to-date masthead rig. Bill, for his part, thought it would be interesting to modify a boat for a trip south down the Inland Waterway and then to take in the Southern Ocean Racing Circuit, a series that no other Concordia had as yet tried. Thus, Bill's *Banda II* became *Gamecock III*, and *Gamecock II* became Bill's *Snow Goose*.

iv

As Mother Luck willed it, Bill had to postpone for a year his plans to take *Snow Goose* south. West and Weekes had already committed her for a 1961 charter, and the charterer wanted no part of a switch of boats, even though each was a Concordia. Quite undaunted by this dilemma, Bill quickly dreamed up a one-year interim project. He and I would buy and operate together one of the older standard Concordia yawls. With a minimum of sails, and our local crew only, we would see what success could be achieved in next season's local regattas, and the NYYC Annual Cruise.

After combing the market, we decided to buy *Suva*, a boat that Bill had last seen in Cuttyhunk during the 1954 hurricane, jammed between the shore and a big barge that had broken loose. She was the oldest Abeking and Rasmussen Concordia yawl, was not in top condition, but did have a lead keel and was available at a modest price. She was brought up to

Concordia Company from the Chesapeake, where we found her, and a program for properly tuning her up was set in motion immediately.

The first step was for the boatyard to strip and smooth her bottom and topsides, and also eliminate any extraneous equipment that created unnecessary windage or weight above deck or friction underwater.

The second step—the most important one, as it turned out—was to design and then create a rig that would move *Suva* most efficiently and handily, and still leave her with a competitive rating. We soon made arrangements to get together with Fenwick Williams at his Marblehead office, where all of our Concordia class design data was neatly filed. Whatever wasn't on paper was in Fenwick's head.

With all of this information at hand, along with a copy of the current CCA Rules, it did not take long for us to develop a new sail plan for *Suva*. Both Fenwick and I agreed with Bill's conclusions. She was to be a sloop, masthead rig, with no bowsprit. Her mainsail was to be smaller than *Banda*'s, but bigger than that of the standard Concordia yawl *Land's End*. Final mainsail measurements evolved at hoist 38 feet, foot 17 feet 6 inches.

During this meeting we determined the new standard sail plans for all future Concordias. Both Thirty-nines and Forty-ones would be masthead yawls. The former would have *Suva*'s new mainsail size, and a mizzen measuring 17 feet on the hoist, 8 feet on the foot. The latter would have a mainsail measuring 40 feet on the hoist and 18 feet on the foot, and a mizzen identical to that of the Thirty-nines, so they'd be interchangeable.

Oddly enough, after 1959, no Thirty-nines or Forty-ones were ordered as sloops, nor were any bowsprits called for. Several boats, including *Dame of Sark*, did, however, remove their mizzens for a serious racing campaign. By making an outstanding record thus rigged, they did prove the efficiency of the sloop rig. Likewise, a few pre-1959 boats retained their bowsprits and carried double head rigs for cruising, and both *Harrier* and *Magic* retained theirs for racing.

Our first move in implementing the planned *Suva* rig was to buy a new aluminum mast for her. This may seem, and actually was, a shocking move for me to agree to. However, the reasoning made good sense. For possible future use, we saw the wisdom of retaining, unaltered, *Suva*'s beautiful original wooden mast and its first-class rigging. At the same time, we both wanted to find out what possible racing advantages might materialize if we went modern with aluminum.

Before stepping and rigging this new spar (which, by the way, we bought from Ted Hood's new spar company), we weighed it and compared it with one of our newest Abeking and Rasmussen wooden masts. As we expected, the aluminum was slightly lighter than the wooden one, but

Sagola (ex-*Banda I*). The big rig (including a mainsail with pronounced roach) was used primarily for racing on Long Island Sound.

221

due to its uniform section its center of gravity was higher, so we concluded that its heeling effect would be about the same. Without any testing facilities to back us up, we just assumed that the oval shape of the aluminum spar might offer slightly less wind resistance than would the bigger square section of the wooden mast. We never found occasion to change these opinions. Thus aluminum might have helped us a little, but not much.

When it came to buying new sails, Bill had complete charge. However, as part of our original plan there were to be only four: main, working jib, number-one genoa, and spinnaker. He spent many hours on these, working them over with Wally Ross to achieve the exact shape and measurements needed for our particular purpose.

As an important companion project, Bill carefully organized the running rigging to make sure that the sails could quickly be hoisted to the right tension or height to suit any given condition, and could readily, with light or heavy sheets, be trimmed to a carefully proven and marked position. Racing success is definitely not all a question of genius and skill. Pre-race preparations often deserve a big share of any credit. This the less experienced sailor sometimes forgets or perhaps lacks time to attend to.

After being measured, *Suva* came away with a rating of 27.7 feet and was as ready as we could make her for the 1961 season.

June 3 came too early for us as a crew to get to Oyster Bay for the NYYC Spring Regatta, but it is doubtful that we could have shone very brightly there, anyway. Bill Luders's unpredictable *Storm* was, for this occasion, sporting a rule-defying ketch rig, which gave her a rating of 25.6 feet, some 2 feet below us. By 28 July, however, we were tuned up and waiting in New London for the start of the NYYC Cruise.

In spite of all our hopes and preparations, this 1961 cruise was not an outstanding one for the home team. It did, however, reveal some interesting comparisons between the performances of the eight or nine Concordias that took part. We on *Suva* more than held our own with the Concordia Forty-ones *Baroda*, *Gamecock III*, and *Snow Goose* (ex-*Gamecock II* under charter to Dudley Johnson), and did even better against our sister Thirty-nines *Malay*, *Rusta IV*, and *Winnie of Bourne*. In essence, this week of racing left us with a feeling that *Suva* as rigged was a great little boat with a lot of potential but definitely in need of more sail for top competition in Long Island Sound and against fast boats like old *Finn MacCumhaill*, old *Dolphin*, and new *Cricket* (an excellent 41-foot centerboard yawl, designed by Aage Nielsen and under charter to Larry Reybine).

Sailing in the stronger breezes of our local regattas, *Suva* showed the excellent performance we had hoped for. At the end of the racing season, the New Bedford *Standard Times* wrote her up as "Number one of the 1961

Snow Goose (ex-*Gamecock II*), Concordia Forty-one yawl #27, rigged with a short aluminum mainmast and sporting white-painted brightwork in anticipation of going to the sunny south for the SORC. As *Windrover*, she later became one of the most widely traveled of all boats in the class.

Big Four of Buzzards Bay." *Malay* was noted as number two. *Juniper*, a William Tripp-designed sloop, was number three. Last of the "Big Four" was the red-hulled Block Island Forty *Swamp Yankee*, another Tripp-designed boat.

Although the 1961 records emphasize that *Suva* took second in the New Bedford Yacht Club's Lloyd Trophy, first in their Stanton Trophy, and first in their Concordia Class Trophy, her crew all remember with more joy and clarity that year's Edgartown Regatta. Entered for this competition were some thirty-four boats of which nine were Concordias. It was a good competitive fleet without any outstanding ringers. As usual, the breezes off Edgartown gave us good sailing for both days of racing.

On Friday, 26 August, *Suva* seemed to be in top form and kept well ahead of other boats of her size and some that were larger. As we neared the finish line we were blissfully confident, but no doubt negligent, because in the end the word reached us that a mysterious boat named *Mambo* had actually beaten us (on corrected time) by five seconds. In both waterline and overall lengths this *Mambo* surpassed *Suva*, yet at the finish line she was so far behind that we could hardly see her. How could *Mambo* have beaten us?

In checking into this terrible miscarriage of justice, we found that *Mambo* was one of Ted Hood's new Robin types, a centerboard yawl rating 2.5 feet below us. You can rest assured that *Mambo* received our full attention during the following day's race. The results were more than rewarding: We beat her by nearly a minute on corrected time. Her second place meant that *Mambo* was tied with us for the Osborn Trophy. This unusual dilemma was settled by Alexander M. Orr, longtime and well-loved chairman of the Edgartown Race Committee and its former Commodore. He dreamed up an ingenious version of flipping a coin. As the *Vineyard Gazette* explained it: "The choice of heads or tails was decided by drawing slips from the Commodore's yachting cap, and the coin itself was then taken from the cap and tossed by a young woman of the club. *Suva*, represented by Basil Stetson, brother of skipper E. W. Stetson, Jr., won the toss, putting *Mambo* (Charles W. Turner) of Marblehead in second place."

So ends this phase of *Suva*'s history. That fall she was sold with her original rig to a good Padanaram neighbor, Calvin Siegal, who politely dispensed with a formal survey, stating that if we had owned the boat she must be in good shape. She was.

By this time, Bill Stetson's plan to campaign the Concordia Forty-one *Snow Goose* (ex-*Gamecock II*) in the SORC was well along; however, upon arriving with the boat in Fort Lauderdale, he learned of an illness in the family and had to turn around and sail back to the Chesapeake. After

Concordia Standard yawl #5, *Suva*, was the first (1950) built by Abeking and Rasmussen and is shown here carrying the masthead racing rig (complete with aluminum mast), with which she competed under Stetson–Howland ownership in 1961.

selling *Snow Goose*—his fourth Concordia—to his brother Charles, Bill slipped into the pattern of other top Concordia racers. Like Harry Sears and Ray Hunt, he went into *America*'s Cup racing. For three years (1962–1964), in company with other members of the *American Eagle* syndicate, he bore the almost killing anxieties of planning and sailing in this type of competition. Then, after a brief and rushed (it never pays) attempt in 1965 to tune up a fifth Concordia for a try at capturing the third leg of the Osborn Trophy, he left the Concordia family to race "newer types" of boats, in one of which he did retire the Osborn Trophy.

More recently, in the early 1980s, Bill discussed buying *Suva* back, but the asking price—twice what he'd paid twenty years before—discouraged the idea. So now, in his beautiful Vinalhaven domain, he and I just discuss the good old days. On occasion, I even hold the stopwatch while Bill starts races for old Herreshoff Twelves and even older North Haven dinghies.

v

Actaea's unexpected successes during the 1952 NYYC Cruise prompted an increasing number of sisterships to become involved in New York Yacht Club-sponsored day racing, as well as, of course, in local day racing up and down the East—and soon the West—Coast. To be specific, an average of eight to ten Concordias took part in the annual NYYC cruises. On the whole, they showed up remarkably well. In spite of continual changes in rules and the introduction of an almost endless series of new designs, this average of eight to ten boats remained nearly constant for the better part of a generation. Naturally, the more Concordias that raced, the better were the chances that some of them would do well. But even following this line of thinking, the question becomes not one of how they fared so well and for so long a time, but rather, why there were so many competing in the first place. My own answer would be that Concordias attracted very special owners—and that the owners, as much as the boats, were responsible for producing these very unusual records.

It was in the fall of 1959 that Commodore George Hinman bought *Banda I*, renamed her *Sagola* (like all his boats past, present, and future), painted her topsides the familiar and easily recognized Hinman light green, and made her flagship of the New York Yacht Club. Because Commodore Hinman's unusually fine racing record is safely preserved in the New York Yacht Club annals and elsewhere, I need only proclaim here that, for six NYYC cruises, the sloop-rigged Concordia *Sagola* remained in the forefront of her class and, often, of the fleet. In 1962 she was awarded the Cygnet Cup, thus creating a special promotion for the Concordia class. For between *Harrier*'s winning of the cup in 1957 and *Sagola*'s win five years later, only the *America*'s Cup defender *Weatherly* (in 1961) was awarded this discretionary prize. No wonder that, if other Concordia owners could beat *Sagola*, they felt a sense of real accomplishment and one they never forgot.

Hinman's victories were not restricted to the NYYC cruise. For instance, during his very first year with *Sagola*, he won an overnight Block

GEORGE R. HINMAN

George Hinman was born in New York City in 1905. His father was an excellent Larchmont Yacht Club sailor and also one of the earliest (1923) members of the Cruising Club of America. His own early sailing career took place on the racing-oriented western end of Long Island Sound. By 1922 he was already part of a winning Sears Cup crew.

After graduating from Middlebury College (Class of 1928), George became involved in optics and electronics, a business that had many boating connections and fitted in well with his life-long hobby of racing. Initially, George raced, and very successfully, too, in such one-design classes as the Atlantics and the Internationals. During the winter months of the 1930s he raced Frostbite dinghies.

After World War II, George's interest turned toward ocean racing, and in 1949 he was elected to membership in the Cruising Club of America. Three years later he bought *Katuna*, a 52-foot Carl Alberg-designed yawl built by Simms Brothers, which had previously raced to Bermuda under its original owner, and which George promptly named *Sagola*. Starting off in 1953 with a spectacular performance on the New York cruise, he won the top-in-fleet Cygnet Cup. Not as successful on the 1954 Bermuda Race, he was beaten in class, as were many others, by a veritable fleet of Sparkman and Stephens yawls. In 1957 he decided to sell his Alberg yawl and, as Vice Commodore of the New York Yacht Club, join Commodore Harry Sears and other Concordia owners in the lively racing in smaller boats of 28 to 32 feet waterline length.

Island Race in which *Finn MacCumhaill* captured second and Stuart Caldara's Concordia *Baroda* took third. Stu sent me a newspaper clipping about this race, because it described *Sagola* as "a new Block Island 40." With this he included a memo note that said only "Good God!!"

Another *Sagola* victory that gave me special pleasure to hear about was in the 1967 Miami–Nassau Race. No other Concordia up until then had participated in Southern racing, and the yachting publications were always so almighty talkative about "wonderful new breakthrough designs" shining their way through the SORC that *Sagola*'s win gave me a real lift.

George not only won races, he was also a wonderful skipper to race with: an excellent helmsman, very steady and quiet, who always knew what he was doing, who planned ahead, and who thus gave confidence to his crew, and allowed them to do their best. I might add that his crew was often made up of family: his wife, Kay, his daughter Pat, and his son George, Jr.

Did George, Sr., make any significant changes in *Sagola* to keep her at such a competitive peak? I don't think so. I believe he just kept her tuned up and in beautiful condition, and equipped her with the best of sails. His rating went up and down along with the ratings of other Concordias, reflecting changes in the CCA Rule. Starting with 29.5 feet he stayed at about that figure until the ratings of all Concordias went down in 1962. Then he crept back up again to 28.0 feet. In 1967 the ratings of almost all boats, including Concordias, went up, and *Sagola* ended with a 30.3-foot certificate. From year to year George did experiment with details of his rig, but the changes were slight. Because he believed in having sufficient sail area for light-weather racing, and because his boat had a lead keel, *Sagola*'s rating tended to stay a little higher than that of other Concordias.

Against my tearful entreaties, George, while racing, tightened up his permanent backstay well beyond what most wooden boats (including Concordias) were built to stand. This caused some leaking, which George partially overcame by lengthening his maststep to distribute the strain and by applying some fiberglass coatings over the stem-and-keel joint. This is my only Hinman complaint. But, really, I can't blame him. It is a fault of the racing Rule that great big genoas are tolerated, and these Rule-cheating demons seem to perform best on a very taut headstay.

When George sold *Sagola* in 1967, he did so to become skipper of the *America*'s Cup contender *American Eagle*. This in turn involved him with the Cup contenders *Intrepid* in 1970 and *Mariner* in 1974. Cup boat racing is an extremely grueling proposition, as anyone who has participated can tell you, and George Hinman's final *Sagola* was quite logically a fine little Grand Banks trawler-type of powerboat, in which he and his wife could watch the races and comfortably cruise, both summer and winter, north and south.

On a final visit to Florida in 1982, George stopped to discuss old times with Bill Stetson. He confided to Bill that the Concordia sloop *Sagola* was the most satisfactory boat he had ever owned and that campaigning her gave him the most enjoyable racing of his career. George and Bill agreed at the time that, for around-the-buoys racing, the Concordia Forty-ones seemed to have a slight edge over the standard Thirty-nines.

Commodore Hinman died in 1983.

16
Ocean Racing
1946–1970

i

Although 1952 was a very special year for Concordia yawls as day racers, 1954 was even more significant for them as ocean racers. I still remember so clearly the excitement of that early morning in June when news of the barely completed Bermuda Race reached my father. He phoned me at my house next door, and, exploding with urgency, insisted that I come over immediately. In bare feet I ran through the wet grass, down the pear walk, to his wisteria-shaded terrace—where he, in his striped seersucker bathrobe, was pretending to eat his breakfast, but was in fact feeding it, little by little, to Bill, the Howland springer spaniel.

Before even attempting a good morning, he sobbed aloud over and over again, "*Malay* won, *Malay* won. My God, boy! She showed 'em!" And he was so right, and he had every reason to be proud of his creation. As Ev (Everett B.) Morris put it in the August 1954 issue of *Motor Boating*: "The smallest boat ever to win the event, Daniel D. Strohmeier's 39-foot yawl *Malay* out of Padanaram, Massachusetts, defeated the largest fleet in Atlantic Ocean racing history, seventy-seven sail...."

Bill Wallace, writing in the August issue of *The Rudder*, described *Malay*'s triumph in a slightly different vein. Noting that *Malay* had been "completely ignored in pre-race speculation," Wallace agreed with the comment of Rod Stephens and Richard Nye that "Bermuda Races are largely a matter of luck," "a lottery" in essence. "By conventional American standards," Wallace went on, "*Malay* is an ordinary cruising yawl, with emphasis on comfort rather than racing ability.... She is a yawl of the Concordia class, designed in the mid-1930s and built in 1939. Strohmeier acquired her ten years later. She has seldom been raced with any great

Class A start, 1948 Bermuda Race. *Baruna* (#98) is in the foreground, followed by *Argyll* (#125) and the schooner *Niña* (#2).

231

Baruna, designed by Sparkman and Stephens and built in 1938. Being 72' overall, she was as big as rules would permit for the Bermuda Race. Winner of the Bermuda Race in 1948, she won other prizes in other years— including, several times, being first to finish.

success.... Both the boat and the skipper were in their first Bermuda run."

It is true. *Malay*—and Concordias generally—did appear to come from nowhere. However, this particular Bermuda Race was not to be the end of Concordia ocean racing, but rather just the beginning. Although not widely known before 1954, Dan was, in fact, already an excellent sailor and racing skipper, and he and his *Malay* were to see more continuous ocean racing together (including fourteen races to Bermuda and sixteen to Halifax) than any other team I have ever heard of.

Twentieth-century ocean racing records are preserved in various forms, so there is little advantage in my trying to recite them in any detail. However, in *A Life in Boats: The Years Before the War*, I did give a brief account of the Bermuda Race from its beginnings to World War II. In this chapter I will do somewhat the same with the postwar Bermuda, Annapolis, and Halifax Races up until 1970, when the International Offshore Racing Rule (IOR) came into being. My object is to bring out another important phase of the Concordia story and, perhaps more important, to emphasize again the basic trends and Rule-prompted changes that affected both boat designs and sailors' attitudes.

ii

The first postwar Bermuda Race took place in 1946 and pretty much picked up where it had left off in 1938. The entries themselves—some thirty-one in all—were generally big boats. Class A boats were 55- to 70-footers, many of them old-guard campaigners like *Highland Light, Escapade* (designed by Rhodes), and *Vamarie.* Then there were the somewhat newer (but still prewar) boats, such as the sloop *Gesture* and the yawls *Good News* and *Baruna.* (I mention these last three not only because they took top prizes, but because they were sound and beautiful boats—all three, I might add, designed by Sparkman and Stephens.) Most of the Class B boats were 45- to 50-footers. Few were new, and no single designer seemed to have an edge on the others.

In 1948 the fleet size grew slightly. The thirty-six entries were, as before, divided into two classes. Class A, numbering fifteen, again consisted of excellent boats, mostly yawl rigged. The leaders were *Baruna, Royono* (designed by Alden), and the schooner *Niña.* John Alden's own 53-foot *Malabar XIII* was one of the few newly built boats in Class B. The fact that she won her class and was a ketch did not suggest any trend; it only indicated that Alden himself was still a top ocean racer. *Malabar XIII*'s competitors were mostly yawls or sloops and included four New York Thirty-twos, which all finished in the top third of their class. As a significant portent, the well-known Long Island sailor Harvey Conover had recently sold his New York Thirty-two to Rod Stephens and was now racing a new (1946) keel/centerboard version of the New York Thirty-two named *Revonoc* (as was his previous boat), whose rating advantages included more beam, less draft, and a yawl rig.

By 1950 the Bermuda fleet had grown to 52 boats, thus prompting the Race Committee to set up a third—or C—class. Class A continued to be dominated in numbers and winnings by Sparkman and Stephens yawls: *Argyll*, a 1948 boat, was winner in class and overall; *Bolero* was second. Not far behind were the old Alden-designed *Royono* and the Rhodes-designed *Escapade*, both yawls. In Class B, *Merry Maiden*, a new Rhodes yawl, had the best corrected time. But, in spite of this, the New York Thirty-twos and other Sparkman and Stephens boats monopolized the winning half of the class. The new Class C was a mixed bag—many rigs, many designers, few new boats. Significantly, the almost-new Sparkman and Stephens yawl *Loki*, built in 1948, placed first, prompting the building of a number of sisterships over the next few years.

Come 1952, there were still no obvious changes. Entries had grown slightly to fifty-eight. Prewar deep-keeled yawls still dominated Class A, and *Royono* took her turn winning first place, followed by England's beautiful Nicholson-designed yawl *Bloodhound* and the brand-new Alberg & Brengle-

The 57' *Gesture*, a beautiful 1941 Sparkman and Stephens sloop belonging to my friend Jimmy Madden, won the 1946 Bermuda Race in Class A and overall. A 1948-built near sistership, *Argyll*, rigged as a yawl, won the same honors in 1950.

designed, Abeking and Rasmussen-built 66-foot yawl *Sea Lion*. In Class B, New York Thirty-twos took first and second places. Class C entries remained a heterogeneous group of keel sloops and yawls, led by the 1940 Rhodes-designed, Richard Nye-owned 46-footer *Carina*, which not only won her class but also had the best corrected time in fleet. *Carina*'s victory was important in that it broke the postwar domination of the race by Class A winners and, in doing so, further focused more attention on the smaller ocean racers of Classes B and C.

By 1954, the first year that Concordias (*Winnie of Bourne* and *Malay*) raced to Bermuda, the larger boats were not changing very much from race to race. Some of the affluent older owners must have been enjoying their sport as it was and thinking to themselves, let's go again with the same old boat, just one more time, win or lose. Certainly the 1950s were not a decade conducive to ordering big, new racing yachts. Boatbuilding in America had become very expensive. Labor was then far more costly than it had been during Depression years and was no longer tuned to producing the fine workmanship of earlier times. Finding, and paying for, good professional skippers and crews had also become very difficult. Meanwhile, during these same years, the number of small family auxiliaries was growing by leaps and bounds.

A look at the 1954 entries in the Bermuda Race's newly created Class D offers a glimpse of what lay ahead. Among the twenty-two entries listed for that class, fifteen were under 40-foot length overall, and at least four of these—two Concordias, two Owens Cutters—were stock one-design auxiliaries. The fact that one of them, *Malay*, not only won in her class, but turned in, by two hours, the best corrected time in the entire fleet, automatically sparked the venturesome small-boat owner to have a go at ocean racing—and encouraged the ambitious yacht designer to dream up more one-design winners.

Of the eighty-nine boats entered in the Bermuda Race in 1956, four were Concordias: *Harrier*, *Wild Swan*, *Malay*, and *Swan III*. Although Ray Hunt in *Harrier* continued his remarkable record by winning a second place in Class D, the main development in the 1956 race within the two smaller classes was the ever-growing number and achievements of keel/centerboard boats. In Class C, first- and third-place winners, and perhaps half of the rest of the class, were of this type. In Class D the keel/centerboarders were not as strong in numbers, but were there in great prominence—especially in the form of *Finisterre*, the overall winner of the race, and her Nevins Forty near-sisters *Indigo* and *Golliwogg* (sixth and seventh). The Concordia yawl *Wild Swan* was fifth in Class D.

The 1958 Bermuda Race proclaimed the ascendancy of the new keel/

235

centerboard 40-footers. Although Class A had its repeaters, along with several new boats, the average size of Class A starters was smaller than ever. Former Class B boats were now racing in Class A—and were themselves being replaced by newer and smaller types. The winner in Class A was a 1954 Sparkman and Stephens yawl, *Legend*. The winner in Class B was the one-year-old 48-foot, Bill Tripp-designed *Touché*. Meanwhile in Class D, *Finisterre* did it again, winning both in class and in fleet. To make her point even sharper, her younger sisters (there were six in all of these Nevins Forties racing) took second, third, and fourth places, and her just-built, fiberglass-hulled, Tripp-designed second cousins—the Vitesse-class yawls (there were three racing)—took fifth, sixth, and seventh. *Harrier*, now owned by Jesse Bontecou, was in eighth place—the best finisher among the eight Concordias entered. But even the lowest-ranking Concordia had a corrected time that was better than any boat in Class A, B, or C. These results prompted the Rules Committee to wonder if perhaps the small boats might not be doing a bit too well. My own concerns were more specifically focused on the centerboard phenomenon, for my firm position of sticking with the keel Concordias as designed was getting very lonely.

The statistics of the 1960 Bermuda Race are both startling and thought-provoking. Here is what happened:

* Sparkman and Stephens-designed boats took first place in every single Class A, B, C, D, and E.
* Except for the new aluminum keel sloop *Cyane* in Class C, all of these winners were keel/centerboard boats.
* Four of the first five boats in Class B were built by Abeking and Rasmussen.
* The first twelve boats on overall corrected time, were in Class E.
* No boat in Class D got to Bermuda as fast as did the first six boats in Class E.
* For a third time *Finisterre* won the Bermuda Race, and she, her sisters, and cousins dominated Class E. (The British sloop *Belmore** placed second, but after that, eight of the next nine boats were keel/centerboarders.) Nevins Forty types (of which there were four) took first and fourth places. The new Tripp Vitesse yawls (of which there were nine) took third, fifth, ninth, tenth, and eleventh places.

Of the eight Concordias scattered in Classes D and E, *Sagola* and *Diablo* did the best; but even they finished (in elapsed and corrected time) some eight to ten hours behind the leaders. For the moment we were competing against boats that had very low ratings.

---

* The British never went in for yawls. I presume that neither tradition nor Royal Ocean Racing Rules favored this rig.

The 46' *Carina*, a fine, able yawl designed by Rhodes and built in 1940, broke the chain of Class A winners by taking first in Class C as well as overall honors in the 1952 Bermuda Race.

DANIEL D. STROHMEIER

Dan Strohmeier, at the wheel of *Malay II*.

Daniel D. ("Dan") Strohmeier was born in Boston in 1911. How he came by his lifelong interest in the sea is hard to figure, because his parents had come from landlocked Pennsylvania with no apparent seafaring background at all. When Dan was eight, his father, a schoolmaster, founded a day camp in Nonquitt, Massachusetts, a summer colony in the town of Dartmouth. Camp White Oak was, like its name, a sound and durable institution that gave an excellent start to two generations of Nonquitt

youngsters. Discipline, enthusiasm, and worthwhile things to do and learn (including a fine boat-modeling program) were there aplenty, and, what was equally significant for Dan, Nonquitt was right on Buzzards Bay. His early sailing experience included Wee Scotts, Beetle Cats, Herreshoff Twelves, and Alden O boats.

I had not fully realized until recently how deeply and how early in life Dan had gone into a study of the various forces that make a sailboat sail. In a recent letter, Dan wrote me that "college included four years at Amherst, where the Physics Department allowed me to build a fairly formidable wind tunnel for testing sail shapes, then two years at M.I.T., where I studied naval architecture. There I contrived a model tank featuring what I'm given to believe was the world's first three-dynamometer carriage for the testing of sailing yachts. At least I was one year ahead of my old friend Ken Davidson at Stevens Institute. Fred Pidgeon (maker of hollow spars), a nabob of the Boston Model Yacht Club, supplied me with test models. My collaborator, Ed Rand, and I were gratified that our selection from the tank later won the U.S. title and represented us abroad." With this background, it is no wonder that Dan seemed to be rather more scientific in his racing tactics than were the rest of us local Padanaram sailors when it came to S boat competition.

After college Dan went to work as a shipbuilder at Bethlehem Steel's Fore River plant in Quincy, Massachusetts. During World War II he was, as he writes, "exiled to New York, where I was assistant to Arthur Homer in charge of Bethlehem's shipbuilding program, the largest such in the history of the world. Fortunately for me, my boss was a sailor and sympathetic to sailor's dreaming." Dan later became Bethlehem's Vice President of Shipbuilding, and Arthur Homer became President, then Chairman of the Board.

Although I would have been proud to have done so, I had little to do with Dan's acquisition of a Concordia yawl. He had, at M.I.T., known Ray Hunt, especially as a great swimmer. And during his sum-

Dan Strohmeier's first Concordia yawl, *Malay* (ex-*Jobiska*), built by Geo. F. Lawley & Son in 1939. The diamond shrouds on her mainmast, the oblong portlights, and the blue sheerstrake made her easy to identify. The yawl rig permits a nice combination of reaching sails, and, as sailors have long been aware, reaching is a wonderful point of sail for both ocean racing and cruising.

mer stays at Nonquitt, he had had ample opportunity to see and admire Father's *Java*. In 1950 (the year Abeking and Rasmussen produced its first Concordia) he bought the prewar, Lawley-built Concordia *Ina* (ex-*Jobiska*) from Drayton Cochran.

Although Dan intended *Ina* (which he renamed *Malay*) primarily to be a family cruiser, he soon entered her in local races with enthusiasm and growing success. In 1953 he enhanced an already fine racing reputation by winning the New Bedford Yacht Club's overnight Whalers Race. The following winter he chanced one Sunday to run across Jack Park-

inson at Jakobsen's yard in Oyster Bay, where both *Malay* and *Winnie of Bourne* were in storage. "With a 'ho-ho-ho,' " as Dan recalls, "Jack boomed forth that he was planning to race to Bermuda." Jack's enthusiasm was catching. Although Dan had never thought of taking such a small boat on such a long race, he figured to himself, "If *Winnie* can do it, so can *Malay*."

In preparation for going offshore, Dan made a number of important modifications to *Malay* details, all of which proved useful and some of which became standard for other Concordias.

239

A Pilot-class sloop. In my opinion, the Pilot is one of the finest small auxiliaries ever built. Designed by Sparkman and Stephens, Pilots have been constructed of fiberglass by Hinckley since about 1965. Their dimensions are 35' LOA, 25' LWL, 9'6" beam, and 5' draft–all moderate and most suitable for general use. In the late 1950s and 1960s both the Pilots and Concordias, with their conventional, full-length keels, faced stiff competition from the newer *Finisterre*-type keel/centerboarders with their low ratings. Yet, when the winds blew and the seas ran high, the Pilots and Concordias proved themselves successful racers in spite of their unfavorable handicaps. In the 1958 Stratford Shoal race, for example, a third of the fleet dropped out because of heavy weather, but the race was won by the Pilot-class sloop *Pony Tail*. Dan Strohmeier's Concordia yawl *Malay* took second, having the best elapsed time in her division and fourth best overall.

To shift for a minute from statistics to theories: My first impulse to credit ratings for all the keel/centerboarders' successes would be neither fair, right, nor reasonable. Especially in *Finisterre*'s case, rating was not all-important in her Bermuda victories. Her success was doubtless more due to her skipper's skill. When you think of it, even a Stradivarius fiddle depends on a good violin player, and a pro tennis racket won't win top matches without a good player to swing it. Carleton Mitchell made a point of being a real professional (in the right sense) as an ocean voyager and an ocean racer. He worked at it summer and winter. For crew he chose men who were excellent skippers in their own right, ones who had the strength, the stomach, and the ability in both light and heavy weather to keep his boat going during his watch below. His organization, navigation, sails, equipment, maintenance, everything, were first class. Mitchell had made all of his preparations years ago, last month, and yesterday. It would be a shame and an injustice, if such perfection didn't create some advantages over other skippers and boats, good though they might be.

iii

The year 1962 was a bit of a shake-up for the Bermuda Race. The fleet had been getting too large—131 starters. Also, newer *Finisterre*-type small boats were doing too well and in certain cases were getting too small for their own safety. The Rules Committee, as we have seen, had by now penalized overly large foretriangles and were already talking about measuring actual stability through inclining tests to lessen the keel/centerboard advantages. The Race Committee for their part, had wisely established a lower limit for size of boat and had restricted the number of entrants by an invitation-only system.

Although the 1962 race turned out to be a light-weather affair, the top corrected-time winners were scattered through the fleet. Some of the old-timers in the top classes did really well. No one had anything but cheers when the thirty-four-year-old *Niña* was declared the overall winner. Two New York Thirty-twos were first and second in Class B, and a Sparkman and Stephens keel sloop won in Class C.

In Classes D and E, however, results were more predictable. The Vitesse yawls (now called Block Island Forties) and other Tripp-designed boats were now showing their potential superiority over the Nevins Forties: the newest were outdoing the new. *Swamp Yankee* won first in Class D and third in fleet. *Burgoo,* a smaller version of the Block Island Forties, was first in Class E and second in fleet. The Concordia yawl *Diablo* held in there with a third in Class E and a seventh in fleet. Her nine participating sistership won no prizes, but with their ratings slightly lowered, and those of the Nevins Forties and Block Island Forties raised, the Concordia yawl's corrected times were again looking more competitive.

In 1964, after the inclining test requirements had gone into effect, conditions began to look even more promising for Concordias. (In general, the rating of Concordias remained at about 28 feet, while the Nevins Forties and Block Island Forties went up about a foot, from 27 feet to 28 feet. With these equalizing rating adjustments, *Nike*, owned by Charles Stromeyer of Marblehead, came very close to being a second Concordia yawl to win an overall Bermuda Race victory. She was second in fleet and first in Class D, only being beaten by *Burgoo*, the smallest boat and the first made of fiberglass ever to win a Bermuda Race. *Burgoo* had squeezed over the low limit restriction by adding a false stern. Ably sailed by her new owner, she saved her time on the fleet.

Even with the win by *Burgoo*, it was a great year for the thirteen Concordias. Following *Nike* in Class D, *Safari* was only nine seconds behind Newbold Smith's Block Island Forty, *Reindeer*, which gave *Safari* a third in class and sixth in fleet. Class D Concordias *Soprano* and *Skye* were fourth and seventh. In Class C, *Malay* was fourth. With such close finishes, tiny variations in ratings were making a real difference in final standings.

Optimism was short-lived, however, for the thirteen Concordias entered in the 1966 Bermuda Race, because this was the dawning year of Bill Lapworth's Cal Forties and other, similar, light-displacement types (see pages 196–198). In Class D there were at least seven of these new fiberglass flyers, which, rating at about 32 feet, took six of the top seven places in those two classes. The first-place Cal Forty *Thunderbird* won the overall Bermuda Trophy, and two others placed fifth and sixth in fleet standings. *Westray* gave the Concordia group some consolation by saving her time on all three Block Island Forties and gaining a fourth in Class D. Other Concordias finished down the line.

The success of the Cal Forties was a certain sign that new design approaches were gaining momentum, that light displacement and fin keels were now taking hold. In Class A several owners were seeking the notoriety of being first to finish regardless of rating. The new Sparkman and Stephens sloop *Kialoa*, long, light, and with a fin keel, proved her point in her very first year, in spite of dropping on corrected time to second in Class A and fiftieth in fleet.

Speed above all else became the spirit of 1968. The newly dubbed "maxi boats" were in great prominence: long canoes with tall rigs, fin keels, trim tabs, and spade rudders, covered with winches and strong young men to twist them; new corporate owners; new skippers. Indeed, all the winners in Class B in 1968 were all-new boats built of fiberglass or aluminum and rigged as sloops. First in Class B and second in the fleet was *Rage*, designed by Charlie Morgan. Overall winner and winner in Class C was Ted Hood, sailing a new *Robin*. And although the Cal Forties no longer monopolized Class D (after the weighing requirement went into effect and their rating rose from about 32 feet to 36 feet), *Thunderbird*, however, was still first in that class, and another Lapworth-designed boat was first in Class E. *Westray* again carried the flag for the Concordias by beating the Block Island Forties and taking first place in Class F.

Light-displacement fin-keeled types now seemed to be having things too easy, and the Rules Committee of the CCA would, in the normal course of events, have studied the matter of wetted surface in their next review of measurement rules. However, the IOR Rule slipped in ahead of them.

Unlike the CCA Rule, the IOR Rule was not a handicap rule. Rather, it was what Professor Evers Burtner called a "spot rule" and led to specific hull shapes. This made it interesting for designers, but difficult for other boat types that tried to compete on favorable terms against boats designed to the IOR Rule. Only if and when a new handicap rule came into general use would Concordias become competitive again.

iv

In summing up ocean racing between 1950 and 1970, it appears to me that participation shifted from a modest fleet of fairly big, one-of-a-kind wooden yachts to a much larger fleet of smaller boats, many of which were one-design class boats in the 40-foot range and built of fiberglass. Each new one-design class, as it came along, enjoyed its day of busy brilliance, then faded into a quieter evening.

Obviously the governing CCA Rule and its changing modifications had a major effect on design trends. However, there were other less obvious influences that should be kept in mind, as they too played their part in encouraging owners to move on to a new boat. An ever-increasing desire to win motivated—almost drove—many a new skipper into deserting the older classes, and, along with his skills and good crew, joining a newer and more promising class. Such switches in themselves were a promotion for any new class, regardless of its design virtue.

Right or wrong, I always felt that brand-new fiberglass boats had very smooth bottoms for the first year or two, and then tended to pit or roughen slightly as they aged. It is certain that new boats had the advantage of having new sails of the latest improved design and sailcloth. (Not always realized, however, is that these sails become gradually less competitive as time goes on.) Almost any boat tends to get heavier after the first season by means of the normal accumulation of gear and the soaking up of water (yes, even fiberglass is a little porous). Especially in light-displacement types, this increase in weight has its disadvantages. Finally, when a new class (or even some one-of-a-kind new boat) is introduced, the designer or sailmaker or other individual with Carleton Mitchell-type abilities is often taken along to campaign the boat and thus promote the designer or the class.

THE ANNAPOLIS RACE

The first Annapolis Race was held in 1939. The race was dropped during the war years, but was reactivated in 1949, thanks mainly to the good efforts of DeCoursey Fales, who, like many others, sensed a healthy demand for ocean racing in the Bermuda Race off-years. As reorganized, the Annapolis Race was and still is jointly sponsored by the New York Yacht Club, the Annapolis Yacht Club, and the U. S. Naval Academy Yacht Squadron. (The Ida Lewis Yacht Club in Newport later became a sponsor as well.) As its promoters had envisaged, many participants in the Annapolis Race were the same enthusiasts who raced to Bermuda. Indeed, conditions were somewhat similar for the two races, until boats in the Annapolis Race rounded the Chesapeake Light Vessel and entered Chesapeake Bay, where the going historically tends to be more variable.

Originally the starting line had been at Brenton Reef off Newport, making the race some 468 miles long. In 1955, the starting line was unwisely shifted to Cerberus Shoal, a tide-ridden spot halfway between New London and Block Island. That year *Actaea* was the only Concordia in a three-class fleet of twenty-seven starters.

The race was a strange, mixed-up affair from the beginning, with the larger boats in particular being penalized by head tides at their earlier start. Light weather prevailed for most of the race, and this, too, favored the smaller boats. Sailing an almost perfect race, Commodore Sears and his crew not only won their division, but were awarded the Blue Water Bowl for best in fleet. *Actaea* saved her time on the Class A schooner *Niña*, winner of second place overall, by over an hour and ten minutes. In her own division, and rating a foot higher than they, she beat the Owens Cutters *Prim*, by ten hours, and *Finn MacCumhaill*, by fifteen.

The Annapolis Race course was reversed in 1957, to allow Chesapeake Bay sailors to make a quick run north for the NYYC Cruise or to spend some time cruising Down East. There were two Concordias entered in what turned out to be a fast race, and *Harrier*, sailed by Ray Hunt, won in class and overall, making it two straight Annapolis Races in succession for Concordias. All the Class C fleet leaders except *Harrier* were new centerboard yawls. (Carleton Mitchell finished third in *Finisterre*, behind George Hinman, who was second in the Nevins Forty *Bonne Amie*.)

Starting in 1959 with seventy-one entries, the Annapolis Race fleet grew over the next few years to one hundred boats, then by 1969 dropped back to under ninety. Concordias, always about four each race, continued to participate, but with modest success. *Sagola* was our most successful representative in the later years: she got a fourth in class in 1961, a second in class in 1965.

The intricacies of Chesapeake Bay made the race very unpredictable, as well as challenging. Owners who knew the Bay seemed to have a real advantage. Increasingly, participants seemed to use the race as a pleasant or quick way to get north, and fewer took the time to really set up for racing and make it a special down-and-back project. Although newer boats often did well, design trends were less noticeable in Annapolis Race statistics than they were in Bermuda Race results.

The second *Actaea*, flagship of the New York Yacht Club and winner of the 1955 Annapolis Race. When the wind exceeds eighteen to twenty knots, a Concordia generally performs best to windward under working jib.

THE HALIFAX RACE

The Marblehead-to-Halifax race, scheduled to follow on the heels of the Annapolis Race, offers all eastbound sailors a sporting and timely start for some fine summer cruising in the beautiful bays of Maine or in the Bras d'Or Lakes of Nova Scotia. Its general course, some 360 miles in length, is an old one, and was followed for several centuries by trading and fishing schooners making their passages between New England and Nova Scotia. Starting from Marblehead, it runs almost due east for some 250 miles to Cape Sable, then turns more northerly for another 110 miles or so into Halifax Harbour.

Probably the first formal yacht race over this course was one run by the Eastern Yacht Club of Marblehead in 1905. It wasn't, however, until 1939 that a formal Halifax Race was organized into an odd-year fixture. The Halifax Race has been run jointly by the Boston Yacht Club and the Royal Nova Scotia Yacht Squadron, except for the years 1953, 1955, and 1957, when it was taken over by the Boston Station of the Cruising Club of America.

Unlike the Annapolis and Bermuda Races, the Halifax Race is a cold-water affair. In July this means fog and lots of it, which, in turn, presents real navigational problems instead of wide horizons. These problems are further intensified by strong (5- or 6-knot) and often unpredictable tidal currents coming out of the Bay of Fundy. As in most ocean races, the wind velocities may vary from strong to nil, but the wind direction is normally southwest, which makes for a reaching-and-running race. Under such conditions good traditional cruising boats have a fairer go against speedy windward specialists.

Dan Strohmeier was navigator aboard Arthur Homer's 54-foot *Salmagal II*, when that boat took fleet honors in the 1953 Halifax Race. In 1955 Dan's *Malay* became the first Concordia to race to Halifax. *Malay* surely gave her sisters that would join this race in later years a fine introduction in how to do it. Leonard Fowle used the word "swift"

in describing *Malay* in his newspaper account of the race, but credited Dan's victory to "a bit of daring, some high-class seamanship and navigation in taking the seldom-used inside passage at Brazil Rock, plus having a well-trained, hard-driving crew." As in his Bermuda Race win the previous year, Dan had a veritable cargo of prizes to take home with him from Halifax.

As for the Halifax Race of 1957, I can only boast that *Malay* just missed first place again, losing by only six minutes to *Galliard*, an Arthur Robb-designed little English boat that was neither new, yawl-rigged, nor of the centerboard type, but rather was essentially an Eight-Meter built in England in 1949 and well sailed by her owner, Newbold Smith.

The 1959 Halifax entry count of forty-five boats grew to some seventy boats by 1969. Likewise over this ten-year period the average number of Concordias participating jumped from two to twelve. Their racing record remained consistently good. In fact, in 1963 *Diablo* was first and *Off Call* second in the overall fleet standings, at the same time breaking, along with other leaders, all previous records for corrected time over the course. Two races later, in 1967, the Concordia yawls *Westray* (first), *Diablo* (second), *Merlin* (third), and *Nike* (fourth) swept Class D, with *Kypris* taking sixth, and *Moonfleet* seventh.

Sentiment prompts me to mention another statistic about these Halifax Races of the 1950s and 1960s. Although eighty percent of the winners were yawl-rigged, the schooner *Niña* remained a shining star. First to finish five times out of six starts, she won the overall best corrected time, as well, in 1967. This says something about two masts for passage-making.

John Robinson's Concordia Standard Thirty-nine yawl #69, *Diablo*, winner of the 1963 Halifax Race. She sets a reaching jib—not a genoa—for this reaching race. Her hull slips easily along, leaving no big wake.

17
A Versatile Boat
for General Use

i

It was the racing successes of the Concordia class that first caught the widespread attention of buyers, whether they were racing-minded or not. But the first Concordia yawl was designed primarily as a daysailer and coastwise cruiser, and it is as an all-around family boat that the Concordia Thirty-nine and Forty-one have seen their widest, longest, and most continuous use. Elizabeth Meyer's fine book *The Concordia Yawls, 1938–1978: Forty Years Sailing* (Edgartown, Massachusetts, 1979) provides biographical sketches of some 60 of the 103 boats in the class. All I can hope to do here is briefly tell the story of several Concordias that I know well and that seem to epitomize the diversity of daysailing and family cruising uses to which these boats are regularly put.

I'll start with *Prettimarie*, a Concordia Forty-one that was ordered from us some thirty years ago by the New York investment banker Hugh Bullock. Thanks to Hugh's perception of his boat, *Prettimarie* has been one of the most meticulously maintained of the entire fleet. I like to feel that Hugh considers her a worthy yacht in the classical sense—and treats her accordingly.

For some nine months of every year since she was built, Hugh has left *Prettimarie* in Concordia's care. Under her own white dustcover, she regularly occupies her own special northeast corner of the main building, a choice position where she is clear of traffic, and where neither drying winds nor direct sunlight can bother her. Coming back as she does in the early fall, and leaving in the late spring, her schedule is such that she re-

Concordia Forty-one yawl *Prettimarie*, a one-owner boat since new, moored off Hugh Bullock's dock at Edgartown. Dressed or not, she has always been maintained to the highest yachting standard. Concordia yawls have been privileged, perhaps more often than any other class boat, to fly a yacht club Commodore's flag.

ceives not only undivided human attention but generally benefits from excellent weather conditions for her painting and varnishing.

During vacation days of July and August, Hugh has, over the years, established her as a notable fixture at the head of Edgartown Harbor. As a Commodore and officer, he himself regularly takes an active part in the yacht club racing affairs. Keenly competitive, he sees to it that his boat has the best of sails, as well as first-class gear and a clean bottom. Often enough he invites Arthur Knapp or other top sailors to race with him, and thus sharpens up an already good crew. Invariably he does well in the annual Edgartown regattas. In the overnight race, "Around the Island," that follows, he has twice been the first prize winner.

Over and perhaps above a racing enthusiasm, I believe Hugh is one of those who takes genuine satisfaction just in owning a fine boat, and that he has been proud to make *Prettimarie* a flagship of the Edgartown fleet.

His summer home sits at the water's edge, a bit beyond the yacht club and right at the bend where the harbor channel swings from a westerly to a southerly direction. By mooring *Prettimarie* directly off his dock and by employing two good boatboys to take care of her, Hugh can, from his porch, have the satisfaction of observing a boat that appeals to his eye, not only for its basic lines and style, but also for its fair and spotless condition—topsides, chamoised brightwork, shined brass, and neatly furled sails. Precisely at eight each morning and again at sunset, he is in the perfect spot from which to witness firing of the yacht club's cannon and the answering fleet colors.

Commodore Bullock's sailing time has been all too limited by business pressures and other interests, but his influence on area yachting has been both significant and most welcome. Any sailor tacking into Edgartown's inner harbor must perforce pass close by the smartly run yacht club and then by *Prettimarie*. In so doing, surely he must at least sense that traditional yachting, and some of its best features, have not altogether faded into the past.

ii

Next is Concordia #71, *Polaris*, built in 1959. For her first eighteen years, she belonged to Roberts Parsons, whom we first met as a regular but apparently casual visitor to our yard. Early on we learned that he was retired, lived in the East Greenwich area of Rhode Island, and had a part-time interest in a small boatyard there. In response to any slight hint on my part that he might buy a Concordia yawl, Parsons invariably explained that, much as he liked these boats, they were just too small for his long legs.

But I kept on trying, and one snowy Sunday morning, he allowed him-

Roberts Parsons's Concordia Forty-one sloop *Polaris* on an afternoon sail. Her distinctive rubrail, roller-reefing mainboom, and (not shown here) jib club all helped to make her an easy boat for two people to handle.

self to be coaxed aboard *Prettimarie.* This did the trick. Although he seemed much surprised by his own decision, he nonetheless knew almost instantly what modifications to specify for his own new Forty-one. To avoid troubling his back in the constant climb over a bridge deck, he just eliminated that structure. To save himself the sheet tending involved with an overlapping jib he added a bowsprit and specified a larger-than-standard working jib on a club. To avoid the confusion of a mizzen and its gear, he called for a sloop rig with a longer-than-standard main boom to be designed for roller-reefing gear. And finally, so that he could come alongside docks without the fuss of fenders, he helped us work out a special guardrail, armored with half-oval brass on its outer edge. The rail's underside was to have a groove so placed as to encourage rainwater to drip directly into the sea rather than streak down the topsides. This same undersurface was also to be artfully painted his chosen red to take the place of the standard decorative covestripe.

For his tender, Mr. Parsons asked us to build him a slighty enlarged bateka, like my father's. He didn't plan to take the tender aboard regularly; he just wanted her to be a good boat that would row well and tow well. (The blades of the oars were to be painted a faded red-lead color, to render them a bit too conspicuous to tempt the unauthorized borrower.)

It was obvious that Mr. Parsons understood completely how he was going to use his new boat, and for once, I had few questions or comments. We merely followed his directions, using tested procedures, designed the A-frame bowsprit to be readily removable, and called for the usual mizzen chainplates and maststep, but not the mizzen unit itself.

From the start, Parsons envisioned making Padanaram his homeport and sailing as often as possible, and every year he signed on a boatboy to be his sailing companion and steady summer crew. At various times my sons Kinny, Tommy, and Waldo, Jr., each had this rewarding assignment.

Like my father, Parsons believed in being rowed to and from *Polaris,* rather than using the yacht club launch. From her dinghy he could admire at leisure the ever-changing shapes that *Polaris* assumed at different angles of approach and departure. Once aboard *Polaris,* setting the main, casting off the mooring, and hoisting the self-tending jib were simple routines for Parsons and his crew. Soon *Polaris* was on her way out the harbor channel. She had just the right spread of canvas to assure a light, steady feel to the helm and a fast, yet comfortable, close fetch across the bay.

As *Polaris* slipped along, there were few sailing chores to interrupt the progress of the ship, and often enough Parsons would bring up the name of a well-known writer and thus slide easily into his favorite subject, classical prose and poetry. For my sons these literary sessions shed exciting new light on what had once been labored schoolroom topics.

For the broad reach back to Padanaram, Parsons often handed the helm to the boatboy and went below to his berth for what he liked to call "a few blessed moments of complete relaxation." I can't help imagining the sunlight as it must have filtered through the skylight overhead onto the cabin paneling—or the water as it slid under the hull and made its own special music.

Once within the breakwater, Parsons again took full charge of *Polaris*, shot the mooring, and helped snug her down for the night. Within a few minutes, he was back ashore and heading home for dinner with his wife.

Just about perfect! If *Polaris* had been any bigger, she would have needed more manpower, more sail, a heavier anchor and gear. Any smaller, and she would have lacked both range and the comforts Parsons insisted upon and deeply appreciated. Any less of a performer, and she'd have failed to provide her master with the exhilaration he cherished. And, according to my son Tommy, if she had been any less well maintained, she could not have been moored in such close proximity to *Java*, Captain Hardy, or my father.

iii

Concordia #57, *Javelin*, has been a valued member of W. Mason Smith's family for twenty-eight years, and she seems to be headed for many more years of the same. Perhaps Mason's satisfaction with her has something to do with the earlier boats in his life.

Mason (along with his two older sisters) apparently caught the boating fever in 1924, when his parents began spending their summers in Mattapoisett. His first boat was one of a class of twelve 14-foot dinghies that had been designed and built by Abeking and Rasmussen. His next boat was a Crane Fifteen, a sleek centerboard sloop designed by Joshua Crane and built by Lawley around 1912, in which he sailed to his heart's content and raced at will in a Mattapoisett handicap class. Several years later Mason acquired the Herreshoff-built *Wahoo*, one of at least eleven Fish Boats then actively sailing and racing in Buzzards Bay.

At about the same time, Mason began crewing on J. Lewis Stackpole's Burgess-designed, Abeking and Rasmussen-built Ten-Meter *Astra*, along with Stackpole's son Dick and other Mattapoisett lads. *Astra*, always strikingly recognizable by her black topsides and her imposingly tall skipper, raced with conspicuous success on NYYC cruises and in local regattas for a decade. At the close of one racing season, Dick Stackpole was granted permission to take Mason and a number of his young friends off for a fall cruise aboard *Astra* and thereby to learn, among other things, how easy it is to run aground when your boat draws seven-and-a-half feet of water.

Mason Smith got equally valuable big-boat experience sailing on the 54-foot, clipper-bowed Crowninshield gaff schooner *Clione*, which his father bought during the deep Depression days of 1930. From *Clione* and her legendary boatman, Ben Waterworth, Mason learned, among countless other lessons, how to use and appreciate a Shipmate stove.

Clione was severely damaged in the 1938 hurricane. Then Mason and his young family chartered Bill Saltonstall's Concordia-designed 37-foot yawl *Arbella* whenever possible until the war intervened.

In 1947, after his release from three years aboard a destroyer-escort, Mason returned to his law practice in New York and his summer vacations in Mattapoisett. It was at this point that he and his wife came to Concordia in search of a small cruising boat. I sold them a Herreshoff-built Fishers Island Twenty-three, which became the Smiths' first *Javelin*. For eleven years Mason, his wife, his son, and his daughter sailed this *Javelin*, and in doing so learned how to obtain and enjoy basic comforts in a boat of great appeal but with modest cabin area.

It was in the fall of 1957 that Mason, with encouragement from a maturing family and an expanding law practice, decided that the time had come to own the cruising boat of his dreams. And so he returned the Fishers Island Twenty-three to us as part payment for a new Concordia yawl.

To me the Smiths are a family who have developed a very special understanding of the simple arts that are so important for genuine and lasting boating enjoyment. They have demonstrated that the thoughtful accomplishment of a well-considered seafaring routine is often more remarkable and rewarding than glamorous exploits or any profusion of shore-side amenities.

As a good omen for *Javelin*'s future, she is being actively sailed more and more by Mason Smith, Jr., and his children, thus making her another three-generation Concordia.

iv

Dr. Graham Pope, a surgeon from Boston's North Shore whom we had the good fortune to meet through Fenwick Williams, has owned, sailed, and cruised Concordia #14, *Saxon*, for thirty-four years as of this writing. What's more, he has, since his retirement to Wiscasset, Maine, some fifteen years ago, maintained the boat himself and done the whole job beautifully. With the help of a Volkswagen engine he operates his own marine railway. With the help of a self-made derrick he steps his own spars. In fact, Graham does everything, including painting, varnishing, and, at times, helping other boat owners.

Graham's wife and *Saxon*'s first mate, Alice, suggests that no sailor would work so much and with such satisfaction on a boat that lacked those qualities that both gratify the senses and give a pride of accomplishment and ownership. But I don't mean to indicate that the Popes enjoy *Saxon* only by working on her. On the contrary, they live year-round in one of the finest cruising areas in the world and know well how to make the most of the privilege. When the spirit moves them, they feel justly confident to venture farther afield, knowing that they need seldom be at the mercy of small problems or employ the services of another boatyard. Maintenance can be a curse to many, but the Popes are living proof that it can be a rewarding operation for others.

v

Tom Hale, whom I knew some years back as a Beetle Cat sailor, bought Concordia #4, *Actaea*, in 1953. Having in mind family sailing, he let us put back her original yawl rig. Naming her *Windseye*, Tom sailed and cared for her long enough to allow him and his wife to raise six children and train them into a fine crew. In fact, two of his boys caught the boat malady so completely that they remained with their father on Martha's Vineyard in a boat business much like Concordia's.

vi

In 1957 two Padanaram sailing friends, Charles Glover and John Bullard, worked out a unique, if potentially hazardous, agreement whereby they became equal partners in the purchase of the two-year-old Concordia yawl #35, *Scone*. They changed her name to *Memory* and then shared her according to a special schedule: first for so many months on Buzzards Bay, where John's permanent home is Nonquitt, and then for so many months on Chesapeake Bay, where Charlie's permanent home is on the Wye River.

As matters worked out, the partnership delightfully widened and lengthened the annual cruising horizons for both owners. Only one difficulty developed. The system necessitated sometimes arduous trips down Long Island Sound and along the Jersey shore. To eliminate this inconvenience, John in 1965 sold his half-interest in *Memory* to Charlie and bought a new sistership, Concordia #100, which he christened *Haven*. By swapping boats at agreed-upon times, they could continue their varied cruising in familiar boats, but without having to undertake time-consuming offshore passages.

Things have, of course, changed a bit in the twenty-nine years since the partners first bought *Memory*, but both of them, I am proud to observe, are

still enjoying their boating aboard Concordia yawls, sharing each one in quite different but complementary areas.

Charlie tells me that *Memory* moors right off his house and dock in a snug Wye Island cove. From early April to late December he and his wife Ginnie are free to set sail at a moment's notice for any one of twenty or so nearby quiet anchorages, something that has become quite impossible during the summer in Buzzards Bay. According to Charlie, the Chesapeake's shallow waters have not seriously limited his sailing, even with 5 feet 8 inches of draft. He does make sure to have a good kedge anchor, however, and a dinghy from which to set it. But the Bay bottom is mostly soft mud, and with a keel that's deeper aft than forward, it is not difficult to swing a Concordia's bow around and into good water. A straight keel of even less draft can present more of a problem.

Memory is undoubtedly a little under-canvased for summer sailing on the Chesapeake, but her divided rig can come in very handy in the Bay's infamous sudden squalls.

The Bullards aboard *Haven* have had from the start to settle on several compromises, especially as to space. Both parents are tall, both sons grew taller, and both daughters did their best. John has had to adjust himself to accept Concordia's position that the luxury of being able to see ahead all day from a seated position at the helm is more important than being able to stand momentarily upright in the cabin while pulling on trousers. And as to extra bunks, John has concluded that a portable one- or two-berth arrangement in an awning-covered cockpit is preferable to overcrowding the four berths below.

With *Haven* moored within rowing distance of their dock, John and Kay make a long season of it and get in a great deal of weekend cruising, as well as a bit of local racing, some of it on weekday evenings and with light sail limitations. In August their vacation plans usually bring them to Maine, a luxury that owners of boats with fin keels, spade rudders, and unprotected propellers have learned to take with some caution. Even without the hazards of lobster traps, Down East cruising is not for everyone. But Maine, Nova Scotia, and Newfoundland present very enticing goals for boats like Concordia yawls that can take the round trip in stride.

I wish I could continue on about daysailing and family cruising in various Concordias, but I have to stop somewhere—and perhaps I've already overstated the point that, with temporary or minor modification, Concordia yawls can be enjoyed in countless ways and by sailors both old and young. In fact, the more I think about it, versatility may well be the strongest and most valuable asset of the Concordia class.

Concordia Thirty-nine yawl #35 *Memory*. Owned jointly by John C. Bullard and Charles C. Glover at the time this picture was taken, she has proven equally at home in Buzzards Bay and Chesapeake Bay waters.

18
Far Horizons

i

From the start, several underlying circumstances have encouraged venturesome Concordia yawl owners to dream of far horizons. The very fact that their boats were built in Germany has automatically given them a practical base of operations in Europe. More important, perhaps, the ocean-racing accomplishments of their class members have spread comforting assurance to others planning offshore expeditions.

Ray Hunt became Concordia's first foreign traveler when in 1955 he raced his *Harrier* in England before she was shipped to the United States. George Nichols with *Magic* followed a similar path a year later, although he spent his first season cruising the waters of Norway, Sweden, and Denmark. In both cases Abeking and Rasmussen carried out all the necessary details of spring outfitting as well as the final ship-to-America procedures that were part of all contracts. The U. S. Customs added monetary inducements for this sail-first, ship-later program by charging a reduced import duty based on the used, rather than new, status of the boat.

David Austen took cruising abroad an additional step, when he bought Concordia #93, *Eden*, in 1962. At the time of his purchase he had been working for a French branch of an American corporation and was living in Paris. His dream was to get off on a boat of his own and, with two or three crew mates, spend several years voyaging: into the Baltic, then to England, Scotland (for salmon fishing), and Ireland, on to Spain and Portugal, and finally into the Mediterranean before sailing via the traditional Caribbean route back to his American homeport in Massachusetts. It was great for us

Winnie of Bourne in the trough of a sea.

259

that a Concordia Forty-one fitted so well into his rather ambitious plans. There were but few modifications that he deemed desirable.

As events turned out, David never had the opportunity to complete his original plans. Nonetheless, as a member of the Royal Norwegian Yacht Club, he did enjoy six summers of sailing in Scandinavian waters, and his boat did receive seven years of excellent winter care from the beautifully run Walsted Boatyard on the island of Thuro, three miles from Svendborg.

In 1970 David wrote me about selling his boat. I, of course, had never seen her, but using the information he sent me, I had no serious reservations about recommending her to potential buyers. My friend Robert Bacon had already inquired about a Concordia Forty-one, to replace his smaller Lawley Weekender, and between us we soon dreamed up a deal based on mutual faith, whereby he put up the money necessary for purchase, duty, and shipment, and I agreed to give it all back to him, if he didn't find *Eden* satisfactory when she arrived in Padanaram.

There were no surprises or disappointments. *Eden* looked just great, as expected. And now, fifteen years later, and with her name changed to *Phantom,* she continues to look as fine as ever, and gives me joy each fall when she returns to Padanaram for winter lay-up.

ii

Even as Ray Hunt was making plans for his English racing campaign in *Harrier* in 1955, two dynamic Concordia owners who had already sailed their yawls in American waters were shipping their boats back to Europe. They were doing so at the invitation of the Royal Swedish Yacht Club, which had invited them to join in its 125th anniversary festivities.

Miss Rose Dolan of Philadelphia was one of these yawl owners. Petite in stature, she possessed a grand and venturesome spirit. During World War I she had been a leader in the famous Red Cross Ambulance Corps. During World War II she engaged in underground activities for her beloved France and paid the penalty by spending several years in Baden Baden as a German prisoner of war. Her favorite nephew told me later, and with tongue in cheek, that this unfortunate experience for her had been a fine turn of luck for him. Aunt Rose, he said, could not get her hands on her money while imprisoned, and so saved the wherewithal to buy good boats in the years to come.

We had first met Miss Dolan in 1950, as a summer resident of Newport, Rhode Island, and as a charterer of small cruising boats. By the fall of 1953 she had ordered Concordia yawl #21—and then, quite contrary to my humanitarian instincts and customary practice, she persuaded me to let her nephew draw up for her what I considered a most impractical cabin

A grand and venturesome spirit—Rose Dolan, at the wheel of the schooner *Defiance*, about 1960. She owned the Concordia yawl *Crisette* before *Defiance* and the Concordia Forty-one *Sea Hawk* afterwards.

arrangement. His design meant that she would sleep in a cramped cubby up forward, while her crew would fare better aft in a location that controlled the galley.

For the first season, and to get acquainted with her new boat, which she had named *Crisette*, Miss Dolan confined her cruising to local waters. The second year she shipped *Crisette* to Sweden, and I wish I could tell that story, but in fact don't have the necessary details. All I am sure of is that she organized her own amateur crew for the summer, had a delightful time of it in the Baltic, and was, while passing under a bridge, hailed from above by an unknown voice sending words of admiration to *Crisette* and greetings to Waldo.

Back in New England the following season and at my suggestion, Miss Dolan made arrangements to hire Captain Pete Culler to help her manage the boats and boating programs that were to come. She expected to keep on the move, and most certainly did. Besides her daysails out of Newport and her frequent short and long cruises, she became much interested in racing, and participated in many local regattas, and in the annual cruises of both the New York Yacht Club and Maine's Northeast Harbor Fleet.

In fact, she became so intrigued with competitive sailing that in 1957 she asked Concordia to design and build for her a modern racer of keel/centerboard design. This would have been an interesting bit of business for us, but the Rule approach to boat design worried me. This being the case, Pete Culler, with a hearty second from me, suggested to Miss Dolan that she go to our mutual friend Aage Nielsen. He had already been successfully designing these types, and he drew up for her a 39-footer that had much the same dimensions and rig as *Crisette*, but additionally incorporated the go-fast, rate-low features that she wanted. Paul Luke in Maine did a fine job of building this *Pellegrina*, and Miss Dolan enthusiastically ventured into the current swim of racing for the next several years.

In 1960 Miss Dolan sold *Pellegrina* and had Paul Luke build for her the 45-foot, shoal-draft, Murray Peterson-designed coasting schooner *Defiance* in which she cruised extensively, including a summer cruise on the Baltic, with Norris D. Hoyt as guest captain. (Pete Culler was on leave that summer.)

Although she was not always the easiest person to work for, Miss Dolan was a wonderful character, and made a life of boating possible and practical for herself and her friends by learning how to acquire and hold on to the very best of professional skippers. Probably making life interesting and active for them was one of her secrets.

Pete Culler not only knew when, where, and how to cruise, but was himself an excellent ship's carpenter, rigger, engine man, and, in an emergency, cook. Tom Waddington, who took over from Pete in 1961, was an equally versatile sailor. For many years a professional skipper in Padanaram, a charter owner and skipper both in New England and the Bahamas, and for several years writer of the *Bahama Guide*, Tom kept Miss Dolan happy and on the move for another eight years.

When Tom announced his retirement as a full-time professional skipper, Miss Dolan made a turnaround with such lightning speed and precision that I have never forgotten it. It happened in 1969. She came into my office early one morning, announced that she was going to sell *Defiance*, and could she please use the phone. Reaching Henry Huidekoper, who had for some time had his eye on *Defiance*, she asked if he still wanted to buy the boat. He said he did. With that settled, Miss Dolan immediately told me that she needed another Concordia yawl.

As it happened, Add Taylor's relatively new Concordia Forty-one #101, *Bequia*, had recently come on the market and was lying in the Concordia basin alongside *Defiance*. A quick look (*Bequia*'s accommodations plan fortuitously included a forward owner's cabin with a special wide bunk, good locker space, and other amenities), and Miss Dolan said she'd take it. She changed the name to *Sea Hawk*, hired Scott Lauermann as boatman, and, seemingly totally oblivious to passing time, was off again on another active yachting stint that lasted thirteen years, until the good Lord suddenly took Miss Dolan from us in 1983.

At her funeral services in France, it was revealed that Miss Rose Dolan had twice been awarded the Croix de Guerre and, for special services, had been given the keys to the city of Soissons. One wonderful lady she was, and I am proud to have had her as a friend, as a customer, and as an owner of two Concordia yawls.

iii

There are so many Concordias that have sailed in distant waters that I almost hesitate to choose among them. There is Ross Sibley's *Hero*, for example, whose adventures in northern European waters Mrs. Sibley wrote up so ably for Elizabeth Meyer's book *The Concordia Yawls 1938–1978**. Dick Thurber's *Whitecap* and, later, his Concordia Forty-one, *Kalua*, have cruised the Great Lakes as well as the length and breadth of the Caribbean. Milton Bergey with *Golondrina* is another Concordia owner who has done his sailing in a warm climate (and has managed for years to maintain his boat's brightwork in top shape throughout the twelve months of hot sun in the Virgin Islands). Stephen Loutrel in *Lacerta* sailed widely in

* Other very interesting, far-horizon stories have been written up by the individuals involved and appear in *The Concordia Yawl, 50th Anniversary 1938–1988.*

Arctic waters. Kennett Love in *Melinda* has sailed to Hawaii and back. In 1969, Glen MacNary in *Westray* and Dr. Hans Rozendaal in *Katrina* made transatlantic passages and carried out special missions in Europe. Some seven and eight years later, Forbes Perkins in *Goldeneye* and Robert Bass in *Madrigal* undertook similar successful voyages across the Atlantic.

But in terms of voyaging, racing, and intensive all-round use, one Concordia and one Concordia owner really stand out: *Winnie of Bourne* and John Parkinson, Jr., who for twenty years were in the forefront of every phase of Concordia yawl progress. Jack, as he was always known, was the second dynamic owner who, with Rose Dolan, shipped his boat overseas for the 1955 Royal Norwegian Yacht Club celebrations. As a champion of Concordias on and off soundings, racing and cruising, in season and out, Jack had no peer.

Urged on by Johnny West, Jack bought Concordia #11 in 1952. Naming her *Winnie of Bourne* in honor of his wife, Winifred, Jack originally intended to use the boat for modest family cruising, but soon introduced her into every worthy sort of boating I can think of.

After satisfying himself that she was "an able little vessel with a turn of speed," he demonstrated his confidence in her by making her the first Concordia yawl to enter a major ocean race. This 1954 Bermuda event was only the first for Jack and *Winnie*. Skipping the 1956 race, they took in the next four. Although never a top winner, Jack set a constructive example for others by making his passages in seamanlike fashion. With real experience prompting his moves, he went prepared with ample provisions and strong offshore gear. His crews, too, consisted of offshore sailors. The older ones were tried-and-true friends, participating essentially for the sport of it. The younger ones, including his son and their friends, shared their strength and agility while absorbing valuable lessons.* On the return trip from Bermuda in 1954 *Winnie* was saved from the wrath of a mammoth waterspout that would have run down and destroyed them all, by a good running engine that drove them barely clear just in the nick of time.

The following spring, Jack shipped *Winnie* to Sweden for a two-year stay. She was off-loaded at Göteborg, and Jack with various members of his family spent the summer revisiting the south coast of Sweden, where he had cruised before with his father. They survived the lively Royal Swedish Yacht Club celebrations and won one of the many prizes awarded in the attendant Gotland Runt race. Then before returning to Göteborg via the Göta Canal, they spent a series of days exploring the Åland Islands that lie off the south coast of Finland. According to Jack, the whole summer was rendered more rewarding in that one of their crew was a young Swedish

---

* My own son Charlie sailed back from Bermuda with Jack in 1958.

sailor who could interpret for them, and because *Winnie* was a type of boat that the local sailors understood and admired.

The following year, Jack and Winnie returned to *Winnie of Bourne* for a second summer of European cruising. They were fortunate in having as companions and crew a most able Dutch yachtsman, Ed Van Rossum, and a young sailing member of the Royal Swedish Yacht Club. Prompted to a great extent by Jack's lifelong admiration for Erskine Childers's epic spy story, *The Riddle of the Sands*, and also by Ed's knowledge of the area, Jack plotted the cruise to Amsterdam to pass across those treacherous shoals that surround the Frisian Islands: these exposed dots of land form a chain that lies several miles offshore and runs for some 150 miles down the North Sea coast of Holland. In their vicinity strong winds and great tides alternately transform stretches of rough water into great expanses of dry sand with only scattered shallow holes and channels in between. The resulting hazards quite understandably deter most yachtsmen from visiting the eerie wonders of this desolate no-man's-land. For a vivid picture of it all, I recommend the reading of Childers's great book.

Once past the excitements of the Sands, the cruise led through quiet canals and lovely countryside to its destination of Amsterdam. From there *Winnie* was shipped home to Concordia.

By 1959 Jack was quite confident that his boat was well able to go to sea, but he was beginning to worry that his own time for venturesome voyages was getting rather short, so he commenced serious planning for a long-envisaged transatlantic passage. Part of his goal was to earn the John Parkinson Memorial Trophy that he and his family had in 1952 set up within the Cruising Club of America to honor his famous and beloved father. Article I of the gift states that the "Trophy shall be in the form of a plaque, awarded to any member of the Cruising Club of America, who in his own yacht makes a transoceanic passage."

During those winter months of 1959–1960, *Winnie* received considerable attention from Concordia Company. It was an awesome thought to me that good sailors and friends were about to trust their well-being and even their lives to one of our boats. For our own account, we refastened and reframed *Winnie* throughout. While the furniture was removed between the bulkheads, Jack and I worked out a few modifications in the cabin, aimed at improving the standard layout for offshore sailing.

As a first leg for the planned passage to Lisbon, Portugal, Jack joined in the 1960 Bermuda Race. For crew he had his old friends and contemporaries Pat Outerbridge, Hugh Bigelow, and Alan Bemis. Due to the advanced age of these gentlemen, their venture was soon dubbed the Junior Cruise.

JOHN (JACK) PARKINSON, JR.

When Jack Parkinson, whose photo is above, bought *Winnie of Bourne* in 1952, he was already an old-timer in the maritime world. His forebears on both sides of the family were New Englanders and well-known seafaring folk. His father had Rotch ancestors and was thereby closely associated with the Nantucket and New Bedford whale fishery. His mother was an Emmons, whose family had in the past owned, operated, and captained Boston-based merchant sailing vessels.

While still a freshman at Harvard, Jack's father, John Parkinson, Sr., was well on his way to yachting fame, having won a season championship in the old Buzzards Bay 30-footer class. Following this notable accomplishment he went on with his brother-in-law, Bob Emmons, to make the Herreshoff sloop *Avenger*, 74 feet LOA, a racing legend by winning, among other trophies, the Astor Cup—not once, but four times. Both men took leading parts aboard *America*'s Cup boats. John was in the afterguard of *Resolute, Rainbow*, and *Weetamoe*. Not confined in any sense to local yachting, he was also one of the earliest members of the CCA and pioneered ocean-

racing events by sailing as skipper of his own little schooner *Mary Ann* and as first mate on larger boats belonging to Frank Paine and other notables.

Young Jack, my contemporary, soon became increasingly involved in the same pattern of life. He learned to sail in a Herreshoff Fifteen, cruised in the Baltic with his father in the Herreshoff-designed Fishers Island Thirty-one e-class sloop *Praxilla*, and continuously crewed for prominent yachtsmen on annual NYYC Cruises and in local regattas. Ocean events saw just as much of him. In 1927 he crossed the Atlantic on the schooner *Nicanor* to take in the season's Fastnet Race. The next year he raced to Spain and then around the Fastnet aboard a similar Alden schooner named *Mohawk.* Come 1932, he raced to Bermuda aboard *Highland Light.* And so it went, year after year. Whatever concerned boats and boating events, you name it, and Jack was probably in on it.

As war clouds gathered in 1940, he sensed conditions to come, and speedily took steps to join the Navy as a reserve officer. By signing up this early, he avoided the likelihood of shore duty and did, in fact, see action at sea well before most of his yachting friends did. Both dangerous and tough action came his way almost immediately. It included patrol, antisubmarine, and convoy duty—first in the North Atlantic, then off the coast of Africa, later in the Caribbean where enemy subs were coming right to our shore to pick off oil tankers, and, finally, out in the Pacific. Jack wrote of his extraordinary wartime experiences in a memoir, *Yarns for Davy Jones*.

John Parkinson, Sr.

His descriptions of the three great storms he survived at sea are simply unforgettable.

It may seem strange that following five years of such tough Navy duty, Jack would, at war's end, rush back into an active life of civilian boating, but this is exactly what he did and with ever-increasing concentration. Once more at the family summer home in Bourne, he bought an old Herreshoff S boat, converted her into a mini-auxiliary cruising boat, and had her rated for racing under the CCA Rule. In the ensuing competition he was outstandingly successful. In cruising with a relatively new bride, however, he found the S boat living space a bit primitive, and therefore went in search of another good sailing boat that had somewhat more accommodation. This was the birth of *Winnie of Bourne.*

Unidentified S boat passing Dumpling Rocks, bound into Padanaram Harbor. Jack Parkinson was one of many Concordia owners whose early sailing experiences included ownership of one of these famous Herreshoff racing sloops.

The Bermuda Race that year was a tough one, and Jack did not fare too well in the standings. He claimed that he made several time-consuming mistakes. First, as stormy weather built up, he himself remained too long at the helm, to the point of becoming overtired. Following compass-light failure, steering became difficult and seas came aboard that resulted in the threat of serious flooding. At this point, they lowered the small genoa and mizzen, the only sails set at the time, and then streamed astern Jack's most efficient drogue, consisting of a metal bucket and a wooden bosun's chair tied together. This combination seemed to have a neutral buoyancy that neither floated too high out nor sank too deep. It was attached to the end of a trailing anchor warp. Thus secured, *Winnie* lay nicely stern-to-wind in the heavy, short seas and sixty-mile-an-hour winds, and gave the crew the opportunity to pump the ship dry and then get for themselves some much-needed rest.

The second mistake that Jack mentioned was that he was altogether too slow in putting sail back on again after the wind commenced to abate. (With an overtired crew, this loss of time almost always seems to take place.)

After Bermuda, the next leg of the passage took them to the Azores, and with fresh southwest winds, *Winnie* made excellent time of it reaching Horta in fourteen days. Because the wind was always abaft the beam, the main was never set; some combination of winged-out jibs and genoas took its place. Unless the wind was too strong, a small genoa was poled out to windward with a spinnaker pole, while the big genoa generally filled by itself out to leeward, although on occasion this big genoa did better with the help of the second spinnaker pole. Having all the sail set forward of the mast, pulling the boat along, she practically steered herself, and problems with chafe never developed. With two headstays* there was no difficulty in setting or changing headsails, and if the wind went light the mizzen and mizzen staysail could be hoisted for extra sail power. All conditions were just about perfect for a fast and pleasant ocean sail.

The final 770 miles from the Azores to Portugal was a very different story. According to Jack, instead of the reasonable reach that he expected, the passage became the toughest beat he ever made in *Winnie* or in any other yacht. I'm glad I wasn't there, and yet I'm grateful that the boat stood up so well to the extremely bad conditions. After ten punishing days they did make Lisbon, but they were hove-to half the time, and pounding against wicked short seas and heavy headwinds the other half.

The following comments about heaving-to as written up by Jack are the

---

* The earlier Concordia yawls were all equipped with double headstays, and Jack kept his for the twin-jib sailing.

most informative ones that I have heard from any Concordia yawl owner: "I have had *Winnie of Bourne* hove-to on many occasions over the years," Jack wrote, "and found she will take care of herself in various ways with no one steering and the tiller lashed. Under mizzen alone, tiller lashed slightly to windward, she lies 45 degrees to the seas and drifts slowly sideways. Under mizzen and a small working jib, both properly trimmed, she fore-reaches slowly ahead unattended about 45 degrees to the seas. I often let her lie with no sail set when she rolls considerably, but takes good care of herself with tiller lashed, stern slightly to the seas due to windage on the mast. In a very bad gale, I stream my drogue on one hundred or more feet of anchor warp over the stern." (Lying stern-to works well with a Concordia because of its narrow, overhanging counter.)

Very few sailors really know what their boat will do under extreme conditions, so these findings of Jack's have to be most helpful and reassuring to those who own or plan to own a Concordia yawl.

This next narrative doesn't concern ocean sailing, but it is all part of the *Winnie of Bourne* saga, and it represents a very fine example of Concordia yawl versatility.

As I suggested earlier, Jack was always one to join in any racing, whether offshore or around-the-buoys. He went at it with great enthusiasm, even though his participation seldom proved to be a real threat to his top competitors. Come 1965, however, he decided to take a new tack, and he approached me one day about "jazzing" *Winnie* up for a program of serious day racing. For any tuning-up project, Ray Hunt was by far the best man we knew of to help, and a meeting with him was soon arranged.

Jack had ideas of possibly changing *Winnie*'s keel shape or the rudder, or perhaps designing a special new rig—anything to improve *Winnie* for racing. Keen as I was to see her win races, I was opposed to radical changes, partly because they got away from the standard and could thus cause confusion within a successful class. If major changes were desirable, which I stubbornly doubted, then it seemed to me that a new boat would be the best solution.

Ray Hunt had, of course, dreamed up, tried out, proved, and disproved many go-fast, rate-low procedures, and he considered each suggestion as we brought it up, and then generously explained his thinking both for and against. In the end we all agreed on the best and most practical procedures to be followed, and they were, fortunately, simple enough.

The first step was to stick with a masthead sloop rig similar to the one that *Suva* had used so successfully. It not only was efficient but was simple in its concentration on only a few sails—basically, main, genoa, and spinnaker. If these sails were of top quality and design, a good small crew

Winnie of Bourne, a most versatile boat, started life as a seven-eighths yawl, with diamond shrouds and jumper struts, the early pulpit configuration and early windlass, double headstays, split backstay, and early fixed gallows frame. She was given a masthead yawl rig in 1960. For serious 'round-the-buoys racing, *Winnie's* mizzen was left ashore, making her a sloop like *Suva* (Concordia #5) and *Absinthe* (Concordia #12). Typically, she sat low in the water because of all the cruising and ocean-racing gear normally carried aboard.

could focus its attention on trimming them correctly, and setting them quickly, all without a lot of running about to set and trim mizzens and mizzen staysails, which confuses things and definitely slows the boat down.

The next move was likewise straightforward and easy enough to accomplish, namely to limit as far as possible weight and windage aloft and on deck, and to render the bottom as smooth and free of dragging elements as we could.

With these decisions settled, Jack had Concordia remove all surplus fittings above deck and underwater, and then polish up the bottom. He also signed up two good boatboys for a steady summer racing crew. Ray undertook to line up a well-designed aluminum mast (as I remember, we supplied the one we had used on *Suva*), then to order and help tune up a new mainsail and spinnaker from Hood, and a new genoa from Owen Tory.

That summer of 1965 *Winnie* appeared at the starting lines, looking her usual unpretentious, innocent self with her painted-out brightwork and her buff decks. Only the lack of a mizzen was a hint of change. At the beginning of the season no one bothered to cover her, or pay her much attention, but after a few weeks—surprise, surprise—she suddenly became the boat to beat.

Much to the glee of many of us, good old *Winnie* had become a sailing Cinderella. Before the arrival of winter, she had won the Concordia Cup at New Bedford and at Block Island, many races off Seawanhaka and in Buzzards Bay, and one race on the NYYC Cruise. The next year she not only repeated earlier victories but added the New Bedford Whalers Race and four prizes on the NYYC Cruise. It was just wonderful! Jack was inwardly thrilled over the winnings for their own sake, and outwardly for the favorable influence they had on the Concordia class.

After enjoying these racing challenges for several years, Jack eased off on competition and drifted on towards the less taxing pattern of cruising with old friends in well-loved waters.

The last time I had the pleasure of going off with him, we picked a good spell of weather and sailed over to Newport just to see all the boats and spend the night once more in the then-quiet of Brenton's Cove. *Winnie* still had her ocean-going cabin and her day-racing rig, but Jack confided in me that he still had the Concordia berth unit and the original yawl rig safely stored in his barn, waiting to be reinstalled when the time was right.

Already, some of the treasured Parkinson gear and equipment was creeping back aboard. During breakfast I noticed that his famous baked eggs again were heated up in the little individual two-egg iron pans and that ample water for shaving, coffee, and dishwashing was kept simmering in the big old teakettle. Among such familiar friends and with the fall sun slanting in on us through the wide open hatch, it was impossible not to linger over our food, and discuss the horrors and wonders of boating life.

Although Jack died in 1973, memories of his friendly, booming voice, his many and various boating accomplishments, and his especial loyalty to the Concordia class, are still invincibly alive.

In Jack's autobiography *Yarns for Davy Jones* (New York, privately printed, 1966), which I have read and re-read, Jack says of *Winnie of Bourne*, "after thousands of miles of ocean cruising and racing through 1966, I have yet to see a yacht for which I would exchange her." After Jack's death, his widow saw to it that *Winnie* was steered into the good hands of one of Jack's favorite crew members, Will Glenn. No later than last winter I heard that *Winnie* was cruising in the Virgin Islands.

19
Quiet Harbor

It must have happened about twenty years ago, very early in the morning, and during that hectic commissioning month of May. Vaguely troubled in mind, I was still abed, drifting somewhere between wakefulness and slumber. Suddenly, quite out of the blue, a vision came to me. The picture is still very clear in my mind and even clearer as recreated for me by that fine and understanding artist Lois Darling.

The season is autumn. The time is evening. Home is on Little Green Island. Across the Sound, not a half-hour's sail away, lies Friendship Village. The church spire rises above the skyline and, all around, soft lights appear in family windows. Somewhat out to the southwest, Lighthouse Point flashes to sailors coming in from the open sea. Above hangs the crescent moon in company with Venus, the evening star.

Our cottage sits back on a grassy point that forms one side of Quiet Harbor. Inland and close by, a sloping patch of ground encourages a small garden in which grow vegetables for the inner man and flowers for the spirit.

Several oaks and an old cedar grow above high water, suggesting good wood for the building of boats, fuel for the open fire on the family hearth, and a center for the evening song of birds.

A few yards up from the water's edge stands a boathouse filled with all the gear that collects during a sailor's life. A few yards off the dock nearby floats a Beetle Cat Boat.

In deeper water a Concordia yawl swings at her mooring, a reminder of boating days gone by and a promise of more to come.

"Quiet Harbor". Pen-and-ink sketch by Lois M. Darling.

Appendixes

Appendix I

SOME CONCORDIA DETAILS

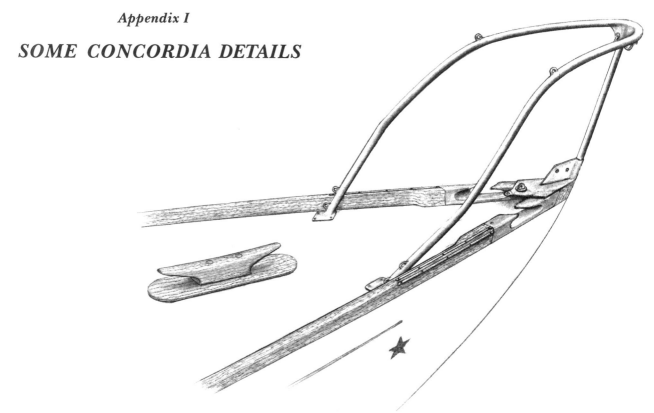

Stemhead Fitting and Pulpit

The stemhead fitting (which, among other things, incorporates the forestay chainplate and the bow chocks) is strong, handsome, and carefully designed to resist a variety of loads and to perform a variety of functions. Basic strength is achieved by extending its long tongue downward along the stemface, where it is securely fastened against the upward pull of the forestay, and by tying the bow chocks together through the stemhead fitting to distribute the stress from dock and mooring lines. Projecting vertically is a centerline flange with holes in it for the forestay turnbuckle and jib tack shackle; forward, the flange widens to become a socket for the bow pulpit. The unit also has a horizontal plate that ties together the mooring chocks and, as it extends aft, takes the jib club swivel. A jibsheet lead block is also anchored here.

The entire unit is made of bronze. The bow chock castings are well rounded, so as to minimize chafe, and large enough for a big mooring line (even when wrapped with chafing gear) or several docking lines. Note that the toerails, upon which the chocks are

mounted, have been widened to match the width of the hardware.

Concordias have locust mooring cleats (one forward and another aft) which, like the bow chocks, are very generously sized. Their shape was copied from our Norwegian-built double-ended pilot cutter *Escape* and, in section, these cleats taper inward toward the top from a wide and stable base. The horns of the cleats are shaped with plenty of space under them for lines. The cleats themselves are set on wooden chafing pads and are through-bolted to oak blocking fitted under the decking and between the deckbeams.

The bow pulpit, fabricated from bronze tubing, has three legs; two terminate as flanges through-bolted to the decking and sheer clamps, and the third one sockets into the stemhead fitting. Brazed-on eyes serve as anchor points for the lifelines, and the upper lifeline, if desired to clear the foot of the genoa, can be pulled downward and lashed to a lower eye of the pulpit. Boats set up for ocean racing generally have their running lights mounted here on the pulpit, where they

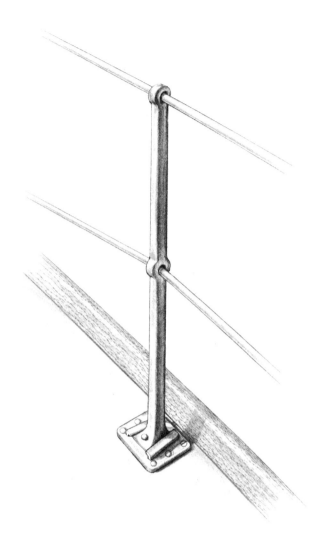

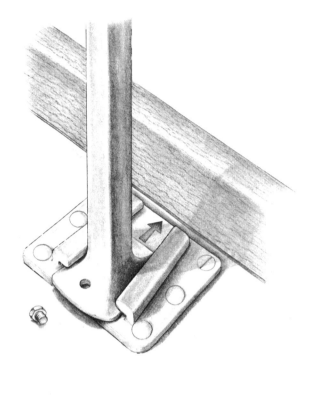

can be more easily seen, instead of on the cabinsides, where a wave or sail might hide them from view.

As far as anchoring is concerned, some boats are fitted with a snatchblock or a roller chock near the top of the pulpit. The thinking is that you can put your anchor line over the sheave, stand up comfortably, and, with the boat coming slowly ahead under power—or, if there's a breeze, under sail—take in the slack until the line is up and down. Then you shift the line down to one of the stronger bow chocks until the anchor is broken out, then back again to the pulpit. From here, you can hoist the anchor until it is washed off and all the way up. Hanging from the pulpit, the anchor can be easily grabbed, carried aft, and stowed in its place on the cabintop, or, when cruising, simply lashed to the pulpit itself.

Lifeline Stanchions

Concordia stanchions are easily removed; you simply back off the set-screws near their bases, and tap them inboard until they are free of the tapered lips of their baseplates. (You may have to slack the lifelines as well.) But, in spite of how easily the stanchions are put up and taken down, there is plenty of strength—coming primarily from the securely fastened baseplates, each of which is bolted through the deck and sheer clamp in four places and screwed down through the decking and into a backing block in two more. Thus, with six fastenings in each baseplate, and beautifully tapered cast bronze stanchions light enough to bend a little on impact (instead of throwing all their load onto the baseplate), loose and leaking stanchion bases are not a problem.

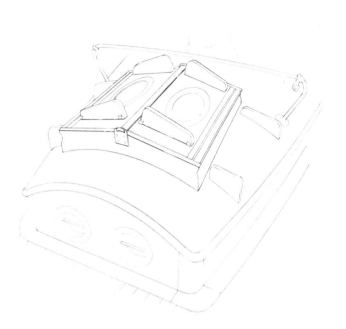
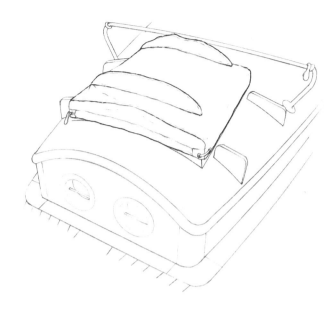

Forward Hatch

The forward hatch is certainly a very special Concordia device. Through it you can gain access to the forward cabin directly from the deck, and you can get out in an emergency (such as a fire in the galley which blocks off the main companionway). What's special is how the hatch is built: with an inner coaming and two hinged covers with fins on them, so that when they are opened, the fins land on sister fins mounted on the cabintop. You end up with a flat, seat-like surface that you can sit on, with your feet hanging down into the opening, and step from your sitting position right down into the forward cabin. There is a conveniently placed small step for this purpose on the cabin bulkhead, and the inside of the hatch has been kept clear of fittings that could snag clothing or sails as they pass through. Normal leakage through the closed covers runs into a deep gutter between the double coamings and out through scuppers cut in the outer one. At sea, with green water coming aboard, something extra is needed, and for this a fitted canvas cover with a drawstring worked into its lower edge hem assures that there will be no leaks.

The hinged covers can be held vertically open by means of two rods that fit into sockets in the fins. The rods act as support bows for a larger canvas cover with zippered flaps forward and aft. You can have either of the flaps open or shut so that you can make the hatch into a scoop and force fresh air down into the cabin; or, if it's raining, you can open only the after flap and let the exhaust air out of the cabin that way. The canvas cover also has transparent windows in the sides to correspond with the windows in the wooden covers so that you get light below. In any case, the hatch, in this mode, turns the forward cabin into a very nice space with full standing headroom, whether it's raining or clear, hot or cold.

One problem that we considered quite seriously was the locking device, that consists of a bar that goes across the peak between the covers and slides through a slotted fitting at each end. Here it can be padlocked to prevent the covers from being opened. Actually, in an ocean race, when security isn't a problem, we eliminate the bar entirely so as to not lock anyone in. The thinking is that, for an emergency escape, you just push up the hatch from below enough to slit the canvas sea-cover with your knife.

Just aft of the hatch lies the jib traveler, bowed outward at the top to allow the club-footed jib as wide a sheeting base as possible and still have the traveler mounting flanges inboard, where they can be well fastened through blocking underneath the cabintop.

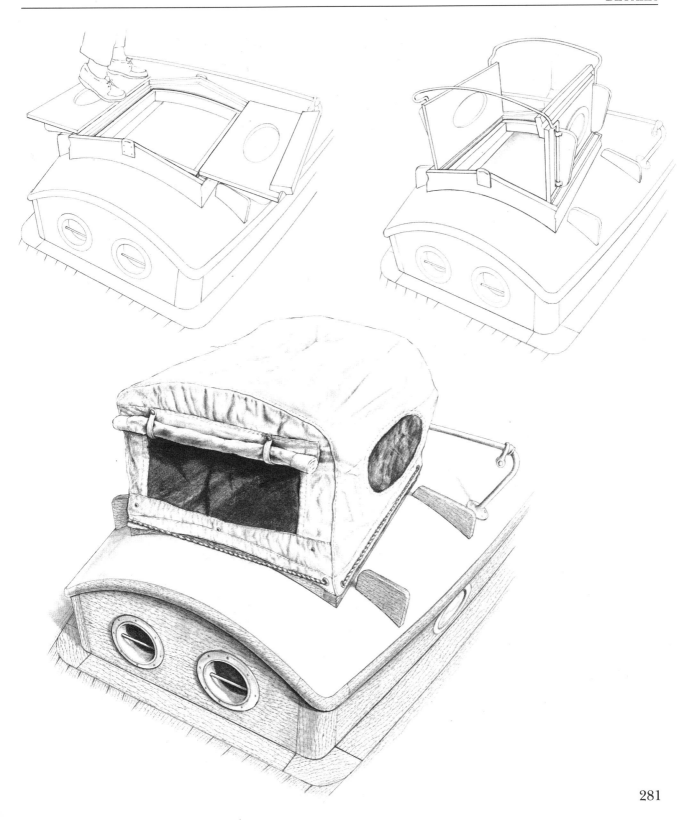

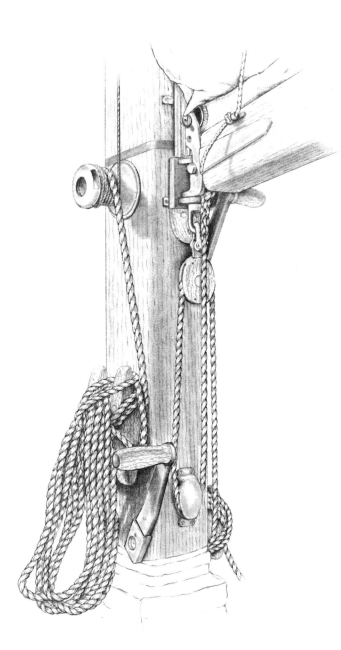

Base of Mainmast

Halyards for jib and mainsail are of wire, with rope tails. Both belay at the mast around specially shaped locust cleats, as shown, whose ends turn inward rather than upward. This tends to hold the halyard more securely, and, although the line is a little harder to get off than, say, the Concordia sheet cleat (see sketch on page 286), there is less chance of fouling clothing or stray lines. Very often a hole is bored through the cleat at its base, through which the halyard's bitter end can be rove and knotted so as not to be accidentally lost aloft. There are six cleats: two on the starboard side (mainsail and spinnaker halyard), two to port (jib and spinnaker), one forward (spinnaker pole lift), and one aft for the main boom downhaul. (There were occasional minor variations, however, as with *Thistledown*'s downhaul tackle, shown here. Most Concordias used a becket block under the boom and a cleat on the after side of the mast.)

Although later boats had main halyard winches like the one shown here, I remain of the opinion that the downhaul, not the winch, should be what puts tension in the mainsail luff. Our halyards were marked with tape to show when the sail's head was hoisted to the allowable limit as marked by a black band at the masthead. During hoisting, the downhaul is cast off so the boom can rise; then the halyard is belayed as shown, after which the downhaul tackle is tightened until the boom is brought to its black band mark (or until the mainsail has sufficient luff tension), then belayed. This results in a more even tension; upward pull—as from the halyard—may put a great tension on the upper portion of the luff, but, because of friction and gravity, very little on the lower portion.

The mainsail attaches to mast and boom with conventional track and slides, and there's a gate in the mast track at about eye level to make it easy to slip on the slides: starting with the slides nearest the bottom, you simply drop them onto the track and let them slide down one by one until they're all in place, then close the gate and hoist the sail. The boom gooseneck is also on a track—a heavier one—so that it can slide up and down, and so that the downhaul can be used as already described.

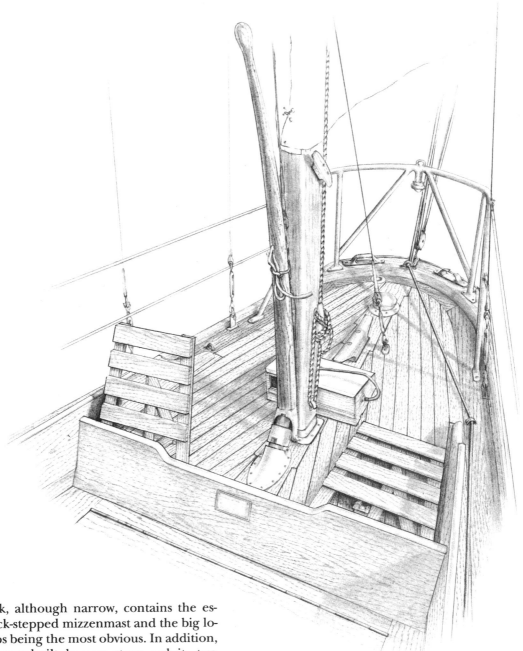

Afterdeck

The afterdeck, although narrow, contains the essentials—the deck-stepped mizzenmast and the big locust cleat perhaps being the most obvious. In addition, there is the custom-built bronze stern pulpit, two chocks (one open for convenience, one closed for security) with taffrail chafing strips aft of them, a mushroom ventilator (to provide fresh air to the space directly below), and a box-type vent hood for the required Coast Guard engine vent ducting. Both vents can be closed off in heavy weather. In port, as shown, the hinged tiller can be swung up against the mast and tied there, out of the way, thus making the cockpit more usable. For sailing or lounging, the hinged backrests can be raised, adding greatly to one's comfort; laid flat, they're made strong enough to walk on.

The mizzen is small and can be hoisted without the need of a winch (the swayhook at the base of the mast works just fine), and, so as not to interfere with the helmsman, the mizzen sheet is led forward to the port jibsheet pad where it is within easy reach of the crew, yet out of the way of guests, who'll customarily be boarding from the starboard side. (The mizzen shrouds, in fact, make good handgrabs for those agile enough to climb over the lifeline. And by hooking the tiller behind the forward mizzen shroud, the helm stays hard over—often a big convenience when you are getting underway short-handed.)

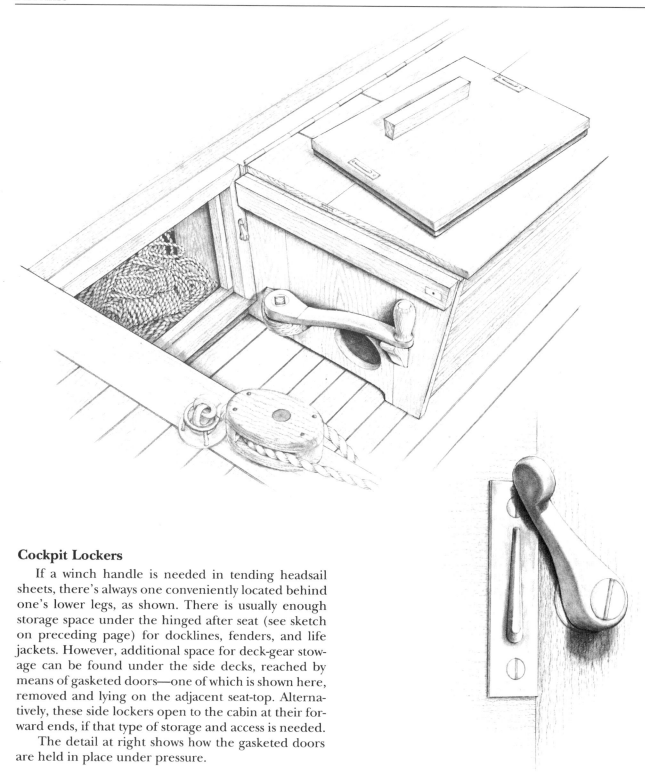

Cockpit Lockers

If a winch handle is needed in tending headsail sheets, there's always one conveniently located behind one's lower legs, as shown. There is usually enough storage space under the hinged after seat (see sketch on preceding page) for docklines, fenders, and life jackets. However, additional space for deck-gear stowage can be found under the side decks, reached by means of gasketed doors—one of which is shown here, removed and lying on the adjacent seat-top. Alternatively, these side lockers open to the cabin at their forward ends, if that type of storage and access is needed.

The detail at right shows how the gasketed doors are held in place under pressure.

284

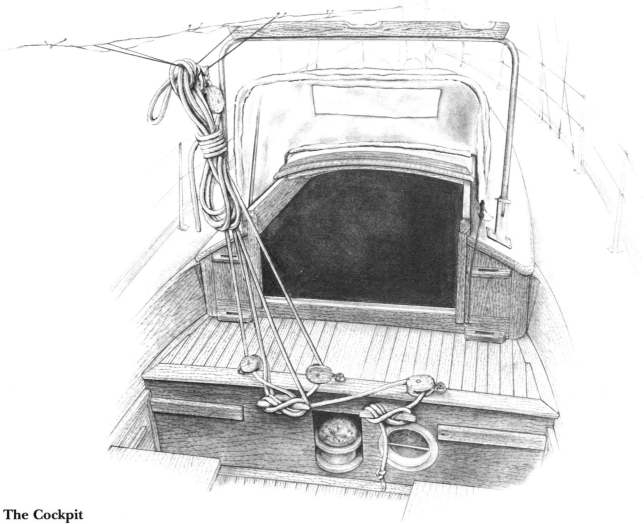

The Cockpit

Whether you are standing or sitting in a Concordia's cockpit, the advantage of the low, narrow cabin trunk becomes pleasantly obvious. You can pretty much see where you're going, even when sitting down. A wide companionway (protected, when desired, by the fold-down canvas "buggytop") helps join the cabin with the cockpit, besides letting in plenty of God's fresh air and sunlight. Although there's a bridge deck between (needed for strength), it is low enough so that climbing over it isn't a problem—and, in port, the mainsheet, rigged off to one side as shown, makes an effective handhold. The compass mounts on the bridge-deck bulkhead where it is easily seen, yet cannot foul lines, legs, or risk damage to itself. Directly over the engine next to the compass is a big opening porthole that can be left open in all but the worst weather, its function being to provide ventilation.

All sheets are within easy reach and can be worked while facing forward, either by the helmsman or crew. The upper mainsheet blocks ride on load-distributing wire bridles attached to the boom. Long-wearing, easily maintained, unfinished teak is standard for the heavily traveled bridge deck, the cockpit sole, and the seat-tops. A bronze half-oval strip protects the coaming's top edges. Because the seats are built within the cockpit's watertight boundary, any accidental leakage or spillage from the tanks they contain falls harmlessly onto the self-draining sole and overboard; the bilge pump discharges into the cockpit as well, cutting by one the number of through-hull fittings.

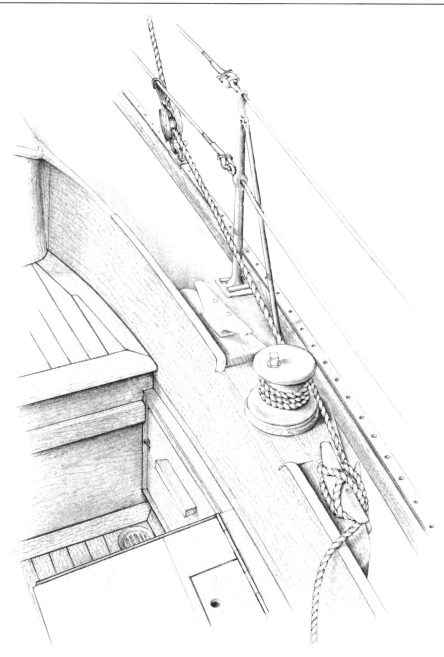

Sheet Tending

The seat-tops on both sides at the cockpit's forward end are removable, allowing more effective, forward-facing sheet tending by crew members. The headsail sheet winch is close at hand just outside the coaming, port and starboard; and the hauling part of the main-sheet lies directly ahead, also port and starboard (the mainsheet is double-ended), passing through its bridge-deck-mounted lead block in such a way that a person seated and facing forward can brace for a hard pull. Concordias are fitted with special locust sheet cleats designed so a line will easily fit underneath; in fact, they're junior versions of the deck-mounted mooring cleats already described.

Concordia Smokehead and Air Vent

Centered on the cabintop just forward of the skylight is the Abeking and Rasmussen-designed water-trap air vent of bronze, which, facing aft and coming from the highest part of the cabin, serves to pull the warm air from the living spaces and allow cool, fresh air (coming in through the companionway or cockpit port) to replace it.

A Concordia-designed bronze smokehead, patterned after the one on our pilot cutter *Escape*, comes through the cabintop (via a water-cooled deck iron) next to the vent and is connected to the coal-fired cabin heater below.

Escape also provided inspiration for the Concordia yawl's opening skylight (although *Escape*'s skylight was not original equipment, but was devised and built by Major Smyth while the boat was under Howland ownership). A fairly conventional unit, it has a heavy gut-tered member running down the middle from which two wood-framed, glass flaps (with water-shedding drip strips) are hinged. There are brass rods for protection against glass breakage, and the frame is well scuppered so that water won't pool on the glass and rot the wood around it. The skylight is low enough that a dinghy may easily be carried (turned bottom up) over it. As with the forward hatch, the skylight's sides and ends have been hollowed slightly to help in securing the drawstring of the fitted canvas sea-cover.

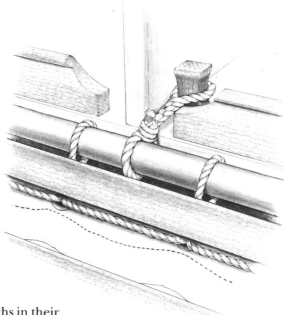

Berth-Holding Post

Holding our swing-down Concordia berths in their normal, upright position as backrests are lanyards and beautifully shaped wooden posts—one for each berth, located about halfway along its length. A similar, but lighter-duty arrangement holds the toilet-room door open and prevents the annoying click-clack of metal latches. The posts are of locust, and the ones for the berths are set into an adjacent shelf, as shown.

Locker Turnbuttons and Striker Plates

When a boat is at sea, heeled and thrashing, it needs locker doors that stay dependably shut; otherwise, life onboard risks becoming unpredictably chaotic. Locust turnbuttons whose positions are clearly visible at all times, even though basic in design, are hard to improve upon. I do feel, however, that the wedge-shaped striker plates against which the turnbuttons land make things a little better, in that (as with the lanyard-and-post arrangement described earlier) they eliminate the click-clack of the usual metal alternative. The turned, wooden doorknobs are a durable, charming, and functional companion to the turnbuttons.

Concordia Båteka
Concordia Co. Inc.   -   -   -   South Dartmouth, Mass.
★   ★   Sole Producers   ★   ★

History

"Jolly Boat," "Pram" and "Eka", as applied to boats, are all words borrowed from the Scandinavian countries. The Danish "Jolle" or yawl boat is a conventional shaped row boat with a plumb stem and of lapstrake construction. A "Pram' in Norway or Sweden may be almost any type of small

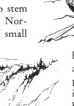

Pilot awaits steamer in Båteka

boat with squared off ends. Often it is a scow, with a flat bottom, and flat sides used for carrying purposes. The "Eka" boat is a special type of pram. She is nicely shaped and of lapstrake construction. Her bow is squared to conserve space for stowing on deck and to make her tow well. She is used by pilots, custom officials, and yachtsmen.

Pram loading hay in fjord

Qualifications Developed

She rows easily, steadily, and dryly in the manner of a first class row boat of longer dimensions. She carries her way in rough water or smooth with a crew of one or four.

She tows unbelievably well, without appreciable drag, and without shipping water, even in extreme rough conditions. She has no tendency to shear or charge in a following sea and her lapstrake construction gives her a steadying and lifting quality not to be found in a smooth sided boat.

She is not difficult to hoist on board or stow on deck and once there she does not present any large flat surface for wind or wave to attack.

She is extremely buoyant and is to be depended on to stay afloat and live under bad conditions of sea.

She is equipped with keel, skeg, and bottom rubbing strakes to withstand constant hauling on float or beach, and her light construction makes her tougher and more able to withstand shock or abuse than many a heavier boat.

She is built up to the best small boat standards of pre-war days and in appearance is a suitable adjunct to the yacht built and maintained in "Ship shape and Bristol fashion".

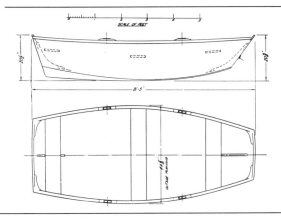

Principal Specifications

Length O. A.	8' 6"
Beam	3' 9"
O. A. depth (allowing for shear)	22"
Weight	80 lbs.
Planking	New England cedar
Keels, frames, skeg, bottom rubbing strakes	white oak
Bow and stern transoms	hard wood
Fastenings	copper

Price with pine rub guard   (   )
With special Concordia Bumper (   )
F. O. B. SOUTH DARTMOUTH
Subject to change without notice
Deposit $25.00 with order
Final payment due on delivery

Round-bottomed lapstrake prams made logical Concordia tenders, as this early brochure, illustrated by Lois Darling, explains.

289

VARIATIONS ON A THEME
Some Changes and Experiments of Particular Interest

(See also Chapter 15, where the Concordia yawls *Eden, Malay,*
***Banda I, Banda II,* and *Suva* are more generally discussed.)**

Modifications to *Malay* and Other Concordia Yawls for Ocean Racing

Just as around-the-buoys racing had led the way to preferred cabin arrangement plans, so ocean racing added its own positive contributions to the final evolution of a Concordia's details.

Going to sea seems to be an infallible way of finding out the weaknesses and deficiencies in a boat as well as its virtues and strengths. Fortunately for the Concordias, desirable and needed seakeeping modifications were neither numerous, difficult, nor especially expensive. Hull and rig were basically finest-kind. Cockpit size and arrangement,* water capacity and tank distribution, lifelines and lights, hull and cabin construction—all passed both Rule and commonsense requirements. No special problems were involved in acquiring and positioning the specified equipment.

However, better provision for keeping man and his materials dry below, and at the same time providing them with essential fresh air, did need extra and thoughtful attention if the crew were to have any comfort for rest or ambition for racing. Dan Strohmeier, with his usual ingenious efficiency, was one of the first to develop seagoing improvements, on *Malay.* We continued on from there, with other early ocean racers helping to work out their choice of details, until a somewhat standard pattern evolved, one that could benefit seagoers and weekenders alike.

To prevent possible forehatch or skylight leaks, we relied on the conventional white canvas covers with translucent plastic panels. These were lashed securely in specially grooved coamings and served well to keep water out and let light in. The design of our forehatch

---

* On the chance of filling, cockpits could not be so big as to cause a dangerous weight situation.

permitted an emergency exit through it, if necessary, by pushing up one of the hinged covers sufficiently to slit the canvas with a knife.

The necessity and desirability of opening and closing the main hatch presented a more complex situation. A standard type of folding canopy worked well as a spray deflector and cook protector, but any heavy water rushing aft along the top of the cabinhouse tended to slosh up under a partially opened hatch. Our solution to this was a carefully fitted bronze cover, under which the companionway hatch could slide, and over the after end of which the folding canopy (buggy top, we called it) could be securely fastened. Such an item could be very expensive, but the cost for us was reasonable because, with only two or three exceptions, all Concordia hatches were of one size. This made it possible for Abeking and Rasmussen's very skilled metal shop accurately to make up a number of covers at one time and over a single mold.

As part of the plan, this bronze cover served a second and very important purpose. It tolerated the stern of a dinghy or other equipment that otherwise would have had to be kept clear of the sliding hatch. In essence it lengthened our usable housetop by several feet.

Our port and starboard under-deck cockpit lockers, which sometimes leaked in rail-down weather, were a third troublesome area. Since their long, narrow spaces could be readily reached from below, we got into the habit of screwing their vertical gasketed cockpit doors closed for any ocean passage.

Adequate ventilation below was very simply aided by installing a Dorade-type water-baffled box at the forward end of the cabinhouse, thus allowing the two standard forward ports to be left open. The baffled ventilator over the toilet room amidships needed no changes, and a metal, eyebrow-type cover over the cockpit port made that usable except in extremely stormy weather. Under sailing conditions, with the buggy top acting like a big chimney, fresh air tended to drop down through the cockpit port, and be drawn aft from the forward ventilator, then up and out the main hatch.

In addition to improvements in watertightness and ventilation, there were a few very simple but helpful alterations worked out for better living at sea. It was not a big or expensive job to modify a standard Concordia yawl for ocean racing.

As a final comment, I'd like to refer to Dan Strohmeier again. He told me what one of his later crew members, a hot young dinghy racer, said: "I had no idea how easy it was to race a boat like *Malay*."

Modifications to *Eden* for Ocean Cruising

To make for effective shortening of sail in boats with the standard double-spreader masthead rig, and in order to reinforce the standard mast against storm conditions, it was necessary only to add an inner headstay and two running backstays, all three terminating at the upper spreaders. This made the use of a short mainsail and small staysail both efficient and practical.

On deck, we had but to supply equipment that was found useful for ocean racing, such as special ventilation, bronze hatch cover, gallows frame, extra bilge pump, etc.

Below decks, the bulkheads were held to their standard locations, but the arrangement of bunks, shelves, and lockers was custom designed to accommodate a mixed crew, some of whom might well live aboard for extended periods, both in port and at sea. Basically, the forward cabin contained a double berth and large stowage bin with dresser top cover opposite; also provision was made for a Root berth above the bin. The washroom became full width with door forward and door aft. The main cabin, in addition to a conventional transom seat to port, had a special built-in pilot berth to starboard that could be made narrow at sea or wide in port.

To provide extra precautionary strength to the hull, Abeking and Rasmussen fabricated and installed three galvanized-steel angle frames that started at the keel and went up the sides, then across the hull under the deck. One was located at the forward end of the cabinhouse, one at the after end, and a special one in the area of the mast, that followed up the cabinhouse sides and across the underside of its top.

Modifications to *Banda I* for Day Racing

There were several factors to consider as we planned alterations to *Banda I*'s rig. As for the actual masthead fitting detail, we gave it a great deal of thought. An obviously important objective, besides strength, was to design all fittings in such a way as to allow for the longest possible luff length between the two measuring points for the headsail: that is, the intersection of headstay and mast aloft and the intersection of headstay and deck alow. To reach this goal, most designers then (and more so now, using aluminum spars) called for double sheaves in the masthead, one for the jib, one for the main. I have always felt (with some experience to back it up) that the double-sheave arrangement has more drawbacks than advantages. It necessitates a wide masthead, unless narrow sheaves for wire only are used. Yet, with all-wire halyards, reel winches are necessary. On a small boat like ours, it is much quicker and more foolproof to hoist a sail hand-over-hand using a wire halyard with a rope tail. This is especially true of a jib you may need to set or lower quickly.

For these reasons, and for a fair, chafe-proof lead, I prefer a jib halyard that hoists through a specially made metal block that has a grooved sheave for both rope and wire and hangs from a strap running over the top of the mast. To be sure, this system does lose a few inches of potential jib hoist. But when I discussed the matter with sailmaker Ted Hood, he agreed that the head of a genoa does, in any case, need a little leeway to clear the mast.

Whatever the conclusions, I stuck with a jib halyard block (Abeking and Rasmussen made good ones with galvanized-steel shell and bronze sheave) and, to gain back some lost luff length, we worked on two other procedures. One of these was to get the sailmaker to make his wire eyesplices (jibs in those days had wire luff ropes, not tapes) to be just within the head of the sail, instead of above it. The second was to supply a special short jib tack shackle that came right to the stem fitting. This eliminated the need for the usual 5-inch swivel-type snap shackle.

For a mainsheet, I favored our bridge-deck lead, but Bill Stetson (*Banda*'s owner) was probably right that for a sloop with a long boom, a stern-deck trim with only the hauling part leading forward and down to the bridge deck was better.

Because a taut headstay on a masthead rig puts more strain on a permanent backstay, Abeking and Rasmussen designed a below-deck bolt, which extended from the deck fitting down through the stern knee.

Modifications to *Banda II* for Day Racing

Bill specified an iron rather than a lead keel for *Banda II*, not because of personal preference or cost, but because the rating would be about .7 foot lower.

For *Banda II*'s sail plan he retained Hunt's latest *Harrier* rig, which had a mainsail with a 40-foot hoist and 20-foot foot (the 2-to-1 ratio that carried no Rule penalty for high aspect ratio). Because the mast was to be in the standard location and because the pending Rule modifications to penalize large foretriangles were not to take effect until 1960, Bill decided to use the 2 1/2-foot bowsprit he had saved from *Banda I*.

Modifications to *Suva* to Establish the Final Concordia Rig

In reviewing with Fenwick Williams the previous standard sail plans and rigs, from the earliest to the most recent, there really had not been many basic changes. We had just stuck to the yawl rig, the same mast location, and the same stemhead seven-eighths foretriangle.

The original 1938 sail plan, adhered to for fifteen years, dimensioned the mainsail at a 42-foot 8-inch hoist, a 19-foot foot, and the genoa luff at 36 feet. By 1954 we had become more race- and rating-minded, and, starting with yawl #24, we had modified the original sail plan by shortening the mast about 30 inches. The mainsail hoist was thus reduced to 40 feet 8 inches. (By using a Rule-permitted painted mastband instead of the centerline of the halyard sheave for a

top measurement, we saved 6 inches of rated hoist.) The mizzen remained substantially unchanged (hoist 18 feet 6 inches, foot 8 feet 3 inches.) Although the jibstay was lowered 1 foot on this shorter mast, details were altered to permit the use of the same 36-foot luff genoa.

Along with the reduction in mast height came an effort to lessen windage and weight aloft. The diamond shrouds were therefore removed and their side support for the top of the mast was taken care of by widening the angle between the jumper struts from 90 to 100 degrees. This 1954 plan also established, once and for all, certain details that we had learned by trial and error. Both Father and Jack Parkinson had been fouled up by jib hanks crossing over from one double headstay to the other, so a single headstay became standard. Likewise, other owners besides Sears had found the divided permanent backstay troublesome, so this became a single stay running right to the deck, only offset enough to clear the mizzenmast and boom.

As to early rig changes on deck, there had been only two of any significance. It had gradually become apparent that the original jib club traveler was not wide enough to permit an efficient trim, and that its bowed shape tended to worsen the problem by binding the traveler block before it reached its maximum slide to leeward. The problem was easily corrected in 1953 by just flattening and lengthening the traveler. Once we canted the two traveler legs outboard, no change in their foot fastenings to the cabintop was necessary.

Likewise, the position of our long genoa sheet track had been found to be too far inboard for efficient trimming of the big genoa, so in 1954 we moved it outboard about 5 inches to the very edge of the deck.* This improved track location exactly fitted in with the 1960 CCA Rule limitation for headsails. The longest-footed genoa that could be used (150 percent

---

* With the track's new position it was no longer possible to bolt it down through the structural shelf, and we all know that having screws down through the edge of the sheerstrake is unsatisfactory. A rather expensive under-deck angle bar had to be designed to not only accept the track through-bolts but also be bolted to the frames. It was worth the extra expense, however, because the new track position not only made a perfect genoa sheet lead but also relocated the toerail upon which it was mounted farther outboard, making the usable deck 5 inches wider.

of foretriangle base) without penalty sheeted with greatest efficiency at a point right on this track. Furthermore, this point came about 2 feet ahead of the after end of the cabinhouse—a perfect location in relation to the standard strongly anchored genoa sheet winches. The genoa sheet could thus lead in an almost straight line from genoa clew to winch, with just a slight downward dip to pass through the snatch block or fairlead on the track. In this way there was practically no friction from the block, there was no reversing in the sheet's direction with resulting double strain on the block or track, and no possible way of any calamitous slingshot action.

From 1954 until the time of our present *Suva* conference, only a few minor changes had taken place. In 1957 Fenwick had, without losing sail area, saved us a slight mizzen staysail penalty. He modified the mizzen masthead assembly so that the existing mizzen sail, boom and all, could be raised 6 inches higher on the mast, where its head was marked with a black band. The measured hoist of the mizzen staysail was at the same time lowered by replacing the block at the masthead with a lignum vitae bull's-eye at a point exactly opposite to the head of the mizzen (at the black band). This not only accomplished its aim of eliminating the small rating penalty but improved and simplified the rig. The higher mizzen boom permitted the permanent backstay to move aft some inches and thus give the mainmast better support, and the bull's-eye for the mizzen staysail halyard saved the weight and cost of a block aloft. In other words, we gained efficiency along with simplicity, and saved some expense as part of the bargain. This was the kind of modification we were always seeking.

Two more rig details were finalized on the 1957 sail plan. *Harrier*-type backstay runner chainplates, specified on a few boats, were eliminated for good in favor of the original type of backstay fittings consisting of slides on the long genoa sheet track. A brief era of trimming the mainsheet to the afterdeck came to an end, in favor of the original bridge-deck location.

It was becoming apparent that in the best interest of the Concordia class, some racing modifications resulted in improvements and should therefore be retained, while others had disadvantages and should be dropped.

Besides consulting these earlier standard sail plans, we studied an experimental masthead plan for the Concordia Standard Thirty-nine yawls. This rig was originally tried out in 1959 on yawl #75, William Okie's *Land's End*, and then the year after on three new standard yawls, #79, *Westray*, #80, *Golden Eye*, and #81, *Kypris*. After watching these four boats in action for a season we came to the conclusion that the masthead rig was good, but that the total sail area was a little on the short side. (We refer the reader back to page 182 for discussion on final sail plan measurements.)

Appendix III

BEETLE CAT CARE

Adapted from text by Leo J. Telesmanick

Storage

Storage under cover, with the boat right-side up on bare ground, is best done with 2-inch blocks under the keel, one just ahead of the centerboard trunk and the other approximately under the middle of the skeg with supports chocked under the bilges to keep the boat upright.

If a boat must be left outside, turn her over, keeping her high off the ground and in the shade. Cover the hull with canvas or perhaps a simple tarpaper roof. Before the hot spring sun opens the seams, she should be turned right-side up.

Centerboards will stay straighter if left right in the boat. Rudders should not be stored in a hot or dry place, but stood upright in a cool, moist area where the air reaches both sides equally.

Spars can be placed on racks or blocking on the floor so as to be supported in two or three places. The sun should not beat directly on them.

Commissioning

Topsides—An extremely good sanding is necessary for a smooth job. Putty bulging from the seams should be sanded off with sandpaper over a block (1/0 sandpaper is perhaps best). Any loose putty in seams or screw-holes should be removed. Don't be afraid to sand. A flat paint can now be applied or, if a color other than white is desired, a thinned coat of that paint can be applied. After a prime coat, any holes can be filled—either with a seam compound, which will not harden solid, or with a trowel cement, which will.

If the seams of a boat are open due to drying out and shrinking of the planking, seam compound rather than trowel cement should be used, since it will squeeze out when swelling occurs. If a boat is in fairly good shape, and the few bare spots are spot-painted, one full coat of flat and one coat of semigloss will look good. If there's a lot of bare wood to cover, two coats of flat will be required under the semigloss. A full-gloss paint is not desirable.

Bottom—Preparation is the same as above. The same compound or cement can be used, even if a different color. Two coats of antifouling bottom paint will be best, with the last one applied very close to the launching time. The centerboard should be lowered and the trunk's interior well painted at least up to the waterline (about eight inches up from the keel), using a rag or sponge on a stick.

The standard Beetle has an antifouling copper paint made by International Paint Co., which is not a hard-finish paint. There are hard-finish copper paints, however, that can be buffed after application. One paint now being used by many is Woolsey's "Vinelast," which can really be polished smooth. However, in many cases, it should be applied directly to the bare wood, since it often acts as a solvent to oil-based paint (although we have found that where the original copper paint has aged enough, there is no unfavorable result when Vinelast is applied).

Deck—As little paint as possible should be applied here, since repeated coats of paint cause the canvas to crack. Give the deck a light sanding with 2/0 paper and apply a coat of deck paint, perhaps thinned down a little.

Cockpit—Give a good sanding with 1/0 sandpaper, and paint one coat.

Bilge—Many owners paint the forward part of the bilge under the deck. This is a practical idea, although not necessary every year or even every two.

Brightwork—An extremely good sanding with 2/0 sandpaper is necessary to get the top surface clean and smooth. The worn spots should perhaps be sanded down to new wood and spot-varnished twice before applying at least two coats of good spar varnish. Sand lightly between coats.

294

Spars—These should have a good sanding and have at least two coats of varnish each year. Don't be afraid to sand heavily for the first coat, but lightly thereafter.

Rigging—The bronze turnbuckles and rigging blocks should be oiled annually. To renew running rigging, use Dacron of 1/4-inch or 5/16-inch diameter. The following information is helpful for establishing required lengths:

      Throat—40'
      Peak—45'
      Sheet line—46'
      Bridle—42"

At Concordia, we do spars first, usually in the late fall. During the winter we paint the deck and cockpit one coat, and varnish the brightwork with two coats, leaving the topsides and bottom until nearer the launching time. However, some yards complete the topsides in the fall or winter and do all but the final coat on the bottom, since they have ideal conditions— the boat neither swells nor dries out while in storage.

Virtually unchanged since the 1920s (this photo was taken in 1928), Beetle Cats have been in nearly continuous production, with well over three thousand built as of January 1988.

Appendix IV

PAINTING A CONCORDIA YAWL

A good paint and varnish job requires both skill and favorable weather conditions. Nick Demers and his crew had the skill. And even when the weather did not cooperate, they did the best they could, using a reasonable day for sanding, a better one for the flat coat, and a good morning for the semigloss. Afternoon dampness always shows up by two or three o'clock, and a glossy coat of paint almost invariably goes flat if it has not set by mid-afternoon. The sign painter, who took care of lettering the name and hailing port on each boat's transom, was one more time-consumer, because he needed, first, to be available, then to have good weather, and finally to have a good scaffold to stand on, before he could even start. And, of course, there had to be a finished hull for him to work on.

Varnished cabinsides and trim (or a varnished hull, for that matter) have always been optional. They are a joy to look at, and, on some yachts and for some owners, they are more than worth the additional cost. However, brightwork does require extra time and special weather conditions. As I've tried to explain to some folks, avoiding brightwork is not a question of saving money; it is that you have it and enjoy it like a beautiful painting, or else you just plain do without it.

Those clear, dry northwest days of September and October are the best ones for varnishing, and Nick's aim was to always get one coat on every boat during the fall. It didn't matter whether it was before or after the owner was through for the season.

The spars routinely, and conveniently, received their two coats of varnish in the fall. Not only did this avoid spring work, but it gave the varnish time to harden before the spars were next stepped and rigged.

For better or worse, the decks were the final item for the painters to tackle. It would have been nice to get painting them over with in the early spring, but, if done then, the subsequent yard traffic would have soiled and perhaps scratched them. By waiting until the last minute, it became an owner's choice whether or not to baby the decks for a day or two while the paint hardened.

I have mentioned the advantages of canvas decks before, but there are a few precautions to be kept in mind about their maintenance. The first is not to build up too much paint: it tends to cause cracking. One light coat a year is sufficient. When trying to do a good job, the painter is apt to run in an excess of paint next to the house or the toerail. In time, this surplus tends to shrink or crack away from the wood, allowing water to get into the void and rot the canvas. If one is then afraid to get paint on the varnish, one may stay too far from this void and make the situation progressively worse. A little varnish crossing over onto the paint may help solve this problem, without being too unsightly. There are many little tricks about painting, and the joker who told me one day that anyone can paint was as crazy as "Dick's hatband."

Needless to say, deck colors themselves are an important consideration. For the Concordia yawls, a light gray or buff seems to look shipshape and does not get too hot in the sun. Although it is very hard on the eyes, white has always been our recommendation for boats going south. Any dark or bright color usually proves to be a big mistake, from all angles.

Below decks, the paint and varnish work requires comparatively little attention, except for a good spring cleaning and an occasional touch-up. The Concordia yawl bulkheads and trim were delivered with many coats of good varnish, the final one being rubbed down to a low lustre with waterproof sandpaper and water. It was durable and didn't show up finger marks or an accidental scratch. The white overhead and cabinhouse sides, because they were high up, seldom got much abuse, and although some paints worked out better than others, these areas never needed annual attention (maybe every ten years).

The bilges of a boat are hard areas to know what to do with. Perhaps it is fair to say that different boats need different treatments. Some people say they should be left unpainted so the wood there can breathe. Our practice on the Concordia yawls was to keep the bilges red-leaded, just as they came from Germany. If nothing else, it kept them looking neat and encouraged cleanliness, and cleanliness is good on a boat anywhere, anytime.

Billing the Customers

Strictly speaking, billing methods are not a part of maintenance procedures, but getting paid promptly for work done can become really urgent. During my brief era of overseeing boat work in other yards, I found that jumbled billing meant slow payment. A long list of miscellaneous items, put together with a 250-hour bottom line, meant little to the owner except that it was too much.

To straighten out situations like this, I had to take the time myself to go back through the workers' original time sheets and sort out what specific jobs took how many hours, and, in essence, make out a new and understandable bill.

When it came time for me to make out bills for our own yard, I was well imbued with the importance of a fair and accurate presentation. With a carefully detailed bill before him, a customer could say to himself, item A took an hour too long, item B appears to be okay, and item C has taken less time than I thought. Adding up the hours, the total probably still seemed a bit on the high side, but the usual reaction was, why fuss about an hour or two?

It was a long, tedious process to make out bills in this meticulous way, but it surely did speed up payment, and, furthermore, it all but eliminated unnecessary complaints. Another unforeseen consequence on the plus side was that future work-estimating became easier and more accurate. On the minus side, Concordia's treasurer, Sally Howland, soon learned that I was so slow in getting out the bills that when payday came around there might well be money on the books, but it certainly wasn't in the bank. When Alden Trull inherited the bill-making job, he was a little faster at it than I had been, but not much.

Consistency was another very important billing consideration. We tried to make sure that no customer got an especially high bill just because his boat was stored outside or because his week for painting came during some spotty weather. No one ever liked to be charged more than his neighbor for the same job.

As a final thought on the subject, we tended for some reason to be the last yard to follow inflation's example and raise labor rates.* This may have helped

to keep us busy (too busy, according to some), but it unquestionably had an adverse effect on our annual statements. I have no sensible explanation for this tardiness in keeping ahead of the shrinking dollar, but I guess boating folks have a certain sympathy for each other that the straight businessman can seldom take into consideration.

* Our labor rates climbed only from $2.00 to $5.50 in the thirty-two years between 1938 and 1970.

Thistle, a 74' LWL yawl designed and built by Herreshoff in 1928 and later owned by Dr. Seth Milliken of New York and East Blue Hill, Maine.

Thistledown, Concordia #62, owned by Alida Milliken Camp of New York and East Blue Hill, Maine.

Appendix V
CONCORDIA OWNERS 1938–1988

Although the main body of our Concordia story is planned to end about 1970, we have tried our best to bring this list of Concordia yawls and their owners up to fall 1987.

A glance at this compilation will reveal that there are one hundred and three Concordia yawls, including seventy-eight of the Concordia Standard 39-foot 10-inch model and twenty-five of the 41-foot 3-inch Concordia Forty ones (indicated by an asterisk). Although not specifically noted, a dozen or so of the fleet sail at times or continuously, as sloops, the mizzen unit merely being removed at the owner's discretion.

As is indicated from the approximate purchase dates listed (there is often a lag between order and final delivery), the oldest boat in the class is now fifty years of age and the youngest is twenty-three. The original four boats were built in this country, two of them just before World War II and two just after. The remaining ninety-nine were built by Abeking and Rasmussen in Germany between the years of 1950 and 1963. To the best of my knowledge, all one hundred and three are still in existence. There has been a strong demand for used Concordias, and new owners tend to return older boats to first-class condition.

As of fall 1987, there have been some four hundred and fifteen Concordia yawl owners, many of whom, to our loss, have seen their last sailing days.

It is of interest to note that some eleven families have had their Concordias for over thirty years. Mr. Parson had his *Halcyon* (#3) for nearly forty years, before his passing terminated the partnership. Some twenty more owners have had their boats for twenty to thirty years. Still others have had two or more Concordias at different times. Bill Stetson has, over the years, had five.

Eleven of the Concordias have had but one owner, while others have sailed under five or more skippers. At least twenty of the fleet have been privileged to fly a yacht club Commodore's flag.

The boat names in themselves seem worthy of some thought in that so many of them suggest a pride of ownership and an awareness of nautical tradition. *Java* set a pattern for naming boats after an important ancestral ship and at the same time initiated a pattern for choosing names of Far Eastern places of nautical interest. Still other boat names hearken back to ancestral homelands or admired characters, family or otherwise. The status of a good boat seems somehow to be enhanced when she displays a carefully chosen name that means something special and suggests a relevant story about her owner.

Addresses or home port statistics are useful to have in that they indicate the wanderings of each Concordia yawl. Congregating first in New England waters, some of them gradually spread to other special cruising grounds: south to the Chesapeake, then to Florida and the Islands, west to the Great Lakes, and on to California and Washington.

The inclusion of Abeking and Rasmussen construction numbers will be of help for identification purposes.

Of course, the list of owners is the most important statistic of all in that it is these folks who have made the Concordia yawl class what it is now and hopefully will be for years to come.

Boat number	Name of boat	A&R construction number	Date purchased	Owner	Fall, 1987 Address/Home Port
1	JAVA	(built by Casey)	1938	Llewellyn Howland	Padanaram, MA
1	KIOWA		1957	Willoughby Stuart	Marblehead, MA
1	KIOWA		1964	C. Andrew Perkins, Jr.	Cataumet, MA
1	KIOWA		1968	Robert T. Clementz	Hollywood, FL
1	JAVA		1973	Z. John Nijitray	Miami Beach, FL
1	JAVA		1978	R. Tuck Elfman	Doylestown, PA
1	JAVA		1986	Mark Scott	Miami, FL
1	JAVA		1987	Weld S. Henshaw and John H. Henshaw, Jr.	Boston, MA and Brunswick, ME
2	JOBISKA	(built by Lawley)	1939	Philip Rhinelander	Brookline, MA
2	INA		1949	Drayton Cochran	Southport, CT
2	MALAY		1951	Daniel D. Strohmeier	Padanaram, MA
2	MALAY		1972	Martin Joy	Beaumont, SC
2	MALAY I		1975	Richard Wertz	Westport, MA
2	MALAY I		1978	David DeLaney	unknown
2	MALAY I		1980	Joseph and Mary Vella	Lantana, FL
2	MALAY I		1983	George and Judy Custard	Cortez, FL
3	HALCYON	(built by Casey)	1946	George A. Parson	Brooklin, ME
3	HALCYON		1984	Frank Walker	Ellsworth, ME
4	ACTAEA	(built by Casey)	1947	Henry Sears	Chestertown, MD
4	WINDSEYE		1952	Thomas Hale	Vineyard Haven, MA
4	TEMPO		1966	August Meyer	Manchester, MA
4	TEMPO		1975	Herbert W. Toms, Jr.	Port Clyde, ME
4	TEMPO		1978	N.C. and Joyce Hawkesworth	Cumberland, ME
4	TEMPO		1980	Jerry Bertetta	Miami, FL
5	SHEILA	(#4612)	1950	Drayton Cochran	Oyster Bay, NY
5	SUVA		1950	Edward Cabot	Westerly, RI
5	SUVA		1957	Robert Foley	Washington, DC
5	SUVA		1960	Eugene W. Stetson, Jr.	Padanaram, MA
5	SUVA		1960	Calvin and Sue Siegal	Padanaram, MA
5	CABARET		1973	Kenneth Abbott	Mattapoisett, MA
5	DUENDE		1974	Stanley W. Brown, Jr.	Belfast, ME
5	DUENDE		1980	Charles Adams	Amherst, MA
6	SHEILA	(#4685)	1951	Drayton Cochran	Southport, CT
6	TABAKEA		1954	William Taussig	Dedham, MA
6	SHEILA		1963	Neil P. Putman	Marblehead, MA
6	TABAKEA		1966	Dr. Benson Snyder	Westport, MA
7	DUSKY III	(#4684)	1951	Hobart J. Hendrick	Saybrook, CT
7	RAYANNA		1956	Dr. Raymond Curtis	Gibson Island, MD
7	RAYANNA		1982	Henry Bornhofft III	Gloucester, MA
7	VERITY		1983	John Anderson	Mattapoisett, MA
8	MOOREA	(#4753)	1951	George Cheston	Wynnewood, PA
8	CIRCE		1961	Gilbert Oakley, Jr.	Bedford, MA
8	WINDHOVER		1963	George Carey and Charles Moran	Tenants Harbor, ME
8	WINDHOVER		1966	George Carey	Tenants Harbor, ME
8	WINDHOVER		1983	Wick Beavers	Tenants Harbor, ME

Boat number	Name of boat	A&R construction number	Date purchased	Owner	Fall, 1987 Address/Home Port
8	WINDHOVER		1986	Salvatore Nicotra	Hamden, CT
9	WHISPER	(#4754)	1951	Frederic R. Pratt	New York City, NY
9	EL HO III		1963	Howard A. Schecterle	Stonington, CT
9	MOANA		1986	Frank Williams	Forestdale, MA
10	RUSTA IV	(#4806)	1952	Standish Bourne	Padanaram, MA
10	INTREPID		1963	John C. Walker	Dalton, GA
10	INTREPID		1967	Leslie H. Quackenbush	Darien, CT
10	INTREPID		1969	Marian Sweet	Rowayton, CT
10	WOODWIND		1969	Donald Lippoth	York, ME
10	CONCORD		1981	Dr. George O. Cummings, Jr.	Portland, ME
10	QUIET THUNDER		unknown	Robert Bristoe	Cataumet, MA
10	QUIET THUNDER		1983	David Myers	Little Compton, RI
11	WINNIE OF BOURNE	(#4828)	1952	John Parkinson, Jr.	Bourne, MA
11	WINNIE OF BOURNE		1973	Mrs. John Parkinson, Jr.	Bourne, MA
11	WINNIE		1976	William Glenn	Oyster Bay, NY
11	WINNIE		1984	Peter Gallant	Stratham, NH
12	ACQUILON	(#4830)	1952	Henry W. Kingman	Boston, MA
12	KAHALA		1954	Joseph Mattison, Jr.	Boston, MA
12	ORSO DEL MARE		1957	J. Hugh McDowell	New York City, NY
12	RACQUET II		1958	William R. Coykendal, Jr.	Padanaram, MA
12	ABSINTHE		1966	Frederick H. Brooke, Jr., and Henry Sears	Padanaram, MA
12	ABSINTHE		1971	Frederick H. Brooke, Jr.	Padanaram, MA
13	PARTHENIA	(#4833)	1952	Parker Converse	Marion, MA
13	MADRIGAL		1957	Robert P. Bass, Jr.	Concord, NH
13	CANDY		1965	Marian Sweet	Rowayton, CT
13	ALERT		1965	W. Eugene Stetson, Jr.	Padanaram, MA
13	PHALAROPE		1965	John E. S. Mitchell	Hulls Cove, ME
13	PHALAROPE		1983	Dr. Allen Webb	Farmington, ME
13	PHALAROPE		1987	Daniel and Sarah Beard	Kennebunkport, ME
14	SAXON	(#4866)	1953	Dr. Graham H. Pope	Westport, ME
15	SKYLARK	(#4867)	1953	W. Perry Curtiss, Jr.	Branford, CT
15	ICRANCA/ABRI		unknown	David P. Heilner	Columbus, OH
15	SKYLARK		1961	Richard Young	Mattapoisett, MA
15	VAHEVALA		1974	J. A. Flanzer	Windham Center, CT
15	SOVEREIGN		unknown	George E. Cook	Woodinville, WA
16	GAME COCK	(#4680)	1953	A. D. Weekes, Jr., and John C. West	Oyster Bay, NY
16	GRAYLING		1954	Concordia Company	Padanaram, MA
16	SUMATRA		1956	H. Addison Taylor, Jr.	New Canaan, CT
16	MALACCA		1963	Jesse D. Wolff	New York City, NY
16	MAELSTROM		1968	John H. Painter	Del Mar, CA
17	*ACTAEA	(#4873)	1953	Henry Sears	Chestertown, MD
17	*DOLPHIN/ GREEN WITCH		1958	Russell Hay	Skaneateles, NY
17	*ANN McKIM		1964	Charles G. Meyer	Oyster Bay, NY

Boat number	Name of boat	A&R construction number	Date purchased	Owner	Fall, 1987 Address/Home Port
17	*OZ		unknown	Robert Wilbur	Michigan
17	*ACTAEA		1974	William Turney	Fort Lauderdale, FL
18	*ARMATA	(#4922)	1954	Moreau D. Brown	Padanaram, MA
18	*JANORAH		1961	Robert Gillette	Quissett, MA
18	*SARA		1971	Stewart MacDougall	Nantucket, MA
18	*SYLPH		1972	Horace C. Sylvester	Scituate, MA
18	*SPICE		1973	Guy Rutherford	New York City, NY
18	*SPICE		1975	Dr. Arthur Burke	Padanaram, MA
18	*CRESCENT		1984	George Helger	Norfolk, VA
18	*CRESCENT		1985	Walter Hobson	Annapolis, MD
19	*SLY MONGOOSE III	(#4923)	1954	Drayton Cochran	Oyster Bay, NY
19	*OTTER		1960	John H. James	Redding Ridge, CT
19	*OTTER		1964	Richard McIntosh	Darien, CT
19	*EDELWEISS		1966	George Wiswell, Jr.	Southport, CT
19	*OTTER		1979	Edward Scheu	Hanover, NH
20	SWAN III	(#4921)	1954	William M. Wood	Padanaram, MA
20	SWAN		1965	Lincoln Davis, Jr.	Friendship, ME
20	SWAN		1968	Herbert J. Kane	Marblehead, MA
20	SWAN		1973	Bruce E. Duclos	Marblehead, MA
20	SWAN		1979	Robert W. Wallace and E.A. and James W. Sargent	Cataumet, MA
20	FLEETWOOD		1985	Ida Galliher	Coconut Grove, FL
21	CRISETTE	(#4944)	1954	Miss Rose B. Dolan	Padanaram, MA
21	AMANDA III		1957	Horace Henriques	Pemaquid Harbor, ME
21	WIND SHADOW		1978	Jack Lockhart	unknown
21	WIND SHADOW		1980	Donald Lockhart	Trumbull, CT
22	LADY EVE II	(#4958)	1954	Raymond Donovan	Warwick, RI
22	HERO		1958	Ross Sibley	Essex, CT
22	HERO		1966	Mrs. Ross Sibley	Essex, CT
23	SCOTCH MIST	(#4963)	1954	James O. Rankin	Southport, CT
23	STARLIGHT		1969	C. Francis Loutrel	Hyannisport, MA
24	NIAM	(#4997)	1955	John T. Ryan, Jr.	Chatham, MA
25	WILD SAWN	(#4999)	1955	Bertram Lippincott	Jamestown, RI
25	WILD SWAN		1969	Dr. Walter A. Wichern, Jr.	Milbridge, ME
25	WILD SWAN		1984	Robert Rodgers	Stonington, CT
25	WILD SWAN		1985	James McGuire	Noank, CT
26	CONDOR	(#5001)	1955	Oliver Robbins	Padanaram, MA
26	CONDOR		1967	Charles G. Shoemaker	New Castle, DE
26	EMIRAU		1976	Nelson H. Smith	Kensington, NC
26	BABE		1977	Arnold Gay	Annapolis, MD
26	ANGEL		1979	Michael Van Kluyne	Washington, DC
26	SUZANNE		1980	Joseph Callaghan	Cheshire, CT
26	MARY ANN		1986	Robert A. and Linda Jones	Boothbay, ME
27	*GAME COCK	(#5005)	1955	Arthur Weekes and John C. West	Oyster Bay, NY

Boat number	Name of boat	A&R construction number	Date purchased	Owner	Fall, 1987 Address/Home Port
27	*GOOSE/ SNOW GOOSE		1960	Eugene W. Stetson, Jr.	Vinalhaven, ME
27	*WINDWARD		1962	Charles Stetson	Westport, CT
27	*WINDWARD		1964	Champe Taliaferro	Oyster Bay, NY
27	*ASTRID		1965	Jerome Margolin	Concord, MA
27	*CANADA GOOSE		1968	Basil Stetson	Edgartown, MA
27	*CANADA GOOSE		unknown	Mrs. Basil Stetson	Edgartown, MA
27	*WINDROVER		1975	Kennett Love	East Hampton, NY
27	*PENARROW		1981	John Wharton	Exeter, NH
27	*PETREL		1983	Allen Vlach	Belmont, MA
27	*SARAH		1986	Robert Gross	Stoneham, MA
28	SAFARI	(#5024)	1955	Alex and Horace Bright	Boston, MA
28	SAFARI		unknown	Cameron Bright	Cataumet, MA
28	SAFARI		1985	Richard Zimmerman	Gloucester, MA
29	*LIAT	(#5026)	1955	Robert Forrester, Jr.	Rumson, NJ
29	*FEATHER		1960	David S. Trend	Padanaram, MA
29	*FEATHER		1985	Eel River Trust	New Bedford, MA
30	*HARRIER	(#5035)	1955	C. Raymond Hunt	Tilton, NH
30	*HARRIER		1956	Jesse Bontecou and W. Harris	Jamestown, RI
30	*HARRIER		1956	Jesse Bontecou	Jamestown, RI
31	HALF MINE II	(#5037)	1955	Chapin Riley and G. Cline	Padanaram, MA
31	GRIFFON		1965	Dr. Orrin Keller	LaSalle, OH
31	GRYPHON		1973	Ben C. Foster	Milland, MI
31	JE-DE-JO		1977	Richard Bell	Michigan
31	GRIFFON		1977	Tom and Penny Carson	Toledo, OH
32	PRISCILLA	(#5038)	1955	John B. Hopkins	Padanaram, MA
32	MIRAGE		1966	John Whitaker	Weston, CT
32	MIRAGE/AKAMAI		1971	Paul V. Converse	East Northport, NY
32	CLAIR DE LUNE		1976	Pierre Wagner	Little Neck, NY
32	CLAIR DE LUNE		1980	John Wheeler	Barrington, RI
32	CLAIR DE LUNE		1984	Dr. Lyman A. Page	Kennebunkport, ME
32	MIRAGE		1986	T. Ricardo Quesada	South Freeport, ME
33	PHOEBE S	(#5043)	1955	Hamilton W. Stiles	Darien, CT
33	SUNDA		1957	Emil Kratovil and W. Jenkins	Greenwich, CT
33	SUNDA		1961	William Jenkins	Falmouth, MA
33	SUNDA		1977	Albert Brown	Savannah, GA
34	HARMONY II	(#5044)	1955	Paul Hanrahan	Marblehead, MA
34	BIANCA		1963	Dr. Jerome Bruner	Gloucester, MA
34	MALACCA		1970	John W. Wheeler	Barrington, RI
34	KITHOGUE		1972	Ann Wulsin and John Walsh	Vineyard Haven, MA
34	SAZERAC		1974	Walter E. Hobson III	Annapolis, MD
34	PELLETREAU		1980	James Maroney	Edgartown, MA
35	SCONE	(#5045)	1955	Arnault Edgerly	Padanaram, MA
35	MEMORY		1957	Dr. John C. Bullard and Charles C. Glover	Padanaram, MA, and Washington, DC
35	MEMORY		1965	Charles C. Glover	West River, MD
35	MEMORY		1986	Richard and Patti Navarro	Eliot, ME

Boat number	Name of boat	A&R construction number	Date purchased	Owner	Fall, 1987 Address/Home Port
36	*MAGIC	(#5116)	1956	Dr. George Nichols, Jr.	Manchester, MA
36	*MAGIC		1973	Thomas Walker	Manchester, MA
36	*MAGIC		unknown	John Phillips	Crescent City, GA
36	*MAGIC		unknown	Hugh Samson	Adamsville, RI
36	*MAGIC		1980	Henry Bornhofft III	Gloucester, MA
37	*WINDSONG	(#5117)	1956	Eugene B. Snydor, Jr.	Richmond, VA
37	*WINDOON II		1962	George B. Drake, Jr.	Port Washington, NY
37	*WINDOON II		1969	Dr. William Kessler	Cedar Point, CT
37	*KESTREL		1976	Robert Nicholson	Avon, MA
37	*SAQQARA		1980	Timothy Jackson	Dedham, MA
37	*YANKEE		1984	Linford Stiles	Wilton, CT
37	*YANKEE		1987	Robert Gorman	Padanaram, MA
38	*DUSKY IV	(#5121)	1956	Hobart Hendrick	New Haven, CT
38	*MOONGLOW		unknown	Gordon T. Arnold	Tenafly, NJ
38	*NEFERTITI		1974	Sibley Smith	Marshfield, MA
38	*NEFERTITI		1978	John Williams Company	Mount Desert, ME
39	LAND'S END	(#5100)	1956	William T. Okie	Darien, CT
39	TRIPOLI		1960	William Bainbridge	
39	FLEDERMAUS		1963	Frank C. McLearn	Bronxville, NY
39	FLEDERMAUS		unknown	Mrs. Frank McLearn	Bronxville, NY
39	FLEDERMAUS		1968	Edward Popper	Marshfield, MA
39	FLEDERMAUS		1972	Herbert W. Toms, Jr.	Port Clyde, ME
39	FLEDERMAUS		1985	Peter Kiely	North Hampton, NH
39	CANDIDE		1986	Philip and Beverly Brazeau	Seattle, WA
40	SKYE	(#5101)	1956	Eldon Macleod	West Falmouth, MA
40	SKYE		1964	Mrs. Eldon Macleod	West Falmouth, MA
40	SKYE		1965	Robert, William, and Eldon Macleod	West Falmouth, MA
40	WHITE WAVE		1981	Lloyd Moulton	Marblehead, MA
41	AUDA	(#5102)	1956	Col. Arthur Herrington	Padanaram, MA
41	PAMEDA		1961	D. Philip Snyder, Jr.	New York City, NY
41	MERLIN		1964	Richard Kerry	Groton, MA
41	NIMUE		1972	William Hefler	Padanaram, MA
41	SISYPHUS		1976	Dr. John F. Towle	Woods Hole, MA
42	ARUNDEL	(#5103)	1956	L. J. Regan	California
42	VETSERA		1957	Douglas Disney	Newport Beach, CA
42	EL CONQUISTADORE		unknown	unknown	unknown
42	MARGARET		unknown	Robert Hovey	San Rafael, CA
43	RAKA	(#5104)	1956	Reginald Saunders	Morgan Bay, ME
43	RAKA		1983	Robert Stuart	Kinderhook, NY
44	SHADOW	(#5105)	1956	Sydney Roberts	Wakefield, RI
44	NIKE		1963	Charles Stromeyer	Marblehead, MA
44	LACERTA		1971	Stephen P. Loutrel	Manchester, MA
45	SYSTOLE/TALOA	(#5106)	1956	Dr. Edward Kline	Shaker Heights, OH
45	FREEWIND		1973	Lt. Cmdr. Fred Purrington	South Dartmouth, MA
45	TALOA		1980	John Hajduk	Niles, IL

Boat number	Name of boat	A&R construction number	Date purchased	Owner	Fall, 1987 Address/Home Port
45	LOON		1985	Wayne Overland	Victoria, BC, Canada
46	JOSEPHINE	(#5107)	1956	Robert Collins	Los Angeles, CA
46	JOSEPHINE		1962	Frank Mead	Orange, CA
46	JOSEPHINE		1967	Michael Meshekoff	Beverly Hills, CA
46	HELENA		1968	Court C. Koener	Olympia, WA
46	ESCAPE		unknown	Geof and Deborah Hobert	Bainbridge Island, WA
46	KODAMA		1982	Stewart MacDougall	Seattle, WA
47	WHITECAP	(#5247)	1957	C. McKim Norton	Princeton, NJ
47	WHITECAP		1962	Richard Thurber	Padanaram, MA
47	CANTATA		1968	Leon Sepuka	Padanaram, MA
47	MARAN		1978	Richard Sciuto	Padanaram, MA
47	ARIADNE		1979	Dr. Charles Stone	Darien, CT
48	BALLERINA	(#5248)	1957	Donald B. Kipp	Edgartown, MA
48	HARBINGER		1970	Richard and Robert Kugler	Padanaram, MA
48	HARBINGER		1975	Robert Gunther	Guilford, CT
48	HARBINGER		1978	Lawrence Warner	Marion, MA
49	MOONFLEET	(#5249)	1957	Robert L. Bortner	Huntington, NY
49	MOONFLEET		1962	Allen E. Whitman	Roxbury, CT
49	DALLIANCE		1970	Eliot Wadsworth II	New York City, NY
49	HAJARI III		1971	Hector Butler	Marblehead, MA
49	LUNE/MOONFLEET		1976	Queene Hooper	New York City, NY
49	MOONFLEET		1986	Gregory Carroll	Biddeford, ME
50	ELECTA	(#5250)	1957	H. Pelham Curtis	New Canaan, CT
50	DJAKARTA		1964	William D. Conklin	New Canaan, CT
50	DJAKARTA		1969	S.W. Labrot	Monroe, CT
50	BANJO		1971	Michael Ferber	Boxford, MA
50	NJORD		1974	Peter and Nancy Engels	Lexington, MA
51	GALA	(#5251)	1957	Dr. J. Alton Edwards	Newport Beach, CA
51	ZAFIR		1960	Bertram Lasswell	Daly City, CA
51	VINTAGE		1964	James R. Phalen	Newport Beach, CA
51	VINTAGE		1965	Edward Isett	unknown
51	VINTAGE		1966	John J. White	Sausalito, CA
51	VINTAGE		1977	Steven Arian	Kentfield, CA
52	*BANDA	(#5252)	1957	Eugene W. Stetson, Jr.	Vinalhaven, ME
52	*SAGOLA		1959	George Hinman	Port Washington, NY
52	*RUNNING BEAR		1967	Robert Young	Rye, NY
52	*LUPINE		unknown	Douglas Baird	Swampscott, MA
52	*BANDA		1985	Lee Davidson	Padanaram, MA
53	*PRETTIMARIE	(#5253)	1957	Hugh Bullock	Edgartown, MA
53	*PRETTIROSE		1987	Rose C. Dana	Padanaram, MA
54	*MELINDA	(#5271)	1957	William Mead	Newport Beach, CA
54	*HORIZON		1966	John M. Wilson	Santa Barbara, CA
55	KIVA	(#5281)	1957	Richard Bewley	Southport, CT
55	KIVA		1976	Saul Gliserman	Northampton, MA
55	KIVA		1982	Douglas Hoffman	Norwalk, CT

Boat number	Name of boat	A&R construction number	Date purchased	Owner	Fall, 1987 Address/Home Port
56	NEREID	(#5283)	1957	Gwynn G. Tucker	Larchmont, NY
56	NEREID		1964	W. Rolf Warner	Larchmont, NY
56	TERN II		1975	Dr. Albert J. Papp	Stamford, CT
56	WHISPER		1986	George F. Henschel, Jr.	Norwalk, CT
57	JAVELIN	(#5328)	1958	W. Mason Smith	Mattapoisett, MA
58	OFF CALL	(#5329)	1958	Dr. Clarke Staples	Boothbay, ME
59	MARY G	(#5360)	1958	Robert A. Green	Watch Hill, RI
59	MARY G		1968	Robert A. Green, Jr., and partner	Watch Hill, RI
59	MARY G		unknown	David M. Pugh and David R. Winans, Jr.	Watch Hill, RI
59	SNOW BIRD		1976	Stevens Peale	Old Lyme, CT
60	*WINDQUEST	(#5362)	1958	A. Justin Wasley	Plainville, CT
60	*ARIEL		1964	Dr. Stephen B. Andrus	Cohasset, MA
60	*LORNE		1970	Wilfred M. Kluss	Stamford, CT
60	*PRINCIPIA		1985	Bruce P. Flenniken	Padanaram, MA
61	TAM O'SHANTER	(#5363)	1958	Frank H. Soule	Portland, ME
61	TAM O'SHANTER		1967	Mrs. Lawrence D. Chapman	Falmouth Foreside, ME
62	THISTLEDOWN	(#5364)	1958	Frederic and Alida Camp	East Blue Hill, ME
62	THISTLEDOWN			Alida Camp	East Blue Hill, ME
63	*BARODA	(#5365)	1958	Stuart Caldara	Stonington, CT
63	*SONNET		1968	James D. Brown	Syosset, NY
64	LIVE YANKEE	(#5366)	1958	Robert Gillespie and Mr. Greenwood	Darien, CT
64	LIVE YANKEE		1963	Robert Gillespie and Chetwood Elliott	Darien, CT
65	LA REVE	(#5375)	1958	Clement McKaig	Sausalito, CA
65	GOLONDRINA		1960	James Emmons	Woodstock, VT
65	GOLONDRINA		unknown	Mrs. James Emmons	unknown
65	GOLONDRINA		1967	Milton Bergey	St. John, USVI
65	unknown	unknown	unknown	Forrest Fischer	California
65	GOLONDRINA		1984	William Rich	St. John, USVI
66	MISTY	(#5435)	1959	Lester McIntosh	Grosse Pointe, MI
66	MISTY		1978	Thomas McIntosh	Long Grove, IL
67	CROCODILE	(#5436)	1959	Mr. and Mrs. U. Haskell Crocker	Manchester, MA
67	CROCODILE			Mrs. U. Haskell Crocker	Manchester, MA
68	BELLE ONE	(#5452)	1959	John Kiley	Wianno, MA
68	EIGHT BELLES		1963	Apthorpe and Hutchinson	Dover, MA
68	BELLES		1975	Richard Hutchinson, Arthur B. Glidden, and Alfred B. Downes	Dover, MA, Dover, MA, and Wellesley, MA
68	BELLES		1983	Richard Hutchinson, Alfred B. Downs, and Allan Cobb	Providence, RI

Boat number	Name of boat	A&R construction number	Date purchased	Owner	Fall, 1987 Address/Home Port
69	DIABLO	(#5453)	1959	John M. Robinson	Portland, ME
69	HOURI		1967	John S. Chatfield	New York City, NY
70	*BANDA	(#5454)	1959	Eugene W. Stetson, Jr.	Vinalhaven, ME
70	*GAME COCK II		1962	John C. West and Arthur D. Weekes	Oyster Bay, NY
70	*PAMEDA		unknown	E. Philip Snyder	Southport, CT
70	*KRISTAL		1977	Robert Drew	Guilford, CT
70	*IRIAN		1980	Darrow Lebovici	Salem, MA
71	*POLARIS	(#5469)	1959	Roberts Parsons	East Greenwich, RI
71	*POLARIS		1973	August Meyer	Belmont, MA
71	*POLARIS		1977	Mr. and Mrs. Louis Siegal	Irvington, VA
71	*POLARIS		1987	Kenneth Brittle	Gloucester Point, MA
72	*ARACHNE	(#5470)	1959	H. St. John Webb	Padanaram, MA
72	*PARAMOUR		1972	Philip A. Hutchinson	Harwood, MD
72	*PARAMOUR		1981	John Stewart	Annapolis, MD
72	*PARAMOUR		1985	Gary Brown	Jonesboro, GA
73	YGERNE	(#5471)	1959	Allen T. Klots	Cold Spring Harbor, NY
73	TYNAJE		1965	Dr. Peter Ross	Mystic, CT
73	WINDEMERE		unknown	Dr. Allen Chamberlain	Greenwich, CT
73	TOSCA		unknown	Rowland and Alexandra Harrison	Halifax, NS, Canada
73	TOSCA		unknown	Dr. G.W.N. Fitzgerald	St. Anthony, NF, Canada
74	SOPRANO	(#5478)	1959	Heywood Fox	Wianno, MA
74	WIZARD		unknown	James E. McHutchinson	Marshfield, MA
74	WIZARD		1983	Seth Pearson and Carl Anderson	Dennis, MA
75	LAND'S END	(#5494)	1959	William T. Okie	Darien, CT
75	PORTUNUS		1968	Augustin H. Parker	Dover, MA
75	PORTUNUS			Mrs. Augustin H. Parker	Duxbury, MA
76	CYMBA	(#5549)	1960	Thomas H. West	Padanaram, MA
76	SUMATRA			Thomas H. West, Thomas H. West, Jr., and F.R. Ballou	Padanaram, MA
76	SUMATRA		1972	Frank Rogerson	Duxbury, MA
76	SUMATRA		1977	James Higson	Newport Beach, CA
76	SUMATRA		1981	Norton Humphreys	Newport Beach, CA
77	CANNONEER II	(#5552)	1960	Basil Stetson	Princeton, NJ
77	MARINETTE		1965	Mrs. Howard R. Sherman	Newport, RI
77	MARINETTE		1971	Robert F. Moser	Padanaram, MA
77	MALAY		1972	Daniel D. Strohmeier	Padanaram, MA
78	BUCKAROO TOO	(#5576)	1960	Willis Shackleford	Wilmington, DE
78	BUCKAROO TOO		1975	Queene Hooper and Elizabeth Meyer	
78	MATINICUS		1975	Elizabeth Meyer	Newport, RI

Boat number	Name of boat	A&R construction number	Date purchased	Owner	Fall, 1987 Address/Home Port
79	WESTRAY	(#5577)	1960	B. Glenn MacNary	North Falmouth, MA
80	GOLDENEYE	(#5578)	1960	R. Forbes Perkins	Manchester, MA
81	KYPRIS	(#5579)	1960	Joseph Mattison, Jr.	Wianno, MA
81	GODWIT		1970	Edward Myers	Damariscotta, ME
81	GODWIT		1973	Dr. M.F. Pettit	Westbrook, ME
81	PAPILLON		1975	Dr. Charles and Phyllis C. Cloutier	Annapolis, MD
81	ENVOLEE		1981	Danielle and Claude Engle	Gibson Island, MD
82	*STARSIGHT	(#5580)	1960	Cornelius Wood	Andover, MA
82	*STARSIGHT		1964	Middlesex School	Concord, MA
82	*CORIOLIS		1966	Gifford C. Ewing	Quisset, MA
82	*CORIOLIS		1980	University of Maine	Orono, ME
82	*CORIOLIS		1980	Edward Gatti	unknown
82	*CORIOLIS		1981	Richard Sciuto	Padanaram, MA
82	*CORIOLIS		1981	Douglas D. Adkins	Seattle, WA
83	FANTASY	(#5667)	1961	S. Prentice Porter	Marion, MA
83	CHRISTIE		1969	Richard S. Robie, Jr.	Marblehead, MA
84	AEOLUS	(#5668)	1961	John E. McKelvey, Jr.	Hyannisport, MA
84	AFTERGLOW		1968	Dr. Arthur Herrington	Cohasset, MA
84	AFTERGLOW		1977	Kenneth Gilbert	Cranston, RI
85	*ARMATA	(#5717)	1961	Moreau Brown	Padanaram, MA
85	*ARAPAHO		1974	Dyer Jones	Warren, RI
85	*ARAPAHO		1980	Norman and Joan Fine	Concord, MA
86	DAME OF SARK	(#5719)	1961	Bruce Barnard	Quissett, MA
86	DAME OF SARK		unknown	Richard D. Hill	Marblehead, MA
86	DAME OF SARK		1983	Stewart MacDougall	Santa Barbara, CA
87	JANIE	(#5720)	1961	Clifton W. Phalen	Shelter Island, NY
87	JEMIMA		1968	Andrew Marshall, Jr.	Marblehead, MA
87	BAHARI		1974	R.M. Sheriff	Stonington, CT
87	ALLURE		1981	Robert Snyder, Jr.	Stonington, CT
87	ALLURE		1983	George Wiltshire	Kennebunk, ME
87	ALLURE		1987	Bejamin Niles	Seattle, WA
88	*ASTRA	(#5599)	1962	Eugene B. Sydnor, Jr.	Padanaram, MA
88	*AEGENA		1968	John Carter	Padanaram, MA
88	*RENAISSANCE		1976	John Lund	Worcester, MA
89	BELVEDERE	(#5768)	1962	Lowell P. Wingert	New York City, NY
89	FREEDOM		1963	D. Brainerd Holmes	Padanaram, MA
89	WOODWIND		1972	Donald W. Lippoth	Cape Elizabeth, ME
89	WOODWIND		1980	Michael and Joan Appel	Guilford, CT
89	WOODWIND		1983	Dr. Frederick Ayres	Norwell, MA
89	WOODWIND		1986	John and Margaret Haskins	Keene, NH

Boat number	Name of boat	A&R construction number	Date purchased	Owner	Fall, 1987 Address/Home Port
90	INGRID	(#5769)	1962	Saul Warshaw	Hawley, PA
90	FABRILE		1984	David Godine	Medomak, ME
91	PAT	(#5770)	1962	John B. Nicholson	Port Washington
91	SHIMAERA		1965	Robert J. Snyder	Stonington, CT
92	*GEISHA GIRL	(#5849)	1962	Cameron H. Morris, Jr.	Osterville, MA
92	*KALUA		1968	Richard Thurber	Charlotte, VT
92	*KALUA		1973	Diane Whitehead	Wickford, RI
92	*FIREFALL		1978	Christopher Page	Hyannisport, MA
92	*AMBIENTE		1985	Robert Deneberg	Philadelphia, PA
92	*WHITE LIGHT		1986	Nicholas Heyl	Thetford Hill, VT
93	*EDEN	(#5900)	1962	David Austen	Paris, France
93	*PHANTOM		1970	Robert Bacon	Woods Hole, MA
94	*WHISPER	(#5955)	1963	Frederic R. Pratt	New York City, NY
94	*KATRINA		1966	Dr. H.M. Rozendaal	Schenectady, NY
95	*RATON	(#5977)	1963	Richard F. Coons	Oyster Bay, NY
95	*DIABLO		1967	John M. Robinson	Portland, ME
95	*BOOTS		1979	Earl A. Maxwell	Metairie, LA
96	*CONNAMARA	(#6067)	1964	Fred J. Foley, Jr.	Portland, ME
96	*CONNAMARA		1967	William Adam	Padanaram, MA
96	*WHIMBREL		1975	Pieter Mimno	Marblehead, MA
97	AQUINNAH	(#6072)	1964	Charles E. Dunbar	Norwalk, CT
97	CHIVAREE		1975	Alden M. Taylor and John B. Parsons	Farmington, CT
97	TAMBOURINE		1987	Barbara and David Wheat	Boston, MA
98	*MADRIGAL	(#6089)	1964	Robert P. Bass, Jr.	Concord, NH
99	PORPOISE	(#6156)	1965	William C. Cook	Hyannisport, MA
99	PORPOISE		1972	Harrison Smith	New York City, NY
100	HAVEN OF PADANARAM	(#6169)	1965	Dr. John C. Bullard	Padanaram, MA
101	*BEQUIA	(#6191)	1965	H. Addison Taylor	Padanaram, MA
101	*SEA HAWK		1969	Miss Rose B. Dolan	Newport, RI
101	*CHRISTINA		1981	Geoffrey Winters	Greenwich, CT
102	ABACO	(#6228)	1966	Mark R. Goldweitz	Padanaram, MA
103	IRENE	(#6244)	1966	William C. Thum	San Diego, CA
103	IRENE			John B. Vincent	Bainbridge Island, WA
103	IRENE		1985	Douglas Cole	Bellingham, WA

* Denotes Concordia Forty one

Credits

All photographs not listed above are from the author's collection.

Index

315